July 1993

The Timing of Voicing in British English Obstruents

Netherlands Phonetic Archives

The Netherlands Phonetic Archives (NPA) are a modestly priced series of monographs or edited volumes of papers, reporting recent advances in the field of phonetics and experimental phonology. The archives address an audience of phoneticians, phonologists and psycholinguists.

Editors:
Marcel P.R. Van den Broecke
University of Utrecht
Vincent J. van Heuven
University of Leiden

Other books in this series:

I   Nico Willems
        English Intonation from a Dutch Point of View

IIA   A. Cohen and M.P.R. Van den Broecke (eds.)
        Abstracts of the Tenth International Congress of Phonetic Sciences

IIB   M.P.R. Van den Broecke and A. Cohen (eds.)
        Proceedings of the Tenth International Congress of Phonetic Sciences

III   J.R. de Pijper
        Modelling British English Intonation

IV   Lou Boves
        The Phonetic Basis of Perceptual Ratings of Running Speech

V   Renée van Bezooyen
        Characteristics and Recognizability of Vocal Expressions of Emotion

VI   Robert Channon & Linda Schockey
        In Honour of Ilse Lehiste

VII   Mary E. Beckman
        Stress and Non Stress Accent

VIII   Cor J. Koster
        Word Recognition in Foreign and Native Language

Gerard J. Docherty
The Timing of Voicing in British English Obstruents

FORIS PUBLICATIONS
Berlin • New York 1992

Foris Publications (formerly Foris Publications, Dordrecht)
is a Division of Walter de Gruyter & Co., Berlin.

⊚ Printed on acid-free paper which falls within in the guidelines of the ANSI to ensure permanence and durability.

Library of Congress Cataloging in Publication Data

Docherty, Gerard J.
The timing of voicing in British English obstruents / Gerard J. Docherty.
  p. cm. - (Netherlands phonetic archives ; 9)
Revision of thesis (Ph. D.) - Edinburgh University.
Includes bibliographical references and index.
ISBN 3-11-013408-X
1. English language-Phonetics. I. Title. II. Series.
PE1135.D6   1992   91-42837
421'.5-dc20   CIP

Die Deutsche Bibliothek Cataloging in Publication Data

Docherty, Gerard J.:
The timing of voicing in British English obstruents / Gerard J. Docherty. - Berlin ; New York : Foris Publ.; 1992
(Netherlands phonetic archives ; 9)
ISBN 3-11-013408-X
NE: GT

© Copyright 1992 by Walter de Gruyter & Co., D-1000 Berlin 30

All rights reserved, including those of translation into foreign languages. No part of this book may be reproduced or transmitted in any form or by any means, electronic or mechanical, including photocopy, recording, or any information storage and retrieval system, without permission in writing from the publisher.
Cover design: ICG Printing, Dordrecht, The Netherlands
Printing: ICG Printing, Dordrecht
Printed in The Netherlands.

Acknowledgements

This book is a revised version of my Edinburgh University Ph.D. dissertation submitted in January 1989. I am grateful to my supervisors, John Laver and Steve Isard for their constructive and challenging comments and for their constant encouragement. I am indebted to their scientific rigour and clarity of thought, not mention their practical understanding of what it takes for a thesis to see the light of day. Needless to say, responsibility for flaws in this work remains my own.

I must also express my gratitude to others who have guided and encouraged me in the preparation of this volume:

to my teachers, colleagues and fellow postgraduates at the University of Edinburgh (and latterly at the University of Newcastle-upon-Tyne) who have read and commented on earlier versions of this work, and who have provided an ideal environment for this study to be carried out (and for this volume to be completed);

to professional colleagues (from UK and abroad) who have taken time out at meetings and conferences to discuss this work with me, and who have forced me to sharpen the focus of many aspects of it;

to Vincent van Heuven who provided detailed and insightful advice regarding the revision of the manuscript;

to the technical staff in the Department of Linguistics at Edinburgh University and the Department of Speech at the University of Newcastle-upon-Tyne from whom expert technical support in running experiments and preparation of the manuscript was always available (and more often than not at short notice);

to my friends and to my parents for their support and patience over the years, and for helping me keep it all in perspective.

My thanks to you all.

CONTENTS

INTRODUCTION	1
1. ARTICULATORY AND ACOUSTIC STUDIES OF THE TIMING OF VOICING IN OBSTRUENTS	4
1.1 Introduction	4
1.2 Laryngeal and supralaryngeal characteristics of obstruent production	4
1.2.1 Laryngeal mechanisms: voicing	4
1.2.2 Laryngeal mechanisms: voicelessness	6
1.2.3 Obstruent supralaryngeal mechanisms	7
1.2.4 Coordination of laryngeal and supralaryngeal gestures	10
1.3 The descriptive apparatus of the timing of voicing	11
1.3.1 'Voiced' and 'voiceless'	11
1.3.2 Aspirated' and 'unaspirated'	12
1.3.3 'Fortis/lenis' and 'tense/lax'	13
1.3.4 'Devoiced'	13
1.3.5 Voice onset time	13
1.3.6 Summary	14
1.4 Limitations of past studies of the timing of voicing	14
1.5 'Physiological' investigations	18
1.6 Acoustic investigations	20
1.7 Single stops	22
1.7.1 Post-pausal syllable-initial position	22
1.7.2 VOICELESS stops in post-pausal syllable-initial position	23
1.7.3 VOICED stops in post-pausal syllable-initial position	29
1.7.4 Stops in intervocalic position	32
1.7.5 Pre-pausal final stops	35
1.7.6 Summary	35
1.8 Fricatives	37
1.8.1 VOICELESS fricatives	38
1.8.2 VOICED fricatives	39
1.9 Consonant sequences	40
1.9.1 Patterns of voicing used in English consonant sequences	41
1.9.2 Instrumental studies	42
1.10 Concluding discussion	49
Notes	50

2. MODELLING PHONETIC VARIABILITY IN SPEECH PRODUCTION — 55
  2.1 Speech production modelling: some general comments — 56
  2.2 Micro-variability in a speech production model — 60
    2.2.1 Micro-variation at the level of execution — 61
    2.2.2 Micro-variation at the level of motor programming — 66
    2.2.3 Characteristics of micro-variability at the level of motor programming — 70
    2.2.4 Micro-variation and the phonetic representation — 71
    2.2.5 Non-universal aspects of micro-variability — 74
    2.2.6 The nature of allophonic rules — 76
  2.3 The status of micro-variability in speech production: summary — 78
  2.4 Modelling the timing of voicing — 79
    2.4.1 Keating (1984a) — 80
    2.4.2 Browman & Goldstein (1986) — 83
    2.4.3 Kohler (1984) — 87
    2.4.4 General problems with the models — 89
  2.5 Summary — 90
  Notes — 94

3. EXPERIMENT 1 — 97
  3.1 Introduction — 97
  3.2 Experimental method — 97
    3.2.1 Linguistic material — 97
    3.2.2 Subjects — 98
    3.2.3 Reading task — 99
    3.2.4 Recording and analysis — 100
    3.2.5 Voicing detection — 102
    3.2.6 Segmentation and measurements — 103
    3.2.7 Consistency of measurements — 109
    3.2.8 Database description — 110
    3.2.9 Data analysis — 113
  3.3 Results — 113
    3.3.1 Effect of phonological voicing category on voice onset time and medial voicing — 113
    3.3.2 Discussion of the effect of phonological category — 127
    3.3.3 Other factors affecting voice onset time — 130
    3.3.4 Other factors affecting the occurrence of medial voicing — 157
    3.3.5 Effect of speaker identity — 167
  3.4 Summary of findings — 169
  Notes — 171

4. EXPERIMENT 2		177
4.1	Introduction	177
4.2	Experimental method	179
	4.2.1 Linguistic material	179
	4.2.2 Database description	181
	4.2.3 Subjects	181
	4.2.4 Recording and measurement procedures	181
	4.2.5 Data analysis	182
4.3	Results	182
	4.3.1 Frequency of occurrence of delayed voice onset	182
	4.3.2 Duration of voice onset time	186
4.4	Discussion	187
	Notes	190
5. DISCUSSION		191
5.1	A descriptive tool for the timing of voicing	191
	5.1.1 A framework for the detailed description of the timing of voicing	192
	5.1.2 Evaluation	198
	5.1.3 Summary	201
5.2	The timing of voicing in a model of speech production	202
	5.2.1 Minimum requirements for an account of the timing of voicing	203
	5.2.2 Incorporating the timing of voicing into the phonetic representation	211
	5.2.3 Towards a 'window model' of the timing of voicing	213
	5.2.4 Evaluation	223
	5.2.5 Summary	227
	Notes	228
CONCLUSION		232
APPENDIX A		235
APPENDIX B		257
APPENDIX C		258
APPENDIX D		260
REFERENCES		268
INDEX		282

Introduction

Two important goals of phonetic theory are the formulation of an explicit account of the detailed phonetic characteristics of languages, and an explanation of their relationship to the linguistic categories which underlie their production and perception.

The first of these goals requires robust instrumental investigation of speech and the elaboration of a taxonomic framework which offers descriptive categories capable of capturing significant phonetic processes.

The second goal hinges on the view that phonetics is a key component of a 'unified cognitive model' (Laver 1988) of speech communication, and that both phonetic theory and other components of that model are enhanced through their integration. This requires phoneticians to focus on the relationship between phonetic observations and other components of the speech 'chain' (Denes & Pinson 1963). More specifically, this task involves assessing the relationship between the phonetic realisation of an utterance and the linguistic representation underlying the production of that utterance. Refining our understanding of this relationship is a central facet of many aspects of speech research, including phonology, speech production modelling and speech technology. Evidence of this can be found in the research which is exploring the so-called 'phonetics-phonology interface' (Ohala & Jaeger 1986, Kingston & Beckman 1990, Docherty & Ladd in press), and in the many years of work addressing the 'invariance vs variability' dichotomy in speech production modelling (Perkell & Klatt 1986).

The aim of this book is to use data from an acoustic study of the timing of voicing in an accent of British English to contribute to both of the above-mentioned objectives of phonetic investigation. There are three strands to this contribution:

(A) to provide a quantitative account of the timing of voicing in British English obstruents occurring in a range of environments. Past studies of this aspect of British English are scarce, and have produced only limited data. The acquisition of such a database therefore contibutes to the first of the goals mentioned above. It also provides an empirical base for consideration of certain theoretical issues associated with the timing of voicing, thereby contributing to the second of the goals mentioned above;

(B) to formulate a descriptive phonetic framework for the timing of voicing in obstruents which has higher temporal resolution than that conventionally used, and which as a consequence is capable of giving a more detailed descriptive account of that aspect of phonetic realisation;

(C) to assess whether there is any evidence in favour of the hypothesis that some fine-grained aspects of the timing of voicing are not explicable in terms of current models of speaker control of voicing timing and yet are not simply 'by-products' of the speech production mechanism, and to evaluate some of the implications of this for our understanding of how variability of voicing timing is produced in a model of speech production:

Chapter 1 outlines the salient articulatory characteristics of the laryngeal and supralaryngeal mechanisms involved in the production of VOICED and VOICELESS stops and fricatives.[1] There follows an evaluation of the descriptive phonetic apparatus most commonly applied to the timing of voicing. I point out a number of reasons why it is unsatisfactory (principally inadequate descriptive labeling, and poor time resolution). The rest of this chapter is a survey of the literature, in which I describe the results of (primarily acoustic) studies of the timing of voicing in stops and fricatives, concentrating in particular on the factors which have been shown to give rise to systematic variability in the timing of voicing. Two principal conclusions emerge from this; firstly, the experimental evidence which is available is extremely limited; secondly, whilst the findings which are reported in the literature are not always consistent, they indicate that the timing of voicing in obstruents varies considerably as a function of a range of factors. This is a feature of phonetic realisation which must receive an adequate account within general phonetic theory and speech production modelling.

In **Chapter 2**, I describe the way in which fine-grained variability in phonetic realisation (the timing of voicing in particular) is commonly handled in work on speech production modelling. I point out that there is effectively a gap in speech production theory. No satisfactory account has yet been given of **systematic fine-grained** variability in phonetic realisation which is **characteristic of a particular language.** This gap is the result of the use of a relatively abstract phonetic representation, allied to an over-readiness to attribute fine-grained variability to factors of utterance execution or motor programming (i.e. to extra-linguistic factors). The chapter concludes with a description of the type of evidence which would confirm the existence of this gap with respect to the timing of voicing in obstruents, thereby providing a link with the experimental chapters which follow.

Chapters 3 and 4 describe the two experiments carried out as part of this study. The first experiment (the larger of the two) investigates variability in voice onset time and medial voicing in obstruents as a function of a number of factors, both inherent in the obstruent themselves, and contextually determined. The second experiment investigates a different type of factor (status of cluster-medial boundary) on the occurrence of voice onset time in stop-sonorant sequences. In describing the results of the experiments, particular emphasis is placed on the implications of the results for the theoretical position outlined in Chapter 2; i.e. to what extent do the findings support the claim that there is a gap in speech production theory.

In **Chapter 5**, in the light of the data gathered in the experiments, I elaborate on the theoretical issues outlined in Chapters 1 and 2. I begin by proposing a parametrically-based descriptive framework capable of providing a detailed account of the timing of voicing in stops and fricatives, and which manages to overcome a number of drawbacks of the conventional descriptive framework described in Chapter 1. In the second half of this Chapter, I outline a set of minimum requirements applicable to any attempt to incorporate a specification of the timing of voicing into the phonetic representation, and give a preliminary outline of one means in which this might be achieved.

NOTES

1. Throughout this book upper case 'VOICED' and 'VOICELESS' are used to refer to phonological categories. Lower case 'voiced' and 'voiceless' are used as phonetic labels applied to intervals when voicing is or is not present.

CHAPTER 1
Articulatory and Acoustic Studies of the Timing of Voicing in Obstruents

1.1 INTRODUCTION

The aim of this chapter is to establish a context for the experimental and theoretical work described in this book. The chapter is structured into three parts. In the first, I outline the principal articulatory and acoustic features of the laryngeal and supralaryngeal activity relevant for giving an account of the timing of voicing in obstruents. In the second part, I provide an evaluation of the terminology most commonly used in attempting to describe significant aspects of laryngeal/supralaryngeal coordination. In the third part, I assess the extent of available knowledge regarding the timing of voicing in English obstruents.

I conclude that further experimental investigation is required (especially for British English) on more global aspects of the timing of voicing (i.e. not just on voice onset time), in order to provide a more complete account of the timing of voicing, and an empirical base for further work on modelling the control of the systematic temporal features of phonetic realisation in a model of speech production. The remainder of this book sets out to broaden our knowledge of the timing of voicing in British English, and to examine its implications for the domains just mentioned.[1]

1.2 LARYNGEAL AND SUPRALARYNGEAL CHARACTERISTICS OF OBSTRUENT PRODUCTION

1.2.1 Laryngeal mechanisms: voicing

The sequence of events which give rise to the production of voicing are embodied in the aerodynamic-myoelastic theory of phonation (Van den Berg 1958, 1968, Broad 1973, Laver 1980, Hirano 1981 and Sawashima & Hirose 1983).[2] A number of conditions are necessary for voicing to take place. The vocal folds must be adducted and tensed, and there must be a trans-glottal pressure drop which is greater than a threshold which varies as a function of glottal resistance (Catford (1977:98) gives a typical sub-glottal pressure requirement for voicing of 2-3 cm H_2O). This pressure drop is normally achieved by a pulmonic egressive airstream. With an open glottis, the airstream generated by contraction of pulmonic volume passes from the lungs through the larynx and through the vocal tract. When the glottis is closed, blocking the channel to the supra-glottal passages, pressure builds up in the sub-glottal passages and a progressively increasing trans-glottal difference is obtained.

Each cycle of vocal fold vibration normally consists of the following stages. With the vocal folds adducted and tensed, (a) sub-glottal pressure gradually builds up; (b) sub-glottal pressure reaches threshold and begins to push the folds apart, from the bottom up, with a 'vertical phase difference' (Laver 1980:96); (c) the folds open completely, thus venting the sub-glottal pressure and allowing air to pass into the vocal tract; (d) due to the Bernoulli effect (a local pressure drop caused by acceleration of a fluid or gas through a narrow constriction) and to the continuing myodynamic tension in the folds, the folds begin to close, once again with a vertical phase difference; (e) the closing motion is far quicker than the opening gesture -- the folds effectively slap back together, and it is the closing gesture which provides the acoustic excitation of the vocal tract; (f) the cycle begins again.[3] The acoustic correlate of voicing is a periodic signal corresponding to the excitation of the vocal tract by the vocal folds.

Vocal fold vibration is not a process which is instantaneously switched on and off by a speaker at the appropriate moment. Intervals of voicing tend to begin and to end somewhat gradually. The laryngeal configuration at the onset of vocal fold vibration may involve the folds being tensed, but held somewhat apart (Catford 1977:97), and in the transition from voicelessness to voicing and vice versa, there is often a stage in which the vocal folds are vibrating but without coming together along the mid-line, thus providing a form of breathy onset/offset.[4] This can be observed in some of the high speed and stroboscopic films that have been made of the vocal folds (e.g. Uldall 1957, Van den Berg et al. 1960). The gradual onset of voicing is also often reflected in the signals produced by a laryngograph or a throat microphone, and in the speech waveform, as a sharp, but not instantaneous build-up in the level of the periodic signal corresponding to voicing. Catford (1977:107) is one of the few investigators who explicitly recognise the gradual nature of laryngeal activity, suggesting that it may be appropriate to think of laryngeal gestures as forming a 'quasi-continuum' ranging from complete voicelessness with abducted vocal folds through to a glottal stop with the vocal folds held tightly together, with voicing located somewhere in between.

The view of voicing which is adopted in this study is a rather selective and simplified one in at least two respects. The fine detail of vocal fold vibration varies both between and within speakers (Catford 1977, Laver 1980, Nolan

1983). This ranges from cycle-to-cycle variability in the fine details of glottal vibration, to the use of diverse phonatory settings by speakers in order to convey particular paralinguistic signals to a listener. However, in the present study, since the timing of intervals of voicing in relation to other articulatory events is the primary concern, rather than the shape of the glottal waveform or the mode of laryngeal vibration, no further attention is paid to this level of variability.

Secondly, despite the fact that the transition from a voiceless interval of speech into a voiced interval is not instantaneous, and that (if we adopt Catford's idea of a 'continuum' of laryngeal activity) there may not be an unambiguous cut-off point between the two, in this study, I identify intervals of speech as being either voiced or voiceless. This requires the imposition of a threshold on the voiceless-voiced 'continuum'. Of course, this is a characteristic of all the work which has been carried out on the timing of voicing, but the fact that this leads to a somewhat simplified view of laryngeal activity is not a factor which is explicitly recognised in the majority of studies. Examples of the thresholds which have been used in the past are given later in this chapter, and that used in this study is described in Chapter 3.

1.2.2 Laryngeal mechanisms: voicelessness

In general, the term 'voiceless' signifies an absence of vocal fold vibration. With regard to laryngeal activity, 'voiceless' is a cover-term denoting a range of laryngeal configurations including:

• complete glottal closure as observed in the production of a glottal stop;

• a near-complete glottal closure as observed in the production of whisper (this is achieved by a glottal configuration which involves an almost complete glottal closure but with a triangle-shaped opening being formed in the cartilaginous portion of the glottis between the arytenoid cartilages. Laver (1980:121) points out that the closure of a large part of the glottis is largely a result of contraction of the lateral cricoarytenoid muscles. The lack of simultaneous contraction of the interarytenoid muscles in whisper means that the glottis is not fully closed along its length, and there is a gap at the arytenoid end through which the pulmonic airstream may pass.)

• an open glottis as the result of a full glottal abduction gesture (mainly achieved through contraction of the posterior cricoarytenoid muscles.[5]).

The articulatory events which are associated with voicelessness are essentially dynamic laryngeal gestures which break up the intervals of voicing corresponding to syllabic nuclei and other voiced segments.[6] The nature of the control of the laryngeal opening gesture has been studied by a number of investigators (including, Kim 1970, Weismer 1980, Löfqvist 1980, Sawashima & Hirose 1983, Löfqvist & Yoshioka 1984). The principal findings of this work are presented below in Section 1.5.

Since the aim of the present study is to examine the timing of intervals of voicing, no distinction is made between unvoiced intervals of speech which are produced in these different ways (one exception to this is the case of glottalised stops -- see comments in Section 3.2.8). A detailed study of laryngeal gestures in speech requires invasive physiological instrumentation. The use of acoustic techniques, as in the present study, allows observations of the relative timing of voicing and supralaryngeal events, but does not permit reliable differentiation of voiceless intervals produced by, for example, glottal abduction and 'whisper'.

1.2.3 Obstruent supralaryngeal mechanisms

The term 'obstruent' emerged from the generative phonology literature and is used as a cover term for the set of oral stops, fricatives and affricates. Since in this study, affricates are not being investigated, the term obstruent is used henceforth to refer to stops and fricatives only.

Stop consonants

Detailed accounts of the articulatory and acoustic properties of stop consonants are provided by Rothenburg (1968) and Zue (1976). The primary articulatory feature associated with stops is that the speaker produces a complete blockage at some point within the vocal tract. Oral stops have a simultaneous closure or near closure of the velic port (in this book the term 'stop' does not include [m, n, ŋ], which are often referred to as nasal stops.)[7] In this study (following Laver forthcoming), for descriptive purposes, stops are considered to consist of three main phases: an **onset** phase during which the articulators involved in producing the stop are coming closer together; a **medial** phase during which there is a complete constriction within the oral cavity; and a **release** phase during which the articulators involved in the constriction move apart.

In aerodynamic terms, oral stops have the effect of completely impeding the passage of the pulmonic egressive airstream out of the oral cavity, and consequently there is a build up of intra-oral pressure behind the constriction. The release of a stop closure is complex, passing through three stages:

• complete closure leading to a build up of pressure -- at this stage, the speech acoustic signal is characterised either by silence (if voiceless) or by low energy periodicity (if voiced);

• the closure is released, giving rise to a short interval in which the articulators are in close approximation at the same time as there is high intra-oral pressure. The release causes a rapid escape of air, which, as a result of these aerodynamic conditions, flows turbulently, giving rise to random pressure variations and a noisy acoustic signal. The noise burst resulting from closure release has a relatively higher intensity in VOICELESS stops than in VOICED stops (Zue 1976), due to the fact that, at the moment of release, intra-oral pressure is lower in voiced stops than in voiceless stops (Brown & McGlone 1969, Prosek & House 1975). The filter properties of the vocal tract during the noise burst of a stop are dependent upon the shape of the vocal tract, both anterior and posterior to the point of constriction. These volumes are determined by the place of vocal tract occlusion;

• the articulators, which are continuously moving apart through the release stage, reach the point at which they are too far apart to cause turbulent airflow (intra-oral air pressure is also dropping continuously from the moment of the release of the stop as a function of the degree of stricture in the cavity). This third phase is discussed in a little more detail below in Section 1.3.2.

Fricative consonants

The articulatory characteristics of fricatives are conventionally characterised as involving an active and passive articulator entering into a positional configuration of **close approximation**, which, in turn, can be defined as a degree of stricture which causes a locally turbulent passage of the airstream, and therefore a noisy acoustic signal.

The definition of fricatives exclusively on the basis of degree of approximation is, however, rather a simplification. 'Close approximation' is typically defined as a degree of constriction which is close enough to cause turbulent airflow of a pulmonic egressive airstream. However, the presence of turbulent airflow is as much a function of the size of pulmonic and intra-oral pressure and of the shape of the constriction, as of degree of stricture. Hence, aerodynamic, as well as articulatory, factors must be considered in devising an explicit definition of fricatives.

A further problem with regard to the definition of fricatives is that the interval of turbulent noise for a fricative does not necessarily correspond to the period of maximally close approximation of the articulators concerned. Noise could set in before the articulators reach their point of maximum proximity, and it could continue for a while during the time in which they are separating (Catford 1977:254, Fraser & Docherty 1990).

The definition of a fricative adopted in the present study is one which is appropriate for an acoustic study; namely a consonant characterised by a sustained noisy acoustic signal, which is the result of a combination of the articulatory/aerodynamic factors just mentioned.

The articulation of fricatives can also be broken down into a sequence of three phases; an onset phase during which the active articulator is moving towards the passive articulator -- this involves not only a carefully controlled movement trajectory, but also, in some cases, a significant alteration in the shape of the active articulator (e.g. the tongue takes on a grooved coronal section for [s], and a cupped shape for [ʃ] -- Hardcastle 1976); a medial phase during which the articulatory constriction gives rise to turbulent airflow -- the point at which turbulent flow sets in may be computed from knowledge of the rate of flow and the cross-sectional area and shape of the orifice (Scully 1990); an offset phase during which the articulators are moving apart, removing the conditions for noise generation.

The acoustic features of fricatives have been investigated by, amongst others, Hughes & Halle (1956), Strevens (1960), Jassem (1965) and Shadle (1990). The key acoustic feature of fricatives is that they are characterised by a sustained noisy signal. The spectrum of the fricative noise is determined by the size and cross sectional area of the constriction, and by the shape of the cavities anterior and posterior to the constriction. Shadle (1990) has pointed out that aerodynamically and acoustically, fricatives can be divided into two main types, differing in the manner in which the turbulent flow is generated. 'Obstacle' fricatives are those (such as [s] and [z]) in which the turbulent airflow (and hence the fricative noise) is produced not at the place of maximum constriction, but by a jet of air forced through the constriction at high velocity striking an obstacle (such as the top teeth) anterior to the place of articulatory constriction. This gives rise to a fricative noise spectrum of relatively high intensity, and with a concentration of energy at relatively high frequencies. 'Non-obstacle' fricatives are those (such as [θ] and [ð]) in which the fricative noise is produced at the point of maximum constriction itself. Fricatives produced in this way are relatively less intense than the obstacle fricatives, and are characterised by a more even spread of energy through the spectrum.

1.2.4 Coordination of laryngeal and supralaryngeal gestures

The vocal apparatus is often described as consisting of distinct sub-systems (e.g. respiratory system, phonatory system, supralaryngeal system). However, there are three main zones in which there are important muscular interactions between diverse sectors of the vocal apparatus; the hyoid muscular system; the linguo-labio-mandibular system; and the linguo-velopharyngeal system. For example, the larynx, tongue and jaw are mutually connected by their respective extrinsic musculature via the hyoid system -- lowering the larynx can pull the tongue down and back, fronting the tongue can raise the hyoid and larynx (depending on the relative fixedness of these vocal structures; Laver 1980:26).

However, even though there undoubtedly are anatomical interactions between the laryngeal and supralaryngeal 'systems', laryngeal gestures are still potentially relatively free to be timed independently of supralaryngeal gestures. Perhaps the major physical constraint on their coordination is that voicing can only be prolonged for as long as there exists a sufficient transglottal pressure drop. This means that in the production of sounds in which there is a gradual decrease in the pressure drop across the glottis, such as stops, voicing ceases at the moment the pressure difference falls below the level necessary for the aerodynamic component of vocal fold vibration.

In practice, in order to maintain voicing in stops, speakers have been found to use a variety of strategies to prolong the interval during which there is a sufficient trans-glottal pressure drop. These are reviewed in Westbury (1979) and Bell-Berti (1975). The three main methods are expansion of the pharyngeal cavity, lowering of the larynx in order to increase the size of the supralaryngeal cavities, and slight opening of the velic port in order to allow some leakage of air and thereby maintain the trans-glottal pressure difference. There is evidence for the use of all three of these mechanisms for prolonging voicing under adverse aerodynamic circumstances, but, as is pointed out by both investigators mentioned, some speakers have a preference to use one means rather than another, and it remains an empirical question to what extent the cavity expansion strategies which have been found to take place are actively controlled by speakers, or passively induced by the high intra-oral post-occlusion air pressures existing during the interval of oral constriction.

Fricatives may be produced with simultaneous voicing. The effect of this is to reduce the overall amplitude of the fricative noise (due to the lower airflow rate during phonation), and to produce a noisy signal which is modulated by the underlying periodic glottal excitation.

1.3 THE DESCRIPTIVE APPARATUS FOR THE TIMING OF VOICING

In the remainder of this chapter, attention is turned more specifically to the **coordination** of laryngeal and supralaryngeal events. As pointed out in the introduction to this book, one of the aims of phonetic theory is to provide a descriptive apparatus which is capable of capturing all of the systematic characteristics of the phonetic performance of speakers of a language or languages. In dealing with the timing of voicing in obstruents, it is possible to identify a number of requirements in this regard:

(a) **detail:** many of the systematic features of the timing of voicing which have to be captured by the taxonomy are very fine-grained. This imposes a requirement for a descriptive apparatus with fairly high temporal resolution.

(b) **parametric:** in dealing with the timing of voicing in obstruents, phonetic theory is essentially required to describe the relative timing of the domains of activation of glottal and supralaryngeal gestures -- a descriptive apparatus which does not allow independent specification of these two articulatory tiers may well be problematic.

(c) **gradience:** whilst, at the phonological level, languages may only have a binary or tertiary 'voicing contrast', the actual realisation of that contrast (at the level of coordination of laryngeal and supralaryngeal gestures) is unlikely to be captured using a categorial scale of that sort (i.e. using 'all-or-nothing' categories).

In the light of these general requirements, how successful is the descriptive apparatus commonly applied to the timing of voicing in obstruents?

1.3.1 'Voiced' and 'Voiceless'

The phonetic denotation of the terms 'voiced' and 'voiceless' has already been discussed in this chapter. If (as is rarely the case) these terms are used **strictly** to refer to obstruents that are produced with (or without) voicing **throughout** their medial phase, then it could be argued that they do not infringe the requirements outlined above. It is clear however, that the strict application of these terms only covers a relatively small subset of all the possibilities of laryngeal-supralaryngeal coordination. It could be argued, then, that these terms would have enhanced value if incorporated into a far richer descriptive framework, but are not in themselves sufficient to meet the descriptive requirements associated with the timing of voicing.

1.3.2 'Aspirated' and 'Unaspirated'

Many descriptive accounts of the timing of voicing in stops supplement 'voiced' and 'voiceless' with the orthogonal terms 'aspirated' and 'unaspirated'. If modal voicing is **audibly** delayed following the medial phase of an obstruent,[8] the obstruent is said to be aspirated. During this delay in voice onset, the oral cavity is relatively unconstricted, and the vocal folds have not yet been adducted, with the result that air can pass relatively unimpeded through the vocal tract. Laver (forthcoming) points out that the resultant phonatory state of the interval between stop release and onset of voicing is occasionally whisper, but normally 'voicelessness' (e.g. glottal abduction).[9] PRE-aspiration occurs when there is an audible delay between the end of voicing in a vowel, and the start of the medial phase for a following obstruent. Voicing ceases due to separation of the vocal folds, thus allowing the continuous pulmonic egressive airstream to pass relatively unimpeded through the vocal tract.

In order for a displacement in voice onset with respect to stop release to become audible, it has been claimed that an interval of approximately 20 ms is required between onset of voicing and the release of the stop (Stevens & Klatt 1974, Pisoni 1977). Therefore, as pointed out by Laver (forthcoming), the term 'aspirated' covers only a subset of cases in which the onset of voicing is delayed with respect to the release of a stop.

Whilst the definition of aspiration given above is based on a combination of perceptual and production criteria, the timing of voicing in the **production** of stops is often described by labelling the stop as being either aspirated or unaspirated. This terminological dichotomy, 'aspirated/unaspirated', implies that aspiration is an all-or-nothing phenomenon. This may be an accurate representation of listeners' perceptual capabilities, but instrumental studies of the timing of voicing (many of which are reviewed below) show that from the point of view of speech production, the situation is more complex. Firstly, there is not always a clear boundary between the delay in voice onset observed for so-called aspirated and unaspirated stops. Secondly, it is necessary to identify different degrees of aspiration; i.e. it is more of a continuous process than the terminology suggests, with longer or shorter intervals of aspiration being found in some environments, and in some languages, than in others (a similar point is made by Randolph & Zue 1987). Therefore, the (widespread) use of these terms to describe the timing of voicing in speech production provides a somewhat simplified view of the timing patterns actually produced by speakers (this point is discussed a little further in Chapter 5).

1.3.3 'Fortis/Lenis' and 'Tense/Lax'

The fact that there are a number of acoustic and articulatory correlates of phonological voicing categories has led some researchers to abandon the 'voiced/voiceless' labels (except for cases when they are truly appropriate as described above), and to adopt more global descriptive labels, such as fortis/lenis and tense/lax, which can be used both at a phonological level to distinguish the sets of homorganic cognates, and at a phonetic level as cover terms for the range of phonetic features which, it is claimed, correlate with the different phonological classes (Malecot 1969, Slis 1970, Kohler 1984). These terms are useful in that they do not imply that the realisational differences between pairs such as /p,b/, /t,d/, /s,z/, etc. reside exclusively in the domain of laryngeal timing, and for this reason they are favoured by many phoneticians and phonologists. However, from the point of view of providing a more detailed descriptive account of the timing of voicing, they are no more helpful than 'voiced' or 'voiceless', since they give no clearer indication of the details of the coordination of laryngeal and supralaryngeal activity.

1.3.4 'Devoiced'

'Devoiced' is the term often used to refer to a segment which is 'normally' accompanied by voicing (usually, by implication, one which is phonologically VOICED) when it is realised without voicing (for example, when it occurs adjacent to a pause or a voiceless segment). Hence, 'devoiced' is a term which is rather different from most other descriptive phonetic terms, since it tends not to be used independently of the phonological category of a segment. It is often prefixed with the qualifier 'partially' when the voicing normally associated with a segment is not completely absent, but occurs during a smaller proportion of the duration of the segment concerned. In strict phonetic terms, a segment that is 'fully devoiced' could also be labelled 'voiceless' (bearing in mind that the term 'voiceless', as described above, covers a range of laryngeal gestures).[10]

1.3.5 Voice onset time

This term was coined by Lisker & Abramson (1964), and it has been widely used since as the major means of describing the timing of voicing in stops. It refers to the interval (in ms) between the release of a stop closure, and the onset of voicing for a following voiced segment. The moment of stop release is assigned the value '0', and any delay in voice onset following the release is assigned a positive value. If voicing commences prior to the release of the stop, the voice onset time is given a negative value. Voice onset time is not strictly speaking a descriptive label, but rather a physical scale along which the realisation of stops (occurring before voiced sounds) can be positioned. It is included in this section merely to indicate the frequency with which it is used as the sole measure of the characteristics of laryngeal/supralaryngeal coordination in stop production (more on which in Section 1.4 below).

1.3.6 Summary

It seems reasonable to conclude that conventional description of the timing of voicing makes use of a rather mixed bag of physical, phonetic, and phonological descriptors. A detailed (perhaps excessively so) account of one aspect of the timing of voicing is certainly provided by a measure of voice onset time but in general, the resolution of conventional terminology is too coarse to capture all the significant characteristics of realisation. A second problem is that only voice onset time and the aspirated/unaspirated distinction really capture the fact that the timing of voicing involves the coordination of two independently controllable parameters. Furthermore, most of the descriptors outlined above are essentially binary, suggesting all-or-nothingness, and they do not facilitate the capture of subtle differences along the same dimension (e.g. 'more or less voiced', or 'more or less aspirated').

In Chapter 5, in the light of the results of the experiments reported in Chapters 3 and 4, I consider again the nature of the descriptive apparatus applicable to the timing of voicing, and outline one possible way in which some of the limitations of the apparatus described above could be overcome.

1.4 LIMITATIONS OF PAST STUDIES OF THE TIMING OF VOICING

This review which makes up the remainder of this chapter addresses the following questions: what is the extent of our knowledge regarding the timing of voicing in English obstruents (particularly in accents of British English), and what factors are known to give rise to variability in that aspect of articulatory coordination?

The available data on the timing of voicing in English obstruents is limited in three major respects; acoustic studies of voicing have concentrated heavily on the perceptual cues for the voicing contrast rather than on the systematic characteristics of the timing of voicing in speech production; the production data that is available relates almost exclusively to voice onset time (i.e. only one aspect of laryngeal timing); there are very few quantitative accounts of the timing of voicing in accents of British English. I now expand briefly on each of these points.

Concentration on American accents of English

In common with many fields of experimental phonetic research, studies of the production of voicing have concentrated to a great extent on speakers of American accents of English. A survey of the literature reveals that there are very few dedicated acoustic studies of the timing of voicing in British English obstruents. The few studies which specifically set out to look at this aspect of phonetic realisation limit themselves to either stops (Suomi 1980), or VOICED fricatives (Haggard 1978), but none match the breadth or coverage of the work carried out by Klatt (1975) and Zue (1976) on American English. By far the greater part of our quantitative knowledge about the timing of voicing in British English is a by-product of studies which have had other more specific aims, and which, consequently, have not placed emphasis on describing and discussing the results pertaining to the timing of voicing (e.g. Bladon & Al-Bamerni 1976, Hanninen 1979, Hawkins 1979, and others described below). One aim of this study is to contribute towards providing a more detailed empirical account of the timing of voicing in obstruents in an accent of British English.

Of course, the need for increased data on the timing of voicing in British English does not stem exclusively from the fact that relatively little work has been carried out previously in this area. Recent work in speech production modelling (reviewed in Chapter 2) suggests that many fine-grained aspects of phonetic realisation are not just a by-product of the speech production mechanism, but may in fact be part of the linguistic control component of speech production. Evaluation of this possibility requires detailed instrumental investigation of phonetic realisation, focusing both on the systematic features of phonetic realisation of particular languages and accents, and on cross-language and -accent variation.

Focus on voice onset time

Even if it were possible to disregard the data imbalance just described, the work which has been carried out on the timing of voicing would still be largely unsatisfactory. The main reason for this is that the reports in the literature concentrate almost entirely on the timing of voicing in stop consonants in pre-stressed syllable, word-initial position (a similar observation is made by Weismer 1980).

This overwhelming interest in the timing of voicing with respect to the release of initial stops, to the exclusion of almost every other instance in which voicing needs to be carefully timed in relation to supralaryngeal activity, is a result of the enormous interest generated by the important work of Lisker &

Abramson (1964, 1967). Their idea that the single parameter of voice onset time could be used to distinguish syllable initial cognate stops in a large number of languages gave rise not only to a new acronym, 'VOT' (Abramson 1977:297), but more importantly, to the situation in which most of the studies that have been carried out on the production and the timing of voicing in English are only concerned with voice onset time, excluding other aspects of coordination of voicing and supralaryngeal activity. The narrow focus of previous work on English becomes even clearer when compared to studies of other languages which have commonly taken a broader view of laryngeal-supralaryngeal coordination (e.g. Dutch, Slis 1986, van den Berg 1988, French, Sock & Benoit 1986).

This in turn has meant that the results of these studies have only provided information on word-initial stops. Voice onset time has not been used as a parameter for categorising word-final stops, or stops occurring before other voiced consonants, since these often lack the burst of wide-band noise in their spectra which marks the instant of the release of the stop, and which is used as a reference point for measuring voice onset time. Of course, voice onset time is not a relevant measure for pre-pausal final stops.

Focus on perception

A further reason why we have an inadequate body of data concerning the timing of voicing is that in the past, a good deal of emphasis has been placed on investigating the acoustic cues for the phonological categories VOICED and VOICELESS, rather than on detailed investigation of the realisation of voicing as a phonetic parameter in speech production. This has meant that researchers have undertaken primarily perceptually-oriented studies, normally involving the manipulation of a range of acoustic parameters (e.g. vowel and stop closure duration, burst spectra, voicing during closure, formant onset frequency, fundamental frequency) which are claimed to be associated with the VOICED/VOICELESS distinction, in order to observe the effects which this produces in the subjects' perception of a target phoneme as being phonemically VOICED or VOICELESS (see Watson (1983), for a review of work on manipulation of the acoustic cues said to correlate with the voicing contrast).[11]

This interest in perception, at the expense of production-oriented work, has received impetus from a number of factors. One motivation is the relative simplicity with which it is possible to carry out experimentation. Before the days of digital speech processing, the availability of the spectrograph meant that it was simple to extract what were judged to be the salient acoustic parameters of speech sounds, and then using pattern-playback synthesis, stylised synthetic utterances could be produced in which the relevant parameters were independently varied (e.g. Delattre et al. 1955). Nowadays, digital signal processing techniques make it even simpler to extract the relevant parameters from the speech signal, and to manipulate and create series of stimuli for presentation to subjects.

Certain developments in the theories of speech production and perception have also contributed to this lack of detailed production information. The long-standing interest in searching for invariant features in phonetic realisation has led investigators to concentrate on analysis of features which might be the source of perceptual invariance (especially spectral features), discarding, in the process, a lot of the detail of the acoustic signal (e.g. context-sensitive variation) which was thought to mask the alleged invariant properties, even though many of these fine-grained phenomena occur in a systematic fashion. It is precisely this fine-grained level of phonetic realisation which is the subject matter of this book.

This perceptually-based approach to experimentation does not just apply to the investigation of voicing, but to the whole range of major acoustic phonetic parameters (e.g. formant frequencies and other quality related features, and a range of temporal features). Consequently, like voicing, these are all areas where further robust quantitative data on speech production is needed to provide firmer empirical foundations for work in speech production modelling.

In the remainder of this chapter, I outline the major results of research carried out on the timing of voicing in single stops and fricatives, and in obstruents in consonant sequences in English. Whilst the goal of this investigation is to study the timing of voicing in an accent of British English, in this review section, I consider work carried out on all accents of English. In this way the paucity of the work carried out on accents of British English becomes clear.

There are two main types of experimentation which provide information on the timing of voicing; acoustic studies and 'physiological' studies (i.e. studies using physiological instrumentation to observe in a relatively direct fashion the timing of laryngeal and supralaryngeal activity). Since in this book I present an acoustic study, I concentrate in this review on the former of these two. However, it is impossible to consider the control of the timing of voicing without making reference to the possible mechanisms of laryngeal control which have been hypothesised by investigators performing non-acoustic studies. Before giving an account of the acoustic studies, I briefly outline the main findings of the physiological studies of the timing of voicing in English obstruents.

1.5 'PHYSIOLOGICAL' INVESTIGATION

There have been a large number of 'physiological' studies of the mechanisms of control and production of voicing, especially for English, Japanese and Swedish. (e.g. Rothenburg 1968, Lisker et al. 1969, Kim 1970, Lindqvist 1972, Hirose & Gay 1972, Yoshioka et al. 1979, Weismer 1980, Löfqvist 1980, Hirano 1981, Löfqvist & Yoshioka 1981, Sawashima & Hirose 1983, Löfqvist & Yoshioka 1984, Löfqvist & McGarr 1986, Yoshioka et al. 1986, Dixit 1987, Bickley & Stevens 1987, Ní Chasaide 1987, Löfqvist 1990). A large part of this research has focused on establishing the principal features of the coordination of laryngeal and supralaryngeal gestures in obstruents (mainly VOICELESS stops and fricatives -- there are very few physiological accounts of laryngeal activity in VOICED obstruents in English).

One point on which all of the investigators appear to agree is that the laryngeal abduction gesture is an integrated opening-and-closing action of the glottis momentarily interrupting vocal fold vibration (although see comments below on Kim 1970). It is not the case that the vocal folds are opened, and then 'held open' before closing again in the production of voiceless segments. This supports the point made above that voiceless intervals of speech are the result of an inherently dynamic gesture of the vocal folds, as opposed to being a uniform 'state', as might be implied by the phonetic label 'voiceless'.

However, beyond this common ground between different investigators, there are disagreements apparent in their consideration of the nature of this gesture. There are three possible components of a glottal abduction gesture which could potentially be controlled (its timing, velocity, and maximum amplitude), and there are (at least) three positions held by different investigators with regard to that control. The first is that described by Weismer (1980). On the basis of an acoustic study of the duration of the 'voiceless interval' in VOICELESS stops and fricatives, he postulates that the glottal abduction gesture used in VOICELESS aspirated stops and VOICELESS fricatives is identical -- in both cases it is timed to commence at the beginning of the supralaryngeal constriction, and in both cases the same maximum amplitude of glottal width is achieved (Weismer makes no mention of gesture velocity differences, but given his argumentation one can assume that this is not thought to vary as a function of manner or place of articulation).[12] Weismer claims that this proposal greatly simplifies our understanding of the control of voicing;

> .. control of voicing in stops (and other obstruents) is simply a matter of whether or not the laryngeal devoicing gesture occurs ... the resulting VOT

> differences are the by-products of the dichotomous laryngeal behaviour.
> (1980:434)

If further experimentation provided support for these claims, this model of voicing timing would indeed be very powerful, since it would provide a transparent link between a linguistic representation of the voicing contrast (such as a binary feature assignment [+/-voiced]), and its surface realisation, with any other variability of the timing of voicing being a 'by-product' of the basic gesture itself. This issue is addressed in greater detail in Chapter 2. The results of the experiments reported in Chapters 3 and 4 allow an evaluation of Weismer's proposal.

A second significant position is held by Löfqvist and colleagues (e.g. Löfqvist 1980, Löfqvist & Yoshioka 1984). Using the results from a large number of studies employing a range of experimental techniques, their view is that the **timing of the abduction gesture** is the crucial control parameter in VOICELESS obstruents. In addition they also note that abduction gestures do not all occur at the same velocity. Both Löfqvist (1986) and Yoshioka et al. (1986) present data which shows slightly higher velocity gestures in fricatives than in stops, leading to wider glottal apertures. This approach differs from Weismer's in two ways; firstly, it allows for greater control of the gesture itself, specifically of the timing of the gesture with respect to supralaryngeal gestures; secondly, it does not claim that there is a relatively transparent relationship between underlying binary phonological voicing categories and their realisation. It does, however, assume that having initiated a laryngeal abduction gesture, speakers have little further control of the way in which the gesture evolves.

This is not the case with a third major position held on laryngeal control in obstruents, emerging from Kim (1970) (more recent data in support of this is given by Ní Chasaide, 1987). Kim's (1970) experimental data suggested that in aspirated stops, the crucial parameter controlled by speakers is not the timing of glottal adduction, but the size of glottal opening at the moment of stop release. He discovered a strong relationship between the size of glottal opening at the moment of stop release and the duration of the period of aspiration;

> instruction to close the glottis is assumed to be simultaneous for all voiceless
> stops (it occurs at the time of release), different aspiration lengths being due
> to different degrees of glottal opening. (1970:112).

Kim's position differs from that of Löfqvist in two ways; he views degree of aperture at release as being the major correlate of different degrees of aspiration, rather than overall gestural timing; and he suggests that the degree of glottal opening is the major controlled parameter in the production of aspirated stops. As pointed out by Ní Chasaide (1987), these two positions are potentially complementary (i.e. timing AND degree of aperture could be controlled), although Löfqvist (1980) argues strongly against the possibility of glottal aperture being independently variable.

Despite the experimental investigations which have been carried out into the detail of the glottal opening-closing gesture in VOICELESS stops and fricatives, there is evidently no consensus regarding the mode of control which speakers use. The reason for this is likely to be the insufficient and somewhat inconsistent data which has been gathered, which makes it rather difficult to evaluate the range of hypotheses which have been proposed. Investigators have used a range of techniques (many of which cannot be used without some perturbation to normal articulation), producing results which are difficult to compare, and most experiments have been performed on a very small number of subjects due to the invasive nature of the techniques involved. In practical terms this a difficult area of research, where there is a large amount of work remaining to be done before a clear picture can be established. Motivation for the use of acoustic rather than 'physiological' techniques in the present study is given at the end of Chapter 2.

1.6 ACOUSTIC INVESTIGATIONS

I now focus on acoustic studies of the timing of voicing. The literature is examined in three stages, dealing with single stops (by far the largest section, for reasons outlined above), single fricatives, and consonant sequences.

In this review, for purposes of illustration, the different patterns of voicing timing are shown in terms of two parameters: (a) a voicing parameter; (b) a degree of approximation parameter (this particular method of illustrating different patterns of coordination was used by, amongst others, Abercrombie 1967). As has been pointed out above, the present study is taking a rather selective view of 'voicing' (shared, tacitly, by all of the studies to be reviewed), by normalising across different voice qualities, and by setting a threshold for dividing speech into voiced and voiceless intervals and indicating when intervals of voicing begin and end. Hence, in illustrating the patterns of voicing timing reported in the literature, voicing is represented in the diagrams as being either present or not. The degree of approximation parameter is considered to have three possible settings; open approximation as in the medial phase of vowels; close approximation as in fricatives; complete closure for stops (of course, this 3-way categorisation of manner of articulation is also a rather coarse representation of the articulatory facts in order to simplify the description). Thus, with time along the x axis, and the two articulatory parameters on the y axis, we might represent a VOICELESS fricative in a V___V context as in Figure 1.1. The advantages of a parametric representation of voicing timing are discussed further in Chapter 5.

Figure 1.1: A parametric representation of an intervocalic VOICELESS fricative. A notional time scale runs horizontally. The top part of the diagram relates to the degree of approximation, and gives a simple representation of the supralaryngeal correlates of the VCV sequence; increasing stricture as the fricative is formed, close approximation of the relevant articulators during the fricative, changing to increasingly more open approximation in the transition from the fricative to the following vowel. The bottom part of the diagram gives a simplified representation of the laryngeal activity during the VCV sequence; voicing (represented by the periodic trace) during both vowels, and voicelessness (represented by the flat line) during the VOICELESS fricative.

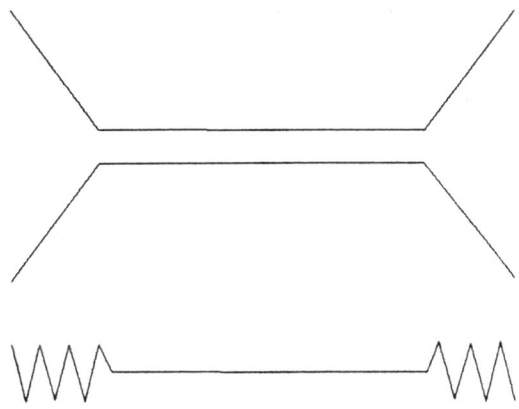

The bulk of the following review consists of a description of observed patterns of timing of voicing in obstruents, and identification of the sources of variability in those patterns. The processes which may explain why certain factors give rise to particular patterns of variability are of central interest to any attempt to account for the timing of voicing in a model of speech production. Discussion of these is deferred until Chapters 3 and 4 so that they can be considered in the context of the experimental results and of the theoretical comments given in Chapter 2.

1.7 SINGLE STOPS

1.7.1 Post-pausal syllable-initial position

In a review of the timing of voicing in stops, it is justified to concentrate on syllable-initial rather than syllable-final stops. The preponderance of voice onset time data over information concerning every other aspect of stop closure/voicing coordination means that more work has been carried out on initial stops than on intervocalic and final stops. A syllable-initial stop with preceding silence or pause, and a following vowel can be represented as in Figure 1.2.

Figure 1.2: A parametric representation of a post-pausal stop. A notional time scale runs horizontally. The top part of the diagram gives a simple representation of the supralaryngeal correlates of the CV sequence; complete closure corresponding to the medial phase of the stop, changing to increasingly more open approximation in the transition from the stop to the following vowel. The bottom part of the diagram gives a simplified representation of three different patterns of the timing of voicing that could be found in the production of the CV sequence; (a) voicing (represented by the periodic trace) commencing during the stop medial phase, (b) voicing commencing at the end of the stop medial phase, (c) voicing commencing after the end of the stop medial phase during the early part of the following vowel. Intervals of voicelessness are represented by the flat line.

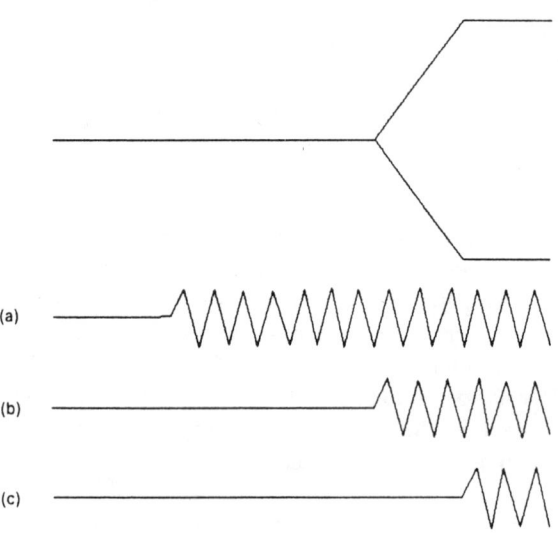

Figure 1.2 also shows the patterns of voicing timing observed to occur in post-pausal, syllable-initial stop consonants in English. In (a), voicing commences

during complete oral closure before the moment of release. In (b), onset of voicing is timed to coincide with the moment of release of the stop closure. In (c), voicing does not start until some time after the release of the stop.

VOICED and VOICELESS stops in English are normally distinguished by their characteristic patterns of timing of voicing onset relative to the medial phase of the stop. In post-pausal VOICELESS stops pattern (c) is observed, with an audible delay between the release of the stop and the onset of voicing (resulting in stops which are aspirated), whereas in post-pausal VOICED stops, patterns (b) or (a) are observed, with voicing commencing at, or around the moment of release, or during the oral closure prior to release.

Given these general trends, which have been noted by a large number of observers,[13] I now consider in greater (quantitative) detail the timing of voicing in relation to the medial phase of initial stops, examining in particular the degree of displacement of voicing onset from the moment of oral release, and how this is affected by certain factors.

1.7.2 VOICELESS stops in post-pausal syllable-initial position

I have stated that voicing in syllable-initial VOICELESS stops normally commences some time after the release of the stop closure. In fact, the timing of voicing in VOICELESS stops is considerably more complex than this suggests. In the literature there are reports of voicing being delayed from a minimum of 28 ms, to a maximum of 90 ms after the moment of release of the stop, with a complete range of values in between these two extremes. Note that these are mean values taken from a large sample, reported in Zlatin (1974) -- the actual minimum and maximum values cited by Zlatin were 10 ms and 220 ms respectively.[14] The degree of delay of voice onset, however, is not a matter of chance, and it is possible to impose a certain amount of order on the wide range of results, and show what factors are likely to lead to a longer or shorter delay. Before considering these factors however, there are a number of procedural matters which must be borne in mind in considering the range of voice onset time measurements reported in the literature.

In the first place, there is a considerable spread of results both within and between speakers. Some of this variability may be accounted for by the fact that only in very few of these investigations was there any control for rate of speech across different speakers, or even within the same speaker.[15] Another procedural source of variation is that the experiments from which the above results are taken, examined stops occurring in a variety of positions and contexts, which, as described below, themselves have an effect on voice onset time, (isolated words read in a list, words embedded in carrier sentences, monosyllabic, and disyllabic words etc.).

A further procedural issue to be considered in this work concerns the measurement criteria employed in the investigation. As was pointed out above, the transition from unvoiced to voiced intervals of speech is not an instantaneous process, and this forces investigators to decide at what point an interval of voicing can be said to have begun or ended. Fischer-Jorgensen & Hutters (1981) have discussed the merits and disadvantages of different segmentation points between voiceless stops and following vowels. They have identified three possible points at which the vowel could be said to have begun; (a) the start of voicing (as indicated by low frequency periodicity in the speech waveform); (b) the start of F1; (c) the start of the higher formants. They point out that all three criteria have been used in studies of voice onset time. Peterson & Lehiste (1960) used point (b) to mark the delay in voice onset, Klatt (1975) and Weismer (1979) used point (c) for the same, and Zue (1976) and Edwards (1981) used point (a).

Fischer-Jorgensen & Hutters were interested in establishing a norm for measuring the onset of vowels in vowel duration experiments, and they argue against the use of point (a), since the presence of low frequency energy does not necessarily mean that the vowel has started; '.. voicing is not a sufficient criterion for vowel start' (1981:86). However, for studies of the timing of voicing, it could be argued that this is a relevant point at which to delimit voice onset time.[16]

In practice, such introspection with regard to the nature and implications of measurements is not common. The measurements performed by most experimenters are, on the whole, constrained by the apparatus which is being used. The presence of vertical striations in spectrograms give a good indication of the occurrence of voicing when the vocal tract is relatively un-occluded, but often, low frequency and low intensity periodicity (such as that found during stop closures and fricatives) is not easily identifiable. Furthermore, measurements based on vertical striations suffer from rather poor time resolution; e.g. to the nearest +/- 10 ms, as acknowledged by Port & Rotunno (1979:655). Measurements taken from a time-waveform can give better resolution, and permit the low frequency periodicity corresponding to voicing to be observed relatively easily. The fact that different experimenters have used a range of measurement criteria must be borne in mind throughout this literature review (further discussion of the means by which the duration of intervals of voicing can be determined is given in Chapter 3).

Effect of place of articulation on voice onset time

There is a sizeable body of data suggesting that one of the main factors influencing voice onset time is the place of articulation of the stop; specifically that the further back in the oral cavity the place of articulation, the longer the voice onset delay. The place-of-articulation effect has been shown in a number of studies (see Tables 1.1 and 1.2).

In one instance, the place effect which has been described breaks down. Peterson & Lehiste (1960) divided their 83 tokens of /k/ (mean voice onset time 75 ms), and analysed the front and back /k/ allophones separately. They discovered that the front allophone had a longer mean voice onset time (78 ms) than the back allophone (72 ms), a finding which runs contrary to the claim that voice onset is delayed longer, the more retracted the place of articulation of the stop.[17]

As confirmation of the point made earlier in this chapter it is noteworthy that the results from Hawkins (1979) and Suomi (1980), shown in Table 1.1, are the only ones pertaining to British English.

Table 1.1: Mean voice onset times (ms) reported for VOICELESS stops in some previous studies of voice onset time in stops.

/p/	/t/	/k/	
34	60	64	(Menyuk & Klatt 1975)
40	43	51	(Baran et al. 1977)
40	55	56	(Suomi 1980)
47	65	70	(Klatt 1975)
47	68	72	(Hawkins 1979)
48	62	78	(Westbury 1979)
53	66	70	(Weismer 1979)
58	69	75	(Peterson & Lehiste 1960)
58	70	80	(Lisker & Abramson 1964)
58	71	74	(Zue 1976)
68	78	84	(Port & Rotunno 1979)
83	87	90	(Zlatin 1974)

Table 1.2: The percentage difference in mean voice onset time as a function of stop place of articulation, as reported in some previous studies of voice onset time in stops.

/p/->/t/	/p/->/k/	/t/->/k/	
5	8	3	(Zlatin 1974)
8	28	18	(Baran et al. 1977)
14	23	7	(Port & Rotunno 1978)
19	30	9	(Peterson & Lehiste 1960)
20	38	14	(Lisker & Abramson 1964)
22	28	4	(Zue 1976)
24	32	7	(Weismer 1979)
29	63	26	(Westbury 1979)
38	49	8	(Klatt 1975)
38	40	2	(Suomi 1980)
45	53	6	(Hawkins 1979)

Effect of vowel quality on voice onset time

Another factor which has been shown to influence voice onset time in VOICELESS stops is the quality of the following vowel. The claim by Lisker & Abramson (1967) that vocalic environment has no significant effect on voice onset time finds support in Zue (1976), but has been questioned in a number of reports. Klatt (1975) noted that voice onset time for /p/, /t/, and /k/ was 15% longer before high vowels than before /ai/ and /ɛ/. Ohala (1981) presents data showing the same effect, and in particular, showing some relatively large vowel-quality induced differences -- e.g. the mean voice onset time for /pi/ is approximately 85 ms, whereas the mean for /pa/ is around 40 ms. Summerfield (1975) found significantly longer voice onset times in /ki/ than in /ka/ (embedded in sentences), with the difference being on average less than 10 ms. He reported no significant difference between /pi/ and /pa/, although there was a tendency for there to be longer voice onset times in /pa/ than in /pi/.

Weismer (1979) set out to test the effect on voice onset time of whether a following vowel was tense or lax. It was found that voice onset times are longer when the following vowel is tense, than when the following vowel is lax, although he did underline that whilst the difference is significant, it is quantitatively quite small (less than 10 ms). In the light of Klatt's results, it is interesting that Weismer reported no relationship between voice onset time and tongue height, except in the case of /k/, which had a longer voice onset time before high than before mid vowels. Weismer's results concerning tense/lax vowels are matched by those of Port & Rotunno (1979), who found that mean voice onset time is 11% shorter before lax vowels than before tense vowels (i.e. a difference of less than 10 ms, based, incidentally, on measurements which were accurate only to the nearest 10 ms). Nolan & Johnson (unpublished ms, cited in Watson 1983) have reported a similar effect for voice onset time in German.

There is some difficulty involved in evaluating these findings regarding the effect of tense/lax vowels on voice onset time. The chief problem is uncertainty about what the labels 'tense' and 'lax' signify in phonetic terms with respect to vowel production. This issue is reviewed in some detail by Catford (1977:204ff) who concludes that:

> tense and lax may, perhaps, be usefully employed as labels to designate phonetically arbitrary classes of vowels that happen to be phonologically distinct. But it should then be made quite clear that the selection of terms may be phonetically vacuous. (1977:208).

Neither Weismer nor Port address this matter in any detail, and as result it is difficult to know which phonetic factors corresponding to the tense/lax label they consider to be the source of their observations.

Effect of position of stop on voice onset time

Voice onset time has also been investigated in relation to the position of the stop in the test utterance, and the type of test utterance produced by subjects. Lisker & Abramson (1964, 1967) asked their subjects to read a list of words with initial stops, and then to make up sentences which contained the same words occurring initially in the sentence and somewhere in the middle of the sentence. They discovered that the voice onset times were considerably longer in the words read in a list than in the same words read in sentences. The results of the sentence condition utterances are shown in Table 1.3, and may be compared with the results for stops in words read as a list shown in Table 1.1. However, whilst the type of utterance did affect the degree of voice onset delay, Lisker and Abramson noted that the position of the word within a sentence, that is whether it is in initial or medial position, had no significant effect on the voice onset times observed.

Further data on voice onset time in words spoken in citation form compared to words embedded in continuous speech is provided by Baran et al. (1977) who found shorter voice onset times for VOICELESS stops, and longer voice onset times for VOICED stops in continuous speech than in words produced in isolation. In citation forms the size of the difference between the mean voice onset times for homorganic stops was (on average) 80 ms, whereas in continuous speech, this difference was reduced to 30 ms.

Table 1.3: Voice onset times (ms) in English VOICELESS stops in sentences reported by Lisker & Abramson (1964).

	/p/	/t/	/k/
Mean	28	39	43
Min:Max	10:45	15:70	30:85
n	24	26	25

Other effects on voice onset time

Two other important contextual factors which have been shown to affect voice onset time are whether the following vowel is stressed, and the number of syllables in a word. Lisker & Abramson (1967) observed that stops with a following stressed vowel had a longer voice onset time than those with a following unstressed vowel. This was the case equally in lists of words, and words in sentences, but in the latter, the degree of unstressed shortening was less. Klatt (1975) presents a rule describing the timing of voicing in VOICELESS plosives which are not 'prestressed' (this term can be interpreted as referring to stops with a following unstressed vowel), in which the voice onset times are shortened by a factor of 60% of their stressed value. This amount of compression is far in excess of that suggested by Lisker & Abramson, but Klatt presents no data illustrating the actual differences in means which this shortening gave rise to.

Most of the test words used in the literature consulted are CVC words with the first consonant being the stop under investigation. In addition to a set of CVC words, Klatt (1975) also investigated some disyllabic test words read in a carrier sentence, and found that the voice onset time was, on average, 8% shorter in a disyllabic word than in the corresponding monosyllabic word. Westbury (1979) is another exception, in that all his measurements on single initial stops were taken from disyllabic words. However, in his experiments, he did not perform comparisons of the timing of voicing in monosyllabic and disyllabic words.

A factor affecting voice onset time, which was not considered in the earlier papers, but which has since received a certain amount of attention from Weismer (1979) and Port & Rotunno (1979), is the effect of the voicing characteristic of the final consonant in a CVC word on the voice onset time of the first consonant. Weismer found that the voice onset time of the first stop in a CVC word was longer if the second consonant was VOICED than if the second consonant was VOICELESS. He pointed out that the effect, whilst significant, was quite small (less than 10 ms).[18] Port & Rotunno set out to ascertain whether voice onset time and vowel duration varied in proportion to one another (as the result of a single 'rule') or whether they were manipulated separately. In a near-replication of Weismer's experiment, they confirmed his results, finding longer voice onset times in CVC words ending in a nasal, than in CVC words ending in a voiceless cluster (/pt/). However, they calculated a shortening factor of 20%, which is rather greater than that suggested by Weismer's data.

Both Weismer's and Port & Rotunno's data suggested that the slight lengthening of voice onset time observed in these experiments was not simply due to the lengthening of the vowel before a syllable-final VOICED consonant (i.e. it was not the case that voice onset time changed in proportion to changes in the duration of a following vowel -- vowel duration changed a good deal across the different conditions, whereas voice onset time changed very little).[19] This is in accord with a finding reported in the earlier study by Klatt (1975:694).

1.7.3 VOICED stops in post-pausal syllable-initial position

Initial VOICED stops in English are characterised by voicing timing patterns of type (a) (shown in Figure 1.2) with voicing commencing during the closure phase (often referred to as **prevoiced** stops), or type (b), voicing commencing at or around the moment of release of the stop.

Table 1.4 shows the principal results concerning voice onset time in VOICED stops which have been reported in the literature. In the table, type (a) is referred to as 'voicing lead', and type (b) as 'short lag.' Lisker & Abramson (1964, 1967) noted that both types of voicing timing occurred in their subjects' performance, but the proportion of stops produced with a short voicing lag was far greater than that of stops with voicing prior to stop release. They also discovered that one speaker out of the four who provided their data was responsible for 95% of the prevoiced stops, suggesting that speakers do not arbitrarily choose one of the two forms of timing, but have a preference for one form or the other. Smith (1978) did not succeed in confirming these earlier results. He found that in a sample of 1200 initial VOICED stops, read by 20 speakers, 52% were produced with a short voicing lag, and 48% were produced with voicing commencing during the closure phase of the stop. Westbury (1979) reported an even greater proportion of prevoiced stops than

Table 1.4: Mean voice onset times (ms) in English VOICED stops as reported in the literature.

		Voicing Lead			Short Lag		
		X	s.d.	%	X	s.d.	%
	/b/	-82.5	31.7	62	11.6	6.4	38
[1]	/d/	-92.6	29.4	55	18.3	4.9	45
	/g/	-68.6	27.3	53	30.0	11.5	47
	/b/	-	-	-	2	4	-
[2]	/d/	-	-	-	7	6	-
	/g/	-	-	-	15	7	-
	/b/	0.7	26.1	-			
[3]	/d/	16.3	8.9	-	(Includes both types of timing)		
	/g/	18.0	19.1	-			
		(Conversation)					
	/b/	8.8	4.3	-			
[3]	/d/	11.4	8.0	-	(Includes both types of timing)		
	/g/	20.7	6.5	-			
		(Word lists)					
[4]	/b/	-114	37	59	-	-	-
	/b/	-	-	-	13	3	-
[5]	/d/	-	-	-	19	5	-
	/g/	-	-	-	30	5	-
	/b/	-	-	-	3	-	-
[6]	/d/	-	-	-	11	-	-
	/g/	-	-	-	20	-	-
	/b/	-	-	-	11	-	-
[7]	/d/	-	-	-	17	-	-
	/g/	-	-	-	27	-	-
[8]	/d/	-79	-	41	15	-	59
	/b/	-	-	-	12	-	-
[9]	/d/	-	-	-	15	-	-
	/g/	-	-	-	23	-	-
[10]	/b,d,g/	-70	-	48	19	-	52
		(Pooled across place categories)					
	/b/	-101	-	23	1	-	67
[11]	/d/	-102	-	21	5	-	79
	/g/	-88	-	25	21	-	75
		(Isolated words)					
	/b/	-65	-	8	7	-	92
	/d/	-56	-	6	9	-	94
	/g/	-45	-	1	17	-	99
		(Word-initial, sentence-medial)					

[1] Westbury (1979), [2] Suomi (1980), [3] Baran et al. (1977), [4] Flege (1982), [5] Zue (1976), [6] Kewley-Port (1982)*, [7] Klatt (1975), [8] Lorge (1967), [10] Smith (1978), [11] Menyuk & Klatt (1975), [11] Lisker & Abramson (1964).

* Kewley-Port's results do not appear to contain any cases of prevoicing. However, this is not explicitly stated in the text of the article

Smith, with 56.6% of his corpus produced with prevoicing, and 43.3% with short lag.

Despite this discrepancy in the observed proportions of the two types of voicing timing, in Smith's and Westbury's results, it was observed that whilst speakers showed a preference for using one type more than the other, in no case did any subject use one type exclusively, and in many cases there appeared to be free variation in the subjects' use of the two types of voicing timing. Surprisingly (in the light of these findings), Klatt's (1975) results do not, apparently, contain any cases of prevoicing, and there is very little discussion of the two different types of voicing timing observed in previous studies. Zue (1976) discards cases of prevoicing from his database, because it is 'not a phonemic determinant of English' (1976:46). On the basis of the figures quoted by Smith and Westbury, it could well be the case that Zue is excluding from his study as many as half the tokens of initial VOICED stops.[20]

It is clear then that there is a bimodal distribution of voice onset times in syllable-initial VOICED stops in English, and that the same speaker may use both types.[21] However, Smith (1978) suggests that there are certain conditions that are more conducive to the occurrence of prevoicing, than to short lag. He noted that both the frequency of occurrence of prevoicing and the duration of prevoicing were higher for labial and dental stops, ('Dental' is the term used by Smith to refer to the place of articulation of [t] and [d]) than for velar stops (56% of labials are prevoiced, 50% of dentals and 39% of velars -- the mean durations of prevoicing were 74 ms for labials, 71 ms for dentals, and 65 ms for velars -- figures not matched by Westbury (1979), see below). On the other hand the frequency of occurrence of short lag went in the reverse order, being greatest in velars, least in labials, and intermediate in dentals.

Smith also noted that the vocalic environment had some effect on the frequency of occurrence of the two types of voice timing. He found that high vowels were associated with voicing lead 54% of the time, but the proportion of voicing lead in stops followed by low vowels was only 43%. Conversely, there was a greater occurrence of short lag in stops with a low vowel context, and fewer cases of short lag in stops with a high vowel context.

In both modes of voicing timing, the place of articulation of the consonant has been shown to affect the duration of the displacement of voice onset from the moment of stop release. Zlatin (1974) noted that the further back the place of articulation, the shorter the duration of prevoicing, and the longer the duration of the short lag (in this second case there is strong similarity with the place effect in VOICELESS stops described above). These tendencies are supported by evidence in Lisker & Abramson (1964, 1967), Smith (1978), Klatt (1975), and Zue (1976), although there is a considerable discrepancy between the results achieved by the different researchers. Westbury's figures, however, suggest that whilst the frequency of occurrence of prevoicing is greater (and consequently, the frequency of occurrence of short lag is smaller) the further back the place of articulation of the stop, the **duration** of prevoicing and short lag increases and decreases respectively in the order alveolar - labial- velar.

1.7.4 Stops in intervocalic position

The timing of voicing in intervocalic stops is an area which has received very little experimental attention. This is possibly because in the case of intervocalic stops, an account of voice onset time only paints part of the picture regarding the timing of voicing, and as was suggested above, areas other than voice onset time have not been the object of very much experimentation. The four major patterns of timing that we might identify in a parametric description of the timing of voicing in intervocalic stops are shown in Figure 1.3.

There is evidence in the literature for the existence of all four patterns in English. The type of voicing timing that occurs is determined by whether the stop is VOICED or VOICELESS, and by whether the VCV sequence occurs within a word, or whether there is a word-boundary between the medial consonant and one of the vowels.

VOICELESS stops in intervocalic position

There is some evidence in the literature that voicing continues from a preceding voiced sound into the early part of the closure phase of a VOICELESS stop. This has been studied instrumentally in British English by Suomi (1980), who noted that voicing continued into the closure phase of VOICELESS stops for around 10 ms. This was the case irrespective of the place of articulation of the stop. Suomi suggests that a place effect would be expected if the cessation of voicing was conditioned aerodynamically, with greater degrees of voicing continuation, the further forward the place of articulation of the stop. That is, if voicing in these sequences ceases as a result of an equalisation of trans-glottal pressure, this would occur more rapidly if the oral occlusion was towards the back of the oral cavity, than if it was it the lips. Suomi interprets his results as suggesting that the offset of voicing is an indication of the beginning of the glottal abduction gesture. This interpretation is examined further in the light of the experimental results reported in Chapter 3.

Figure 1.3: A parametric representation of an intervocalic stop. A notional time scale runs horizontally. The top part of the diagram relates to the degree of approximation, and gives a simple representation of the supralaryngeal correlates of the VCV sequence; increasing stricture as the stop closure is formed, complete closure corresponding to the stop medial phase, changing to increasingly more open approximation in the transition from the stop to the following vowel. The bottom part of the diagram gives a simplified representation of four different patterns of timing of voicing which could be found in the production of the VCV sequence; (a) voicing (represented by the periodic trace) taking place throughout the stop medial phase; (b) voicing terminating after the start of the stop medial phase; (c) voicelessness (represented by the flat line) throughout the stop medial phase; (d) voicing commencing before the end of the stop medial phase.

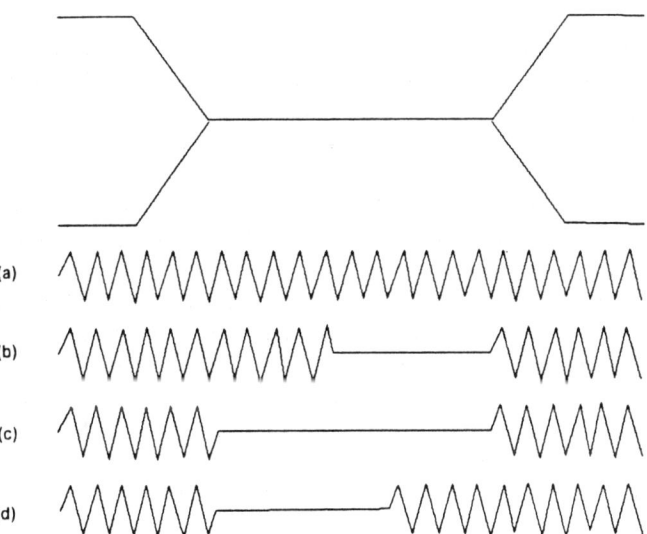

As for American English, Westbury (1979) reported a greater degree of incursion of voicing into a VOICELESS stop closure phase than Suomi. He examined single stops in the medial position of nonsense disyllables (see Table 1.5). In common with Suomi's findings, Westbury's results do not suggest that the amount of voicing continuation is proportional to the distance between the vocal folds and the place of occlusion. Westbury also found that the vowel environment has some effect on the amount of voicing continuation. Voicing would continue for longer when the preceding vowel was /I/ compared to when the preceding vowel was /a/. Edwards (1981), and Keating (1984b) also reported a certain amount of incursion of voicing into intervocalic stops, averaging 25 ms, across 10 speakers in the former case, and averaging less than 10 ms, across 6 speakers in the latter case.

Table 1.5: Mean duration (ms) of intervals of medial voicing in intervocalic VOICELESS stop medial phase, as reported in Westbury (1979).

	/p/	/t/	/k/
Mean	20.0	27.3	27.0
s.d.	10.7	10.3	11.0

VOICED stops in intervocalic position

In word-medial intervocalic VOICED stops, voicing normally continues unbroken throughout the medial phase of the stop. Flege & Brown (1982) reported unbroken voicing in 82% of their cases of intervocalic VOICED stops. Westbury (1979) found that only in 15 cases out 432, was voicing interrupted in intervocalic VOICED stops. Suomi (1980) looked at British English VOICED stops preceded by vowels, not only in word-medial position (disyllabic words), but also in word-initial, and word-final position (in monosyllables in the carrier phrase 'Say ____ loudly'.) In line with Flege & Brown and Westbury, he found that in word-medial position, there were very few cases of voicing ceasing before the end of the stop closure (only 11 out 144 - 7%). However, he found a considerably higher occurrence of interrupted voicing in word-final intervocalic VOICED stops (76 out of 213 cases - 36%), and especially in word-initial intervocalic VOICED stops (201 out 294 cases - 68%). In the instances in which there was a break in voicing, periodicity would continue into the stop medial phase for a longer interval than in VOICELESS stops. Normally, voicing would continue for the first 50% to 60% of the closure duration before stopping.

Hanninen (1979)[22] has produced similar results regarding the timing of voicing in intervocalic word-medial stops. In data from three speakers of British English, it was found that word-medial VOICELESS stops had no incursion of voicing, on average, whereas word-medial VOICED stops were almost all completely voiced throughout (mean duration of stops = 68 ms: mean duration of voicing continuation = 65 ms). Edwards (1981) in a study of the acoustic characteristics of intervocalic VOICED and VOICELESS stops found that voicing would continue into the medial phase of VOICED stops (which had a mean duration of 96 ms) for an average interval of 78 ms. These results suggest that not even in intervocalic position are VOICED stops inevitably fully voiced in English.

1.7.5 Pre-pausal final stops

If we consider the case of a final stop consonant in which the closure is released, three main categories of voicing timing can be identified; (a) voicing continues throughout the stop closure and into the release phase. (b) voicing ceases completely at the onset of oral closure for the stop. (c) voicing continues during the stop closure, and ceases at some point before the release (see Figure 1.4). Whilst text-books describing the pronunciation of English make claims about the nature of voicing in final stops (see example below), this area has scarcely been the object of the sort of instrumental investigation which would permit us to say which of the three categories outlined above occur, how frequently they occur, and under what circumstances.

Auditory analysis suggests that pre-pausal VOICED and VOICELESS stops in English cannot be reliably distinguished on the basis of the existence and/or the duration of voicing during the closure phase.[23] This is a reflection of the fact that type (a) is rarely observed in English. Jones (1960) notes that final VOICED plosives are often totally or partially 'devoiced'. In a similar vein, Roach (1983) points out that final VOICED stops in English contain little voicing, and that if it occurs at all, it is normally only in the early stage of the closure phase.

A certain amount of instrumental confirmation of what has been discovered by auditory analysis has come from work carried out to investigate the cues to the phonological voicing category of a final stop (Denes 1955, Chen 1970, Raphael 1972). However, whilst these reports provide good evidence that voicing in a final VOICED stop may not be as perceptually salient in English as other cues, such as vowel duration, they do not really advance our knowledge regarding the types of voicing timing which are characteristic of the phonetic **realisation** of final VOICED and VOICELESS obstruents in English. One of the aims of the experiments reported in this study is to obtain data which goes some way towards filling this gap.

1.7.6 Summary

This review of studies of the timing of voicing in relation to the pre-closure, closure, and release phases of stop consonants shows that the following factors are sources of significant variability; whether the stop is VOICED or VOICELESS, its place of articulation, whether the following vowel is stressed or not, position of the stop in a word, number of syllables in a word, speaker identity. The following factors have given rise either to inconsistent findings or to differences that are extremely small (in some cases within the resolution of the measurements taken); speech rate, vowel quality, whether the second consonant in a CVC word is VOICED or VOICELESS, whether a word is produced in isolation or in a sentence. This suggests that, in general, there are three types of factor that can affect the timing of voicing in stops; properties of the stop itself (whether it is VOICED or VOICELESS, and its place of articulation), properties of the adjacent context, and more global temporal and prosodic factors such as rate and stress. The experiments described later in this book investigate the effects of the first two factors on the timing of voicing in SBE.

Figure 1.4: A parametric representation of a pre-pausal stop. A notional time scale runs horizontally. The top part of the diagram relates to the degree of approximation, and gives a simple representation of the supralaryngeal correlates of the VC sequence; increasing stricture as the stop closure is formed, complete closure corresponding to the stop medial phase, changing to increasingly more open approximation as the final stop is released (indicated with a broken line due to the fact that final stops are not always released). The bottom part of the diagram gives a simplified representation of three different patterns of timing of voicing which could be found in the production of the VC sequence; (a) voicing (represented by the periodic trace) taking place throughout the stop medial phase; (b) voicing terminating after the start of the stop medial phase; (c) voicelessness (represented by the flat line) throughout the stop medial phase.

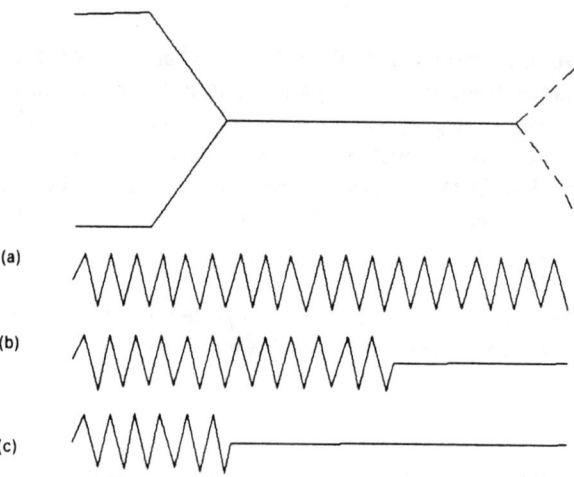

1.8 FRICATIVES

The timing of voicing in relation to supralaryngeal activity in fricatives has received far less attention than that given to single stops. The set of fricatives may be represented parametrically as in Figure 1.5. The bottom section of the diagram depicts some of the types of voicing timing which could hypothetically occur in VOICED and VOICELESS fricatives.[24]

Figure 1.5: A parametric representation of an intervocalic fricative. A notional time scale runs horizontally. The top part of the diagram relates to the degree of approximation, and gives a simple representation of the supralaryngeal correlates of the VCV sequence; increasing stricture as the fricative is formed, close approximation of the articulators during the fricative, changing to increasingly more open approximation in the transition from the fricative to the following vowel. The bottom part of the diagram gives a simplified representation of four different patterns of timing of voicing which could be found in the production of the VCV sequence; (a) voicing (represented by the periodic trace) taking place throughout the fricative medial phase; (b) voicelessness (represented by the flat line) throughout the fricative medial phase; (c) voicing terminating after the start of the fricative medial phase; (d) voicing commencing before the end of the fricative medial phase.

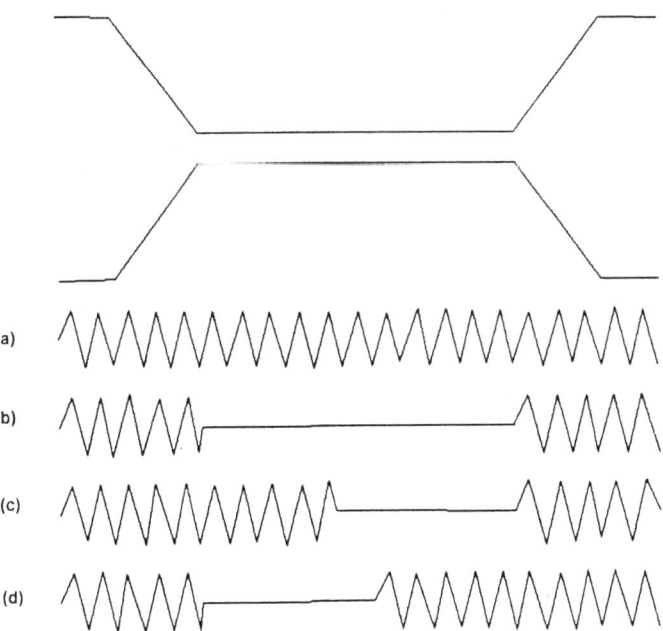

1.8.1 VOICELESS fricatives

There are virtually no reports in the literature on the timing of voicing in English VOICELESS fricatives. Klatt (1975) noted a short period of what he terms 'aspiration' (lasting 12 ms), in the transition phase between a word-initial /s/ and following vowel. However, as Klatt (1975:693) himself points out, it is quite possible that there is alveolar frication during that period, but that its level has fallen below the detection threshold of the spectrograph, and therefore it is not visible on the spectrogram.

An alternative explanation is that this interval of 'aspiration' appeared merely as a function of the measurement criteria adopted by Klatt. As has already been pointed out, Fischer-Jorgensen & Hutters (1981) suggest that the onset of energy in the higher formants (the criterion used by Klatt for marking voice onset) is a reasonable point for marking the onset of a post-stop vowel, but that in some instances, vocal fold vibration will have started prior to this instant in time. So the very short delay in voice onset described by Klatt may well have disappeared if a different segmentation point had been chosen. The difficulties involved in defining the class of fricative consonants have already been discussed, in Section 1.2.3. It is clear that the voicing timing patterns that are observed in this case depend on the definitions of 'fricative' and 'voicing' which are adopted.

Scully & Allwood (1985) carried out a study of the timing of voicing in /s/ and /z/ in British English, in order to compare the results with the same fricatives produced by an articulatory synthesiser. Their five subjects were asked to repeat the words his and hiss six times in a carrier phrase 'a ___ it said'. Their results showed that for all speakers, the VOICELESS fricative was consistently produced without voicing during its medial phase (results for the VOICED fricatives are given below). Hanninen (1979) investigated the timing of voicing in fricatives in word-initial, word-medial, and word-final position. In accord with the findings of other researchers, it was found that the VOICELESS set were consistently produced without any voicing during their medial phase.

There are no other reports of a delay in the onset of voicing in English syllable-initial VOICELESS fricatives, and likewise, no reports of any encroachment of voicing from an adjacent vowel or sonorant into the interval of high frequency noise associated with the fricative. The experimental results reported in Chapter 3 allow some consideration of why there appears to be a certain amount of incursion of voicing from a voiced context into the medial phase of VOICELESS **stop** consonants, whereas in VOICELESS **fricatives** in the same environment, no voicing incursion takes place.

1.8.2 VOICED fricatives

The timing of voicing in VOICED fricatives is rather more complex. Auditory analysis of initial and final VOICED fricatives suggests that they are not voiced throughout the period of close approximation, and in some cases hardly at all (Jones 1960:203, Abercrombie 1967:137). The only instrumental investigation dedicated to voicing in English VOICED fricatives was carried out by Haggard (1978). He examined word-initial, word-final,[25] and intervocalic VOICED fricatives, occurring before stressed and unstressed vowels, and adjacent to a VOICED or VOICELESS stop. His results showed that there was a good deal of variation in the mean percentage of the fricative that is voiceless,[26] ranging from 100% in every case of a VOICED fricative occurring before a VOICELESS stop, to only 8% in /v/ occurring intervocalically before an unstressed vowel. In not a single case were all the tokens of a fricative voiced throughout the duration of the interval of close approximation.

Haggard concluded that the timing of voicing in VOICED fricatives could not be attributed entirely to free variation. He identified a number of factors which influenced the duration of intervals of voicing associated with VOICED fricatives. The place of articulation of a fricative was a significant factor with /dʒ/ (presumably Haggard is referring only to the fricative component of this affricate) showing shorter intervals of medial voicing than /z/, which in turn had a consistently less medial voicing than /v/. Haggard's data also showed that the context and position of the fricative had an effect on the timing of voicing. In all cases, there were shorter intervals of medial voicing when the fricative occurred after a VOICED stop, than when it occurred intervocalically. Likewise, VOICED fricatives were completely voiceless when followed by a VOICELESS stop, and between 90-100% voiceless when they occurred in a word-final position. VOICED fricatives in intervocalic position produced the longest intervals of medial voicing, and word-initial fricatives showed intervals of medial voicing of intermediate duration, slightly shorter than the intervocalic set. Whether surrounding vowels were stressed or unstressed proved to have no systematic effect.

Haggard's findings have been backed up in more limited investigations by Hardcastle & Clark (1981), Scully & Allwood (1985), and Hanninen (1979). Hardcastle & Clark carried out a range of physiological and acoustic measurements on VOICED fricatives in intervocalic and pre-pausal position (they used only two subjects, and nonsense words). Their acoustic results indicated that the intervocalic fricatives showed 'strong periodicity' (:76), whilst the final fricatives showed little sign of periodicity. Scully and Allwood, looking at intervocalic /z/, found that the fricative was produced with varying amounts of voicing according to the subject. One subject consistently voiced the entire medial phase of the fricative, whereas another subject, on average, 'devoiced' 95% of the duration of the /z/ medial phase. Hanninen's results confirm those of Haggard which relate to the effect of fricative position on the timing of voicing. It was found that the shortest intervals of medial voicing were found in word-final fricatives, with an average of only about 25% of the fricative being accompanied by voicing. VOICED fricatives occurring word-medially and word-initially showed longer intervals of medial voicing, with, on average, 93% and 89% of their respective medial phase being voiced.

To summarise these findings of the small number of studies of voicing in VOICED fricatives, the shortest intervals of medial voicing seems to occur in final VOICED fricatives, and in VOICED fricatives followed by a VOICELESS stop (greater than 90% voiceless in both cases). In word-initial position, intervocalically, and following a VOICED stop, there are longer intervals of medial voicing (greater than 50% in all cases). In all cases, the place of articulation of a fricative can affect the duration of any medial voicing which takes place.

1.9 CONSONANT SEQUENCES

In describing the timing of voicing in sequences of consonants many writers use terms such as 'assimilation' of voicing or voicelessness (which can be progressive or regressive), or 'devoicing'. The use of different terms to refer to the timing of voicing in single consonant and consonant sequences (e.g. vowels which follow aspirated stops are never referred to as 'devoiced') does not seem to be motivated out of descriptive and theoretical rigour, since in both cases, the object of the description is the same; namely the timing of intervals of voicing with respect to supralaryngeal gestures. Hence, in describing the timing of voicing in consonant sequences, I adopt the same procedure as in single obstruents, and discuss the temporal coordination of intervals of voicing with respect to the medial phase of the two consonants concerned, without invoking different terminology. Given a sequence of two consonants, one VOICED and the other VOICELESS, there is a variety of possible patterns of voicing timing which could hypothetically occur. Some of these are shown in Figure 1.6.

There is a good deal of between-language and -accent variation regarding which types of voicing timing occur. The types which are normally observed in Southern British English are described below. Abercrombie (1967:136) discusses some of the differences between accents of English spoken in

England and Scotland, Laver (1968) provides further examples of accentual variation from educated Nigerian English, and Kerswill (1984) notes differences between the accent of English spoken in Durham and 'R.P.'. There has been scarcely any controlled instrumental investigation of this type of coordinatory activity in English consonant sequences. However, a review of what little has been carried out permits the following conclusions to be drawn.

Figure 1.6: A parametric representation of some possible patterns of timing of voicing in sequences of VOICED (+V) and VOICELESS (-V) consonants. In (i) C1 is VOICED and C2 is VOICELESS. In (ii) C1 is VOICELESS and C2 is VOICED. The vertical line represents the boundary between C1 and C2. In (a), each consonant is voiced according to its phonological voicing category; in (b) the VOICED consonant is completely 'devoiced'; in (c) the VOICELESS consonant is completely voiced; in (d) the VOICED consonant is partially 'devoiced'; in (e) the VOICELESS consonant is partially voiced.

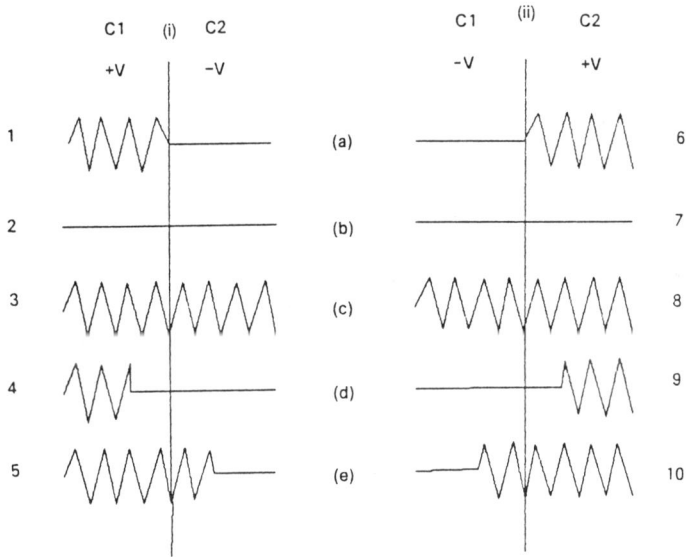

1.9.1 Patterns of voicing used in English consonant sequences

Speakers of English use more than one type of voicing timing in their production of mixed (i.e. VOICED/VOICELESS) consonant sequences. Late[27] onset of voicing in a VOICELESS-VOICED sequence is the most frequently noted; for example, by auditory phoneticians such as Jones (1960) and Gimson (1980). Jones (1960:217) notes that 'particularly breathed' varieties of /m,n,l,r,w,j/ are used when they follow a VOICELESS obstruent in a stressed syllable (by 'particularly breathed' Jones can be understood as meaning that there is a delay in voice onset after the medial phase of the obstruent). As is pointed out below, the occurrence of voice onset delay in such sequences is not as restricted as Jones suggests (it may also occur across a word boundary, or when the first consonant is VOICED). This type of voicing timing has been investigated instrumentally to a certain extent by Klatt (1975), Bladon & Al-Bamerni (1976), Zue (1976), Barry & Kunzel (1978), Hawkins (1979), and Dent (1984).

Early offset of voicing in a VOICED-VOICELESS sequence is another type of voicing timing which has been noted by auditory phoneticians (for example by Jones 1960) in cases of 'juxtapositional assimilation of voicing' as in George can, with some, newspaper (see discussion in 1.8.2 of final VOICED fricatives occurring before VOICELESS consonants). This has been the subject of an instrumental investigation by Westbury (1979) which is discussed below.

1.9.2 Instrumental studies

Studies by Thorsen and Westbury

One of the most notable studies of voicing in sequences of VOICED and VOICELESS consonants in British English is that reported by Thorsen (1971). Thorsen draws the following conclusions which conform to what has been noted in other less-specific studies. Intervals of voicing in the medial phase of VOICELESS consonants, whether spreading from a preceding or following context, are of short duration. Early offset of voicing for VOICED consonants (timing pattern 4 in Figure 1.7) only affects VOICED fricatives, whereas late onset of voicing (timing patterns 7/9) occurs frequently, affecting stops and fricatives. Thorsen also noted that a consonant 'preserves its voicing characteristic better' (1971:25) when it is adjacent to a stressed vowel than when it is adjacent to an unstressed vowel.

Westbury (1979) has provided one of the most important studies of the timing of voicing in sequences of stops in (American) English. His investigation focused on intervals of voicing during mixed word-medial stop sequences ('mixed' means that the cluster consists of a VOICED and a VOICELESS element). His results come from 10 subjects who produced a list of English disyllables of the form C'VCCV(C). He classifies the patterns of voicing timing which he observes by identifying internal and external voicing components. The former are delimited by any change from voiced to voiceless (or vice versa) within the medial phase of the stop sequence concerned. The latter are defined by changes in voicing during the onset and offset phases of the sequence concerned (this useful descriptive framework breaks free from the idea that voice onset time is the only interesting descriptor of the timing of voicing -- see Chapter 5 where I explore a similar approach to the description of the timing of voicing).

In VOICED-VOICELESS clusters, he found that late offset of voicing (timing pattern 4) took place very regularly, but there were only a small number of cases in which the medial phase of the VOICELESS consonant was completely voiced (5%), and that in all cases (including those with complete 'assimilation'), there was a long delay in voice onset time following the second element of the cluster ensuring a VOICELESS percept. (The fact that there was consistently a long voice onset time, even after fully 'assimilated' realisations suggests that, despite the way in which the VOICELESS sound was realised, there was still no alteration of its underlying form - i.e. it was still phonologically VOICELESS.)

Westbury found that the duration of voicing during the cluster medial phase was longest when the second element was an alveolar, and shortest when the second element was a velar, with labials falling between these two extremes. He concluded that clusters of this sort consisted of two internal voicing components (voicing, followed by voicelessness), and one external voicing component (a long delay in voice onset).

In VOICELESS-VOICED sequences, Westbury found much less regularity. There was a large amount of between-speaker variation regarding the timing pattern used. However, there were no cases of early onset of voicing (timing pattern 8). The results were best explained by relating them to the results of single post-pausal VOICED stops. Speakers who prevoiced these also had some prevoicing in VOICED stops in VOICELESS-VOICED sequences. Speakers who tended not to prevoice their single VOICED stops, did not prevoice their VOICED stops in these sequences. It was concluded that there were two main types of voicing timing in VOICELESS-VOICED stop sequences, analogous to those observed for single stops. Subjects who prevoiced their stops would have three internal timing components (voicing continuation, silent interval, prevoicing), whereas those who produced VOICED stops with a short delay in voice onset would have two internal components (voicing continuation and a silent interval), and one external component (short delay in voice onset time).

Studies of obstruent-sonorant sequences

Most of the work carried out on the timing of voicing in consonant clusters deals with obstruent-sonorant sequences (once again chiefly in accents of American English). In VOICELESS obstruent-sonorant sequences there is a period following the release of a stop or a fricative, in which the following VOICED sound is not accompanied by vocal fold vibration (experimental data showing the nature of this process in SBE is presented in Chapters 3 and 4). In VOICED stop-sonorant sequences there is also a (shorter) interval following the release of the stop for which the onset of voicing is delayed. It seems then that the timing of voicing with respect to the release of a stop is approximately the same, regardless of whether the following segment is a vowel or another consonant (although, in all of the stop-sonorant sequences, this delay in voice onset is longer than that found in the same stop occurring in a stop-vowel sequence).[28] The delay in voice onset observed following VOICELESS fricatives in fricative-sonorant sequences is, however, rather different to the pattern of voicing timing observed in fricative-vowel sequences.

It has been shown that there is a large amount of variation in the timing of voicing which occurs in these sequences, and that two factors which are important in determining that variation are the identity of both the first and second element of the sequence, and the nature of the boundary that lies between the two elements.

The effect of stop voicing category and sonorant identity can be seen in data from Hawkins (1979), Klatt (1975) and Zue (1976). Hawkins (1979) measured voice onset time in initial stop-/l/ and stop-/r/ clusters, and found a range of onset delays, from 51 ms in /pr/, to 104.3 ms in /tr/. Klatt (1975) measured the voice onset time in approximately the same set of clusters, and found a similar pattern of results, with the smallest delay in /pr/ 59 ms, and the longest in /tw/ 102 ms (not examined by Hawkins). Zue (1976) compared the voice onset times for single VOICED and VOICELESS stops when they occur in a cluster before a sonorant, with the voice onset times of the same set of stops occurring before a vowel. In VOICED stops in clusters, the mean voice onset time, averaging across place of articulation was 26.3 ms, which represents an increase of 28% on the mean voice onset time of the stops occurring singly. The greatest percentage increase was in the alveolar stops (i.e. in /dr/ sequences) - 37%. In VOICELESS stops, the mean voice onset time in clusters, averaging across place of articulation, was 85.6 ms, an increase of 27% on the mean voice onset time of the stops occurring singly. As in the VOICED stops, the greatest percentage increase was recorded in the set of alveolar stops - 40%.

The effect of the manner of articulation of the obstruent in VOICELESS obstruent-sonorant sequences has been described by Jones (1960:220) who suggests that there are greater delays in voice onset in this type of cluster when the first consonant is a stop than when it is a fricative, a claim which has found some instrumental confirmation in the work of Bladon & Al-Bamerni (1976) and Dent (1984).

It has also been claimed that the timing of voicing in stop-sonorant sequences is sensitive to the boundary which lies between the two consonants. This is the subject of the study described in Chapter 4 of this book. Gimson (1980:287) claims that delayed voice onset in VOICELESS stop-sonorant sequences only occurs when the sequence is word-internal, except when 'the sequence of words forms a close knit entity - a phrasal word or a rhythmic group'. Brown (1977:69) states even more categorically that there is no 'assimilation of voicing' across word boundaries, the only exception cited being the case of VOICED consonants becoming voiceless as a result of the elision of an adjacent schwa. Both these positions can be traced back to a paper by Jones (1931), where he essentially makes the same point and lists pairs distinguished by, amongst other features, the presence or absence of a delay in voice onset (e.g. my train vs might rain; grey trout vs great rout; lie quiet vs like Wyatt.

A further claim which has been made concerning boundary-sensitivity of this aspect of voicing timing is that the (phonological) syllable is the key factor which determines whether a delay in voice onset occurs or not in stop-sonorant sequences. Kahn (1976) states that aspiration only occurs if /p,t,k/ 'are both syllable-initial and non-syllable final' (1976:45), and specifically points out that this applies equally to stop-vowel and stop-sonorant-vowel sequences. Evaluation of this particular claim is dependent on the definition of the syllable which is adopted, and more specifically on the means used to determine syllable boundary location in connected speech. Whilst work on defining the phonetic correlates of the syllable has largely concentrated on the correlates of the syllable nucleus (Lass 1984:250), phonologists have tended to define syllable margins on the basis of allophonic variation which is assumed to occur either only syllable-initially or finally (i.e. a somewhat circular procedure -- examples of this can be found in a review of the role of the syllable in phonological theory in Nespor & Vogel 1986, Chapter 3). Without a clear procedure for identifying syllable boundaries (especially in connected speech) it is difficult to assess the extent to which this claim is an accurate account of boundary sensitivity of the timing of voicing in English consonant sequences. The experimental results presented in Chapter 4 shed some light on this issue.

Hence, there are essentially two (potentially complementary[29]) positions regarding the domains in which voice onset delay in obstruent-sonorant sequences takes place. One which claims that it normally only occurs word-internally, and another which claims that it only occurs in sequences in syllable-initial position; i.e. late voice onset for a sonorant is predicted not to occur across a syllable boundary or across a word boundary (except in the cases mentioned by Gimson and Brown).

Reservations about treating aspiration as an all-or-nothing process have already been expressed above. They are equally applicable to claims such as these (Randolph & Zue 1987), and are supported by the fact that the very small amount of experimental work that has been carried out on this aspect of the timing of voicing has produced somewhat inconsistent results.

Dent (1984) has carried out one of the few instrumental studies of the timing of voicing in obstruent-sonorant sequences in British English as a function of different boundary conditions. In an acoustic study of /sl/ and /kl/, it was discovered that voice onset for /l/ was delayed in both cases when the sequence occurred word-internally, and when there was a word-boundary intervening between the obstruent and the lateral. In word-internal sequences, there was a longer delay in the stop-sonorant sequence than in the fricative-sonorant sequence, but when a word-boundary intervened, the opposite effect was found. The presence of an adjacent stressed syllable also played an important role. When the sequence occurred across a word-boundary, there was a shorter delay in voice onset for /l/ if the following vowel was stressed than if the following vowel was unstressed.

These results are slightly different to those reported a few years previously in a study by Bladon & Al-Bamerni (1976). The main aim of their study was to carry out an acoustic analysis of the coarticulation between allophones of /l/ and a vowel environment. However, part of their work involved looking at the timing of voicing in obstruent-lateral sequences occurring in word-initial position, and across syllable and word boundaries. They found that voice onset for /l/ was delayed under every boundary condition. The duration of the delay in stop-lateral sequences was slightly less across a word and syllable boundary than in a word-internal sequence, but for fricative-lateral sequences there was little difference. They also found that in all cases, there were longer delays in laterals following stops, than in laterals following fricatives.

These results however require cautious interpretation. The authors pooled data from two different experiments, in one of which they used spectrography, and the other of which was based on measurements of airflow. It has already been suggested above that the measurements performed by many experimenters are greatly influenced by the instrumentation which they employ. It is not possible to gauge whether this is the case with this work, since no description is provided of the segmentation criteria which were used, and to what extent measurements with one technique could be equated with those obtained using the second technique.[30] However, in all fairness to the authors, the timing of voicing in obstruent-lateral sequences was far from being the main focus of their paper.

Lehiste (1960) in one of the earliest studies of the acoustic correlates of juncture provides data on only one sequence that is relevant to the present work - night rate, Nye trait, and nitrate. It was found that there was a similar delay in voice onset for /r/ in the last two cases, but in the first sequence, Lehiste states that there is no voice onset delay for /r/. However, figures are presented for the duration of the (voiceless) release of the stop in the /t#r/ case (ranging between 20 ms and 60 ms), and the stop release is clearly visible on the exemplar spectrograms presented by the author. Therefore, it may be that the difference between the word-internal and word boundary cases is not so much in the laryngeal timing with respect to the stop closure (a relatively long delay in voice onset is observed in all three conditions), but in the amount of overlap between the supralaryngeal gestures for the stop and approximant.

Barry (1981) investigated the pairs lamb play and lamp lay, and right sleeve and Wrights leave, and found that the Jones/Gimson/Brown claim was confirmed in the second pair, but in the first pair, there was a delayed onset of voicing to the lateral in every case. However, it was significantly longer when the sequence occurred word-internally than when it occurred across a word-boundary.

Barry & Kunzel (1978) in a short study of 'devoicing' in English and German /s/ - nasal sequences occurring word-initially and across a word boundary, found consistent late onset of voicing for the nasal in every case in both languages, irrespective of the boundary condition.

Hence, there is some inconsistency in the literature regarding the extent to which the status of the boundary between two elements in a stop-sonorant affects the timing of voicing within that sequence. One of the aims of the experiment reported in Chapter 4 is to provide some clarification of this issue.

The timing of voicing in /sp/, /st/, /sk/ sequences

One aspect of the timing of voicing in English consonant sequences which has received a certain amount of attention, is the delay in voice onset following VOICELESS stops in /$-s-stop-V/ or /$-s-stop-sonorant/ sequences (where $

stands for a syllable boundary). As is pointed out in many of the standard texts on English phonetics (e.g. Gimson 1980:53), in this environment, /p/, /t/, and /k/ are realised without the interval of aspiration which is, in other contexts, associated with prevocalic VOICELESS stops. This means that the timing of voicing in relation to the stop medial phase is very similar under these circumstances to that which is found in pre-vocalic VOICED stops.[31]

This has been confirmed instrumentally by Davidsen-Nielsen (1974). Whilst one must have reservations about data pooled from a number of speakers of widely varying accents of English, Davidsen-Nielsen's experiments showed very clearly the differences in voicing timing according to the presence or absence of a preceding /s/. Furthermore, they showed that the presence of the syllable boundary before the /s/ was crucial for this process to take place. He found that in /$spl/ sequences, the /p/ would be unaspirated, whilst in /s$pl/ sequences, the stop would be aspirated as normal, with a delay in voice onset for the following lateral. This is further evidence for the importance of medial boundary status for temporal coordination.

However, Gimson (1980:154) provides examples which suggest that the effect of the positioning of the syllable boundary in /s-VOICELESS stop-V/ sequences may not be as clear-cut as suggested by Davidsen-Nielsen. He agrees that in /$sCV/ sequences (where C is a VOICELESS stop) the stop voice onset time is very short, unlike the situation in /$CV/ sequences in which long voice onset times are found. Gimson diverges from Davidsen-Nielsen by pointing out that in /s$CV/ sequences, it possible that VOICELESS stops may also only be 'weakly aspirated ... *discussed* may be distinguished from *disgust* only by the fortis nature of /k/' (1980:154). He also indicates that word-initial VOICELESS stops with a preceding word-final VOICELESS fricative (not just /s/) may be subject to a certain shortening of voice onset time (e.g. *push past* vs *go past*). The data from the experiments performed as part of this study allow Gimson's assertions to be tested.

To summarise this brief survey of the state of our knowledge of the timing of voicing in English consonant sequences, it is possible to identify three principal findings.

(a) whilst late onset of voicing in VOICELESS-VOICED combinations has been the most remarked upon in the literature, a range of patterns of voicing timing are observed in different types of sequences.

(b) a significant factor affecting the frequency of occurrence of a particular type of voicing timing may be the status of the boundary which lies between the components of the sequence.

(c) in consonant sequences in which stops and fricatives are followed by sonorants, a wide range of voice onset delays is expected, with the longest occurring in clusters of /t/-sonorant, and the shortest occurring in clusters of voiced stop-sonorant. The duration of voice onset time (for stops) in these sequences is longer than that found in the corresponding stop-vowel sequence.

1.10 CONCLUDING DISCUSSION

This review set out to address two questions; what is the extent of our knowledge regarding the timing of voicing in English, and particularly in accents of British English? What are the major factors determining variability in the timing of voicing? It has served to demonstrate that what information there is available on the timing of voicing in English, is heavily weighted towards analysis of voice onset time in post-pausal pre-stressed-vowel stops, largely related to accents of American English. Furthermore, there are instances in which claims made about the timing of voicing have not been backed up by the small amount of experimental work which has been performed (e.g. the effect of medial boundary status on voicing in stop-obstruent sequences). Consequently, our knowledge of this aspect of phonetic realisation is limited in scope (dealing mainly with voice onset time), coverage (with very few studies based on British English), and consistency, and as a result we have a rather incomplete picture.

The information that is available in the literature demonstrates that the timing of voicing in VOICED and VOICELESS obstruents is a complex aspect of phonetic realisation. Two features of this are particularly noteworthy. Firstly, there are considerable asynchronies between the laryngeal and supralaryngeal activity corresponding to VOICED and VOICELESS obstruents. Secondly, despite having some potential for relatively independent activity, the fine-grained coordination of laryngeal and supralaryngeal events is systematically constrained by a number of factors (including phonological voicing category of the obstruent concerned, phonetic context, and more global aspects of temporal and prosodic organisation such as rate and stress). These are features of phonetic realisation which are of central concern to general phonetic theory and speech production modelling, since both areas have the task of accounting for all of the systematic characteristics of speech production. In later chapters of this book an attempt is made to reach a deeper understanding of the processes which give rise to fine-grained systematic characteristics of voicing timing.

NOTES

1. The accent of English which is studied in the experiments reported in this book has been variously labelled Received Pronunciation (R.P.) (e.g. Gimson 1980:91), mainstream R.P. (Wells 1982:279), Southern British Standard (Wells 1982:301), and General British (Windsor-Lewis 1987). The accent is regionally unmarked, in that it does not identify the speakers as being from a particular area, and also due to the fact that the same accent can be heard outside the South-East of England. Henceforth, the term 'Southern British English' (SBE) is used to refer specifically to the accent being focused on in this study. The use of 'Southern' should not be understood to be implying anything other than the geographical origin of the speakers involved.

2. The detailed anatomy of the larynx is not dealt with here, since the emphasis in this study is more on the nature of the conditions necessary for voicing to take place, than on a detailed account of the characteristics of the laryngeal structures themselves. Accounts of laryngeal anatomy can be found in Zemlin (1968), Broad (1973), and Laver (1980).

3. The aerodynamic-myoelastic theory is the dominant model of phonation. Husson's (e.g. 1965) proposal of direct innervation of the vocalis muscle is the most salient alternative account. This so-called 'neurochronaxic' theory suggested that the movement of the vocal folds is the result of innervation of the vocalis muscle, rather than the result of a combination of aerodynamic properties and muscular tension. This approach met with much criticism, and is generally regarded as being untenable. Laver (1980) outlines the principal arguments against this alternative account of phonation.

4. Occasionally, in cases of 'glottal attack', the starting position for phonation involves a completely closed glottis.

5. During abduction, contraction of the posterior cricoarytenoid muscles coincides with suppression of the activity of the adductory interarytenoid muscles. (Sawashima & Hirose 1983:15)

6. The term 'segment' is used in this chapter largely for descriptive convenience. The problematic theoretical status of the 'segment' is discussed in later chapters.

7. Air flow traces of oral stop articulation often show an incomplete velic closure during the closure phase of the stop. Warren (1976:128ff) points out that a velic opening of 2-3 mm^2 may occur during the production of VOICELESS stops. Even when velic closure is achieved in the production of a stop, this is often some way into the interval of oral occlusion, and often just before the instant of stop release (this can be observed clearly on airflow traces). It seems then that the build-up of pressure behind the occlusion is dependent more on the relative sizes of the openings in the oral and nasal cavities than on the existence of a complete closure at the velic port. The velum only has to be raised high enough in order to allow the build up of pressure behind the oral occlusion (Bell-Berti 1980:296).

8. The term 'obstruent' is used because whilst aspiration is normally associated with stops, it is also possible for fricatives and affricates to be aspirated. Ladefoged (1971:12) gives examples of aspirated fricatives in Burmese.

9. Sawashima & Hirose (1983) illustrate the time course of glottal aperture with respect to stop release in VOICELESS aspirated and unaspirated stops.

10. One phenomenon which 'devoiced' is not used to refer to is an attenuation of the amplitude of voicing, as seen for example when voicing occurs during the medial phase of stops and fricatives. There is no single term commonly used to describe this aspect of voicing.

11. Watson (1983) points out that the study of the perception of the voicing contrast was also (unjustifiably) dominated for some time by the notion that voice onset time was the overriding perceptually relevant acoustic parameter. The term 'voicing contrast' is being used in this study (as in Watson 1983) merely as a convenient means of referring to the distinction between cognates such as /p,b/ /t,d/ /k,g/. It is not intended to suggest that the nature of that contrast lies entirely in the voicing patterns associated with the distinction.

12. Weismer's is not, strictly speaking, a 'physiological' study, but it is included in this section because of the strong physiological conclusion which is drawn. By 'voiceless interval' Weismer is referring to the interval between voice offset and voice onset in an intervocalic VOICELESS obstruent, as measured on spectrograms from the final to the first vertical striation visible in F2 and the higher formants. The problem with this definition is that closure voicing does not give rise to vertical striations in F2, so effectively what Weismer is measuring is stop closure duration plus voice onset time, not the duration of the 'abduction gesture', as he claims. Furthermore, it might be argued that Weismer's interpretation of his results is open to question due to the fact that a consistent 'voiceless interval' duration is really only apparent when the means of the 9 subjects are pooled, but there are considerable within- and between-subject differences in 'voiceless interval' duration which do not seem to conform to a uniform glottal gesture across place and manner differences, as claimed by Weismer.

13. Whilst this review is essentially of quantitative instrumental studies of voicing, it should not be forgotten that many of the findings which are reported have also been observed by phoneticians whose only analysis tool was their auditory skill. For example, the general trends regarding the timing of voicing in English stops are discussed by Jones (1960:154), and Heffner (1950:121).

14. Zlatin's results, based on a large number of repetitions of a very limited set of words, should be treated with a degree of caution, since her voice onset time measurements are by far the highest reported in the literature, and similarly they show the widest range, well outside the ranges observed in other researchers' results, and in the results of the present experiments.

15. Surprisingly little is known about the effect of varying rate on voice onset time. Lisker & Abramson (1967:15) report that 'no correlation could be established between VOT values and rate of syllable production'. On the other hand, Summerfield (1975), Diehl et al. (1980) and Miller et al. (1986) have shown that there are smaller mean voice onset times in VOICELESS stops at higher rates of speech, but that in VOICED stops there is very little difference (only the data from Summerfield (1975) refers to British English, but it is not clear how similar the six subjects' accents were: their 'first language was English learnt in England' 1975:62).

16. Paradoxically, Lisker & Abramson (1964:416ff) also chose to mark the onset of voicing in voice onset time measurements at a point after the onset of voicing. This is because they chose to disregard what they call 'edge vibrations', on the grounds that they are not audible ('There is no point ... in speaking of the distinctive relevance of a phonetic feature that is not perceptible' 1964:416). It would appear then, that even voice onset time was originally conceived not exclusively as an articulatory/acoustic measure, but as a measure with an auditory/perceptual component (c.f. Fischer-Jorgensen & Hutters:84-85).

17. Whilst the pooled data from Suomi's (1980) subjects shows the conventional place of articulation effect, he found that some subjects actually had lower mean voice onset times for velars than alveolars. In all subjects the means for alveolars and velars were quite close and frequently not significantly different.

18. In fact, the difference was very small indeed. In cases where the vowel in the CVC sequence is tense, the mean difference between words with final VOICED and VOICELESS consonants was 3.87 ms $p < 0.05$. When the vowel is lax, the mean difference was 5.14 ms $p < 0.02$.

19. It is, therefore, rather an overstatement for Port et al. (1980:238) to describe these findings as showing a 'direct correlation of voice onset time with the duration of the following vowel.'

20 The fact that speakers show a preference for one type of voicing over another in post-pausal VOICED stops may be a useful feature for incorporation into speaker identification/verification systems. Wolf (1972) reported that this was quite a successful parameter, when used as part of a vector of acoustic features characterising a particular speaker.

21. The conclusion that this is a bimodal distribution and not simply a unimodal one with a wide spread of values is supported by the finding of Flege (1982) that there is consistently a 'gap' in the voice onset time 'continuum' characterised by the fact that voicing is never observed to begin just before the release of the stop (his data indicate that voice onset times of 0 - ⁻30 ms (approximately) are not observed). Flege also observed that glottal adduction in initial VOICED stops always took place more than 50 ms before the stop release.

22. Hanninen's work is potentially of some importance for the study of the timing of voicing in British English, since it is one of the few experimental studies of voicing in that accent of English reported in the literature. However, the results of the study have to be treated cautiously. The first

reason for this is that no segmentation criteria are presented in Hanninen's report. Given the inconsistencies in experimental technique which I have discussed earlier in this chapter, it is important to be aware of exactly what measurements are being carried out in studies of this type. The second source of uncertainty with regard to this work concerns the statistical analysis carried out by Hanninen, and the results which are presented. The problem is that the results are pooled from words produced under three different experimental conditions; single words, word-pairs, and sentences. Evidence from the literature suggests that these conditions have a significant effect on the timing of voicing observed, so pooling the results in this way may conceal significant between-group effects.

23. One feature of the production of final VOICELESS stops in many accents of English, is that the stop closure may be accompanied by a glottal closure -- a process known as glottal reinforcement (Roach 1973). The nature of glottal reinforcement is discussed in Chapter 4.

24. As with stops, most of the studies carried out on fricatives have been oriented towards identifying the cues which can be used in distinguishing VOICED and VOICELESS fricatives. Voicing during the noise portion of the fricative has been shown to be of perceptual relevance (Massaro & Cohen 1977), but, as is pointed out below, this is hardly a consistent feature of English VOICED fricatives. Probably the two most consistent features correlating with the voicing contrast are fricative duration (Denes 1955, Cole & Cooper 1975), and in post-syllabic fricatives, duration of the preceding vowel (Denes 1955, Raphael 1972). Harrington (1988:105) provides further details on the acoustic cues for the voicing distinction in English fricatives.

25. It is not clear whether the word-initial and -final fricatives were also post- and pre-pausal. Haggard had subjects produce lists of sentences incorporating words containing the fricatives being investigated, but he does not indicate the position of the words in the sentences.

26. When VOICED fricatives are realised as 'voiceless', this is normally with whisper phonation (Abercrombie 1967:137). This distinguishes them from VOICELESS fricatives which are realised with a glottal abduction gesture.

27. 'Late' and 'early' (used later in this section) are defined with respect to the 'boundary' between the two consonants in the sequence (e.g. the release of the stop in stop-sonorant sequences, the onset of fricative noise in stop-fricative sequences).

28. If the VOICED stop is prevoiced or voiced throughout its medial phase, then there is no delay in the onset of voicing; instead, the stop release is superimposed upon continuous vocal fold vibration.

29. Most of the examples given by Gimson (1980) involve transparently syllable-internal sequences. However, in describing the occurrence of a (partially) voiceless allophone of /r/ he points out (1980:206) that 'a partially devoiced variety of /r/ occurs: when /r/ follows an unaccented fortis plosive in a syllable, and in rapid speech, at syllable or word boundaries.'

Gimson, therefore, seems to qualify the 'word-domain' hypothesis described above, and describes instances of devoicing which would presumably not be predicted by the 'syllable-domain' claim.

30 There are two particular measurement issues which cloud interpretation of Bladon and Al-Bamerni's results. The first relates to their measure of voice onset time for the lateral. This is defined as the percentage of the duration of the lateral that is unvoiced. The onset of the lateral in stop-lateral sequences is presumably marked at the release burst corresponding to the stop. In fricative-lateral sequences, marking lateral onset is a far more difficult task, since both the fricative and the unvoiced lateral signals are characterised by a high frequency aperiodic signal. Similarly, the end of the lateral in a lateral-vowel sequence is not a particularly easy point to mark. Without some knowledge of the criteria used, it is difficult to evaluate the results.

31. This fact leads to problems in both the phonetic and phonological domains. It is a problem for the traditional phonetic labels used to describe voicing, since exactly the same pattern of laryngeal-supralaryngeal coordination tends to be labelled voiced when it occurs with a VOICED sound, and voiceless, when it occurs in conjunction with a VOICELESS sound. From the point of view of phonological description, it is important to determine to what extent it is justifiable to treat these stops as VOICELESS, when they are indistinguishable in their realisation from VOICED stops. In the light of recent studies of other types of neutralisation which have shown that so-called neutralised forms may be differentiated in realisation (e.g. Port & O'Dell 1984), it would be interesting to investigate whether the same applies in this case of neutralisation; i.e. whether the underlying difference between the cognate stops is maintained in some way. Wingate (1982) describes one such study, and concludes that 'the English stop [p] after word-initial /s/ is both acoustically and perceptually different from the voiceless allophone of word-initial /b/' (1982:24).

CHAPTER 2
Modelling Phonetic Variability in Speech Production

In Chapter 1, I pointed out that what data is available on the timing of voicing in English obstruents shows that the coordination of laryngeal and supralaryngeal gestures is rather complex, and that variability in patterns of coordination occurs systematically, often at a very fine-grained level, as a function of a number of contextual and structural factors. A full account of the timing of voicing in a model of speech production must give an explanation for the fine-grained variability which is observed to occur. This is the area which is focused on in this chapter. I begin by considering the success with which systematic fine-grained aspects of phonetic realisation, in general, are dealt with in speech production modelling. In the second half of the chapter I review some recent attempts to clarify the relationship between linguistic aspects of voicing and the surface realisation of voicing timing.

The following is a summary of the position to be outlined. I consider three components of a speech production model which are possible sources of fine-grained systematic variability of phonetic realisation (utterance execution, motor programming, phonetic representation). I suggest that whilst aspects of 'micro-variability' which are **common to all languages** may be accounted for by appealing to physical properties of the vocal apparatus and to general strategies of speech motor programming, fine-grained patterns of variability which are **characteristic of a particular language or accent** must be a feature of the phonetic representation which drives the speech production mechanism. However, models of the linguistic control of speech production are largely incapable of dealing with this level of variability. This is because, as it is commonly envisaged, the phonetic representation is rather abstract, lacking the temporal resolution necessary for specifying fine-grained temporal coordination of different articulators.

Consequently, in models which have a phonetic representation such as this (the vast majority), no adequate explanation is given for fine-grained variability which cannot be accounted for in terms of universal phonetic processes. This means that there is a significant gap in many of the models which have been proposed in the literature. I conclude that an account of the detail of phonetic realisation (how it differs across languages, and how it is represented in the phonetic 'plan' for an utterance) is an important area which has not received sufficient attention in speech production modelling. In particular, I suggest that models which attribute systematic variability of the timing of voicing to a conjunction of underlying phonological contrast and universal phonetic processes are inadequate.[1]

2.1 SPEECH PRODUCTION MODELLING: SOME GENERAL COMMENTS

As has been pointed out by a number of writers (e.g. Abbs 1986), the main task which is undertaken in attempting to model speech production is to arrive at an account of the processes which underlie the mapping between a linguistic representation of an utterance, and the realisation of that utterance as a complex, continuous sequence of interwoven articulatory gestures and corresponding acoustic signal.

The nature of the realisation of an utterance may be empirically observed by using a number of different experimental techniques. These differ in degree of accuracy and appropriateness for diverse types of investigation, but on the whole they permit a fairly clear picture to be built up of the acoustic and articulatory characteristics of speech production.

On the other hand, the nature of the linguistic representation of an utterance is a matter of some dispute. This is mainly for two reasons. Firstly because it exists at a level which is not easily accessible for the purposes of objective investigation. This means that the strategy used to determine properties of the concealed processes relevant to speech production is to infer them from observations which can be made at the periphery (Laver 1970, Abbs & Eilenberg 1976). This gives rise to differences in interpretation of the available data and a range of different conclusions. The second reason is inherent in the nature of the topic being studied. It is possible to study speech production from an exclusively motor control perspective without attributing any special attention to the fact that speech may be different from other types of motor activity -- i.e. by attempting to deduce the properties of speech motor control without making *a priori* assumptions about the nature of the goals that a speaker is trying to achieve (Moll et al. 1976). But in practice, what most investigators do is to carry into their investigation a framework of assumptions regarding the nature of the linguistic representation which then moulds their experiments and the judgements which they make regarding the speech production processes. Dispute arises from the fact that different views are held regarding the nature of that linguistic representation, and the frameworks which are imposed on speech production research are therefore of different types. A good example of this is found in the differing views held over the years concerning the domains of the linguistic primes underlying speech production -- proposals have included context-sensitive allophones (Wickelgren 1969), phoneme-sized segments (e.g. Perkell 1980), demi-syllables (Fujimura & Lovins 1978), and syllables (Kozhevnikov & Chistovich 1965).

Not only is a framework of linguistic assumptions 'carried into' speech production modelling, the framework in most cases forms part of the model itself (Fowler 1985:193). Typically, then, the aim of speech production modelling is conceived as being to provide an account of the mapping between the output of a speaker's grammar (the nature of which depends on the particular approach to linguistic theory which is adopted), and the level of the articulatory and acoustic realisation of an utterance. This is a characterisation of the so-called 'translation' approach to speech production modelling (Fowler et al. 1980). This strategy is adopted by the vast majority of the work on speech production. The difficulty inherent in this task, and the reason for the rather limited progress that has been made, lies in the immensity of the gap existing between the cognitive level of hypothesised discrete linguistic primes and the surface level of continuous, real-time phonetic realisation (Ladefoged 1980, 1988, Hammarberg 1982, Nolan 1982b, Fowler 1985, Laver 1988).

A review of the general strategies adopted in speech production modelling would not be complete without pointing out that the need to account for such a 'translation' is not universally accepted. Since the late 1970's a number of investigators (working principally at the Haskins Laboratories within the paradigm of 'Action Theory') have been attempting to show that the notion of a 'translation' is not a relevant issue from the point of view of speech production modelling. Detailed reviews of the Action Theory approach to speech production modelling are given by Fowler et al. (1980), Nolan (1982b), Kelso et al. (1986), Harris et al. (1986), and Kelso & Tuller (1987), and the implementation of Action Theory within a framework of 'Task Dynamics' is described by Saltzman & Kelso (1987) and Hawkins (in press). Fowler et al. (1980) summarise their stance vis-a-vis 'translation' thus:

> ... the mismatch between abstract linguistic units and articulatory categories may be only an apparent one. Such a mismatch may arise when an immutable assignment of values (e.g. discrete, static) to linguistic units is assumed by production theorists ... our suggestion is that linguistic units, as they are known to a language user, and as they are spoken or perceived by him, are *qualitatively separate*, and serially-ordered (but not discrete), *dynamic* and *context-free*. Their dimensions and their values seem to us to do no violence to the essential *linguistic* properties of segments. Yet they permit the claim that there is no

> essential difference between the segments that a language-user knows, and those that he speaks and hears. (1980:375)

Initially (probably as a result of the fact that the foundations of this approach lie in studies of other types of motor activity) this line of enquiry was developed in a rather limited way, concentrating on speech motor programming, rather than on demonstrating the compatibility, or indeed the identity, of a linguistic representation of an utterance and its realisation. Two specific proposals which emerge from this work are the idea that in complex motor tasks, muscles are grouped together in task-specific 'coordinative structures' thereby reducing the degrees of freedom requiring independent control, and the idea of 'intrinsic timing'; i.e. that temporal aspects of the production of an utterance are exclusively the result of dynamic properties of muscular organisation. These two proposals are discussed in more detail later in this book (later in this chapter, and in Chapter 5, respectively).

Whilst proponents of Action Theory and its Task Dynamics implementation categorically reject the need for a 'translation', it has been argued by Laver (1988) that when an attempt is made to link this view of motor programming to the linguistic specification of an utterance, it will be necessary to consider questions that are essentially 'translationist' in nature.

> Given that eventual appeal to a concept of an interface between symbolic representation and neuromuscular implementation is necessary, even though Action Theory as applied to speech developed out of discontent with a translation theory approach, it could be argued that the two approaches are complementary rather than incompatible. The competitive issue between the two approaches then reduces to the question of the location of the interface between the symbolic and the implementational components of the model. (1988:97)

Indeed, much of the recent work which has been carried out attempting to demonstrate the compatibility of a task dynamical model of motor programming and the phonological representation of an utterance (chiefly by Browman & Goldstein' 1986, in press -- this work is discussed in more detail later in this chapter) does find itself considering issues such as the extent to which phonetic realisation can be attributed to aspects of the execution and motor programming, as opposed to being part of the phonetic plan of an utterance specified upstream of the motor programming stage of production.

The question of whether 'translation' is an appropriate means of modelling speech production is still an extremely live issue. This study does not attempt to provide evidence for one approach or another, although it does effectively assume that some form of translation is required in order to provide a full account of phonetic realisation. In doing so, and in common with many other investigators, it leans on the rationale summarised by Nolan (1982b:288) that 'as a way of limiting the class of hypotheses to be entertained, it seems reasonable (since after all speaking is a realisation of linguistic structure) to try to incorporate into models of speech production the insights of linguistic description.'

In attempting to unravel the nature of this 'translation' there are many aspects of the production of an utterance which could serve as a base for hypotheses concerning the nature of the processes which underlie speech production. At a macroscopic level it is possible to investigate aspects of phonetic realisation which have relatively long domains, such as tempo, phrasing, and rhythm (Fletcher (1988) provides an extensive review of results of research in these areas). The focus of this chapter is at the other extreme, at a microscopic level -- on the systematic fine-grained characteristics of phonetic realisation.

There are at least two classes of phenomena which are relevant at this level of analysis. The first is context-sensitive variability -- the way in which articulatory gestures and their timing alter as a function of the context in which they are embedded. The second is interarticulator coordination -- the timing relationships between articulatory events which are involved in producing a particular articulatory or auditory goal. There is some overlap between these two categories of course -- no sound is ever made in isolation (since even silence provides some context), so interarticulator coordination is always to a certain extent context-dependent. The review of the factors affecting the timing of voicing in Chapter 1 suggests that both of these areas are relevant in devising a full account of the observations (many instances of late/early offset/onset of voicing are affected by adjacent context -- other factors which affect the timing of voicing such as phonological category, manner of articulation, speaker identity etc. are not presented by the context but do have a significant effect on interarticulator coordination).

Two important characteristics of the variability to be considered here should be borne in mind; firstly, it occurs systematically in a speaker's performance (as opposed to being random and unpredictable -- this is discussed in a little more detail below); secondly it is non-distinctive, that is, the fine-grained nature of the variability means that it is not crucially involved in guaranteeing the systemic distinctions of the accent concerned. So, the focus of this chapter is on how speech production models account for systematic, non-distinctive, temporal and configurational variability at a fine-grained level of vocal performance.[2]

One matter which should be broached before proceeding with this review, is that use of the term 'micro-variability' begs the question 'micro-variability of what?' As was mentioned in the introduction to this volume, arriving at an understanding of the nature of the primes underlying the production of an utterance is one of the major tasks of those investigating speech production. A number of different proposals have been made on the basis of empirical data, but there is as yet no consensus on this matter. What is more, as pointed out by Laver (1988), there is a certain amount of, probably inevitable, circularity in the argumentation used to justify opting for one type of prime rather than another:

> ... given that the search for organising entities is conducted with the help of these primes as basic descriptive tools, it is hardly surprising that the entities discovered might then be describable in terms of those a priori units of description. (1988:93)

Since in the present study the nature of the linguistic representation which drives the speech production mechanism is very much at issue, it seems reasonable, at this stage, to adopt as neutral a definition as possible. Therefore, the term 'micro-variability' is used to refer to fine-grained systematic variation in the realisation of 'a phonetic unit that constitutes an integrated event -- an organised set of articulatory gestures or auditory cues -- in a temporal flow of speech' (Fujimura & Lovins 1978:107). This leaves open the precise size of the organisational unit (it could be a phoneme sized segment, or a syllable, for example) until the question can be addressed in the light of the experimental data which is gathered.

2.2 MICRO-VARIABILITY IN A SPEECH PRODUCTION MODEL

In this section, I discuss the extent to which different components of a speech production model may account for micro-variability. The discussion focuses on three aspects of speech production: execution, motor programming, and the phonetic representation (definitions of each of these aspects are given in the appropriate section).

Micro-variability in phonetic realisation can be sub-categorised as shown in Figure 2.1. A primary division can be made between random variability and systematic, conditioned variability (Laver 1988). Vocal performance is characterised by a core of random variability. This reveals itself in the fact that no two repetitions of the 'same' utterance/word/syllable in the same conditions, by the same speaker are absolutely identical. Random differences may reside, for example, in temporal coordination of articulators, in articulator velocity, in fundamental frequency. One possible cause of this is the means by which muscles implicated in speech gestures are innervated. For example, Baer (1979) points out that:

> Since ... the outputs of many motor units consist of asynchronous pulse trains, they cannot sum to a perfectly constant result, although the result is nearly constant on average. There are some perturbations that must be left over as the result of single motor unit twitches. (1979:19)

Whilst there are some accounts in the literature of random variation in phonetic parameters (e.g. F0 perturbation -- Baer 1979, Hiller et al. 1983), little is known about the extent of such variability in speech production and of the factors which give rise to it. However, I intend to concentrate in this study on the second type of variability, that which is systematic and predictable.

Figure 2.1: Diagrammatic summary of the sub-classification of phonetic variability adopted in this review. The lower tier of the figure shows (in parentheses) the different stages of a speech production model which are the sources of the two types of variability.

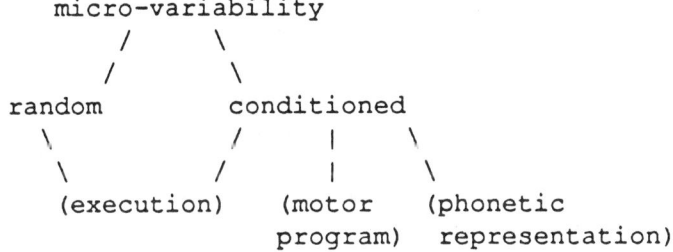

2.2.1 Micro-variation at the level of execution

It is likely that some aspects of systematic micro-variability are the result of bio-mechanical and inertial factors present in the execution of an utterance (the motivation for the somewhat qualified nature of this statement is outlined below). The term 'execution' is being used to refer to the final stages of speech production -- the muscular innervation and resultant articulatory movements and gestures which constitute the physical realisation of an utterance.

There are (at least) three features of the vocal apparatus which could conceivably give rise to micro-variability at the stage of utterance execution:

(a) the fact that there are physical connections between diverse parts of the vocal organs (this was mentioned briefly in Chapter 1; examples are yoking of the larynx and tongue/jaw system via the hyoid bone, interaction of the tongue and velum via the palatopharyngeal muscle, etc.) means that an articulator may be induced into activity merely as a result of such a connection without directly being implicated in the current articulatory goal; (b) the performance of a particular gesture or collection of gestures may result in side-effects in a different part of the vocal apparatus to which there is no physical connection (e.g. the occlusion for stop closures results in a rapid rise in intra-oral air pressure and a progressive equalisation of trans-glottal pressure leading to difficulty in maintaining voicing); (c) a third feature of the vocal apparatus which is a potential source of micro-variability is the mechano-inertial characteristics of the vocal organs; i.e. 'sluggishness' of the vocal organs might lead to a delay between receipt of neural commands and the articulators' response to those commands (Harris 1974:2293).

Certain observations do seem to fit into this category of phenomena. All else being equal high vowels have higher pitch than low vowels (Hombert et al. 1979). This seems to be a result of the muscular connections between the larynx and the tongue. The larynx is raised as result of the elevation of the tongue and the upward pull which this has on the hyoid bone. Raising of the larynx generates a slight increase in tension of the vocal folds, and hence the higher pitch (Ohala 1978).[3] Another example is to be found in the small but systematic differences in pitch at the margins of VOICED and VOICELESS stops. On the whole, pitch is slightly higher at the margins of VOICELESS than of VOICED stops. Ohala (1978) reviews a number of possible accounts, concluding that the most likely explanation lies in the fact that there is greater tension in the vocal folds in VOICELESS stops since the larynx tends to be relatively higher than in VOICED stops (the difference in larynx height may be due to larynx lowering in VOICED stops in order to maintain the trans-glottal pressure drop, and hence glottal vibration). This difference in laryngeal tension may lead to the slight differences in fundamental frequency. A somewhat different example is outlined by Kent (1983:66). With regard to the fact that on the whole, temporal spreading of lip-rounding and nasalisation has a relatively long span in comparison to other types of coarticulatory accommodation, he points out that some researchers believe that this could be due to these articulators being inherently more 'sluggish' than others.

Physical features of the vocal apparatus such as these have frequently been invoked by investigators as a means of explaining surface variability, (e.g. Lindblom 1963, Stevens & House 1963, Daniloff & Hammarberg 1973). Indeed, an important characteristic of much of the work in speech production modelling is the adoption of the idea that a good deal of the opacity in the relationship between the linguistic representation of an utterance and its physical realisation is the result of physical, mechanical and inertial properties of the vocal organs.

This approach is exemplified by Daniloff & Hammarberg (1973). They envisage the linguistic plan for an utterance to consist of a string of 'canonical forms' (idealised, uncoarticulated, discrete, phoneme-sized target units). The execution of this plan is carried out through the mediation of 'built-in strategies of operation' (this presumably refers to motor programming) and *'mechano-inertial, anatomical and neuromuscular constraints'* (my emphasis), resulting in a merging together of the features of adjacent segments, and a displacement in time of the gestures associated with any single segment. A further example comes from Smith (1971), cited in Abbs & Eilenberg (1976:141);

> It would be hypothesised that although the neuronal commands to the muscles are essentially the same in most of the muscles involved in the production of a phoneme, the inertia and damped response of the articulators themselves could produce different observed gestures depending upon the different positions of the articulators in the immediate phonetic context. (1971:69)

This is an appealingly simple idea. It suggests that a significant portion of the complex surface variability in articulation can be accounted for by a set of universal physical principles inherent in the physiological properties of the vocal organs. The implication is that in vocal performance, the vocal organs strive to achieve a relatively invariant target for each segment, but are prevented from doing so by their own inherent physical constraints, and presumably by the overall rate at which they are being driven.

However, despite the frequency with which an explanation of this type is used to 'account for' micro-variability in phonetic realisation, it remains very tentative. The principal reason (Abbs & Eilenberg 1976) is that it has not received a significant amount of empirical support.

> ... in large part these (peripheral mechanical) properties have not been measured, simulated or synthesised into a functional model. Few, if any, studies have evaluated these properties in relation to their actual physical influence upon speech movements, particularly in the articulatory system. Most often, experimenters in speech production have taken the view that mechanical properties limit a speaker's ability to move the speech structures in consistent correspondence with an underlying phonological or phonetic unit.(1976:141)

Take the notion of inertia for example. Whilst there are certainly boundary conditions defining the maximum and minimum velocity at which a given articulator can move, it is clear that speakers are capable of manipulating the allegedly 'sluggish' articulators at a range of different velocities (e.g. certain instances of labial activity are far from 'sluggish'; the lips are capable of responding very rapidly indeed in order to compensate for unanticipated perturbation introduced just before, or during, a bilabial closure gesture: Gracco & Abbs 1987). So, another interpretation of the evidence cited above is that it is as much a reflection of preferred patterns of neuromuscular control (possibly based on an articulatory economy constraint such as that described below) as of articulator sluggishness. It is evident that this matter is in need of a good deal of investigation, but equally, it is clear that the way in which articulator inertia has been invoked in accounts of variability in phonetic realisation may well be something of an over-simplification.

A further reason little empirical support has been given to this possibility is that it is not a simple task to identify micro-variability which is produced as a result of properties of the execution phase of speech production. One way of attempting to quantify the effects of peripheral, mechano-inertial effects on vocal performance and on the acoustic signal, would be to use a digital simulation of the vocal tract. It could be argued that the current lack of understanding of the fine-grained realisational detail of speech production is due to the fact that there is not yet in existence a model which approximates the vast complexity of the human vocal apparatus, but that when such a model is obtained it will provide a clearer picture of the processes which give rise to low level timing and coarticulatory effects. However, since even the most sophisticated articulatory models fall some way short of the comprehensiveness which would be required in order to confirm whether a particular phenomenon was exclusively the result of peripheral properties of the vocal apparatus (e.g. Scully 1990), a full evaluation of bio-mechanical accounts of variability is some way off.

Whilst it may be that we cannot fully reject factors such as these as an explanation for certain types of micro-variability, many models of speech production can be criticised for the readiness with which they have adopted this explanation (in many cases without pointing out its weaknesses)[4], and for their failure to adopt a more balanced approach by considering a possible alternative explanation.

One alternative has been described by Keating (1985:129). Rather than adopting as the null-hypothesis a mechano-inertial account of fine-grained variability, one might adopt a hypothesis that there are no aspects of systematic micro-variability which are **entirely** passive, and that the control of speech production, leaves little to chance other than the random variability mentioned above. This would mean that an explanation for processes that appear to be common to all languages such as those mentioned above would then have to be sought at the level of motor programming; i.e. why do certain patterns of articulatory coordination tend to recur in languages? Are there perceptual or production explanations? (e.g. Bell-Berti (1980:298) takes this approach in accounting for observations of velum height in different vocalic environments). This paints a rather different picture of speech production. Rather than being characterised as an imperfect response to (relatively) invariant neural commands, vocal performance is considered to be an efficient, skilled behaviour, subtly tuned to achieve its task (see discussion below on motor programming). However, an approach of this sort implies that the linguistic and motor control underlying the production of an utterance is more complex than suggested by a simple mechano-inertial account, and involves addressing questions such as, what are the relevant control parameters, and how is temporal variability controlled?

It seems, then, that a large degree of caution should be exercised in the use of a mechano-inertial account of micro-variability. However, if at least some aspects of systematic variability do have their roots in the bio-mechanical properties of the vocal apparatus, it is possible (without having to await the results of future generations of vocal tract modelling) to predict three characteristics that they might have, and which thereby give some means of identifying them.

Firstly, one might expect the same effects to be found across most, if not all, languages. There are, of course, between-speaker differences in the absolute size and shape of the vocal organs and their relative proportions (giving rise to variability on an individual basis -- see Nolan (1983) for a review and discussion of these factors). However, on the whole the same types of individual differences should be found across languages. As well as these individual organic differences giving rise to uniform types of variability across languages, there is a common core of properties of the vocal apparatus which one would expect to find across all speakers; e.g. regardless of the physical size of the velum, it still interacts with the tongue through the intermediary of the palatoglossus muscle. Hence, one characteristic of variability generated in this way is that it should be (quasi) universal, since it is the result of properties of the vocal apparatus which are themselves (quasi) universal.[5]

A second feature which it seems reasonable to attribute to this level of variability is that it should involve relatively short-span interactions (this feature is particularly relevant from the point of view of modelling intersegmental context-sensitivity which can often operate over quite a long span; Kelly & Local 1986). This is because all of the sources of this type of variability are essentially transient; the effects of articulator inertia (if this is in fact a relevant factor) are overcome within a finite length of time, and the other factors, resulting from particular conjunctions of circumstances associated with specific gestures or articulatory configurations, are relatively short-lived. Therefore, it could be argued that any long-span context-sensitivity cannot exclusively be generated in this way.

A third feature is that the variability which is induced in this way should occur automatically, all else being equal. Whenever a given set of circumstances arises (e.g. a particular sequence of segments) the same effect should occur.

In summary, it is conceivable that an account of systematic micro-variability in phonetic realisation should make reference to the bio-mechanical and inertial properties of the execution stage of speech production. However, there is little robust experimental evidence quantifying the extent to which fine-grained variability can be attributed to those properties. Variability which arises in this way is predicted to have the following characteristics: it should be quasi-universal, automatic, and of relatively short span. Hence, one important conclusion from the point of view of this study is that properties of utterance execution have rather limited explanatory power, and an alternative account must be provided of variability which is non-universal and/or non-automatic (e.g. context or boundary dependent), and/or capable of spreading over long domains.

2.2.2 Micro-variation at the level of motor programming

The motor programming stage of speech production involves conversion of the linguistic goals of an utterance (which are probably at least partially acoustic or auditory in nature -- Ladefoged et al. 1972, Gay et al. 1981, Nolan 1982a) into a motor program for the successful realisation of that utterance. Numerous different proposals have been made for this stage of speech production (e.g. MacNeilage 1970, Lindblom et al. 1979, Perkell 1980, Fowler et al. 1980). One characteristic of motor programming common to these different proposals is that it is governed by a number of general principles. These include economy of effort, encoding efficiency and plasticity (each of these are discussed in more detail below). The overall result of this is a delicate trade-off of auditory requirements and motor capabilities (Lindblom 1983, 1987, 1990).

Another characteristic shared by the various models of motor programming is that it is seen as a process which interprets linguistic goals, but which does not in itself generate the linguistic goals. Motor programming in speech production is, of course, driven by the phonetic representation, but the phonetic goals themselves are established as a result of the phonological and phonetic rules of a given language. Motor programming is the process common to all speakers of optimally converting those goals into a motor program for their successful realisation.

There are two characteristics of speech motor programming which give rise to micro-variability in phonetic realisation; firstly, the need to achieve motor equivalence (i.e. the phonetic context in which a given production goal is embedded means that different gestures have to be used in order to achieve the 'same' target)[6]; secondly, variability can arise as a result of the application of the above-mentioned principles of economy and efficiency of effort, and plasticity in computing the optimum motor sequence for the achieving of goals in a given set of circumstances. Each of these is now considered in turn.

Motor equivalence

Various mechanisms have been proposed for motor equivalence in speech production.[7] MacNeilage (1970) proposed that speakers make use of a 3-dimensional mental representation of their vocal apparatus. Each articulatory target is coded as complex of points or vectors within the articulatory space. Articulation involves an on-line comparison of the desired target configuration and the current position of the relevant articulators. An appropriate set of motor commands is then computed in order to produce the correct configuration for the next target. In other words different strategies are used to reach the same target as a function of the context in which the target is embedded.

A conceptually-related approach (labelled 'predictive simulation') was proposed by Lindblom et al. (1979) and elaborated in Gay et al. (1981). The nature of the target specification is rather different to that proposed by MacNeilage (auditory rather than articulatory), and the mechanism is slightly different (involving an internal simulation of the candidate motor commands, a distance measure between the simulated feedback and the target feedback, and then appropriate modification of the motor commands prior to articulation), but the result is rather similar. Articulatory organisation for a given target varies as a function of the context.

A coordinative structure is the tool by which motor equivalence is achieved in the Action Theory account of speech production. A 'coordinative structure' is defined as a set of muscles (not necessarily located in the same area of the vocal apparatus) coupled together into functional units in order to achieve particular motor tasks -- 'functionally specific units of action defined over groups of muscles and articulator degrees of freedom.' (Fowler 1985:265). The action which results from the formation of a particular coordinative structure is not stereotyped, since one of the key features of a coordinative structure is that some of the parameters which specify the relationship between the components of a coordinative structure may be modulated without degrading the functional efficiency of the structure. It is more appropriate to say that a particular coordinative structure gives rise to an 'equivalence class' (Fowler 1980:123) of actions which have certain invariant properties in common, but which differ along certain other dimensions. Fowler (1980) lists a number of possible coordinative structures used in speech. One of these involves a linkage over a relatively long time span of the inspiratory and expiratory musculature during speech-mode respiration with the goal of producing a quasi-constant sub-glottal pressure. Another example is linking of the laryngeal musculature to produce particular modes of phonation (this example can be extended to include long-term supralaryngeal settings: Laver 1988). So, within Action Theory (and its implementation in Task Dynamics), coordinative structures are seen as the main vehicle for constraining the multiple degrees of freedom of the articulators involved in a particular movement or gesture in order to achieve motor equivalence.

Regardless of the approach to modelling motor equivalence which is adopted (the debate concerning the relative merits of these various approaches is still being hotly pursued; Kelso et al. 1986, Lindblom & MacNeilage 1986), it is possible to conclude that they all have the effect of generating one specific type of variability; the need to achieve speech production goals in a wide range of different contexts gives rise to a different organisation of gestures as a function of reigning contextual conditions.

Economy, plasticity and efficiency

General principles of economy, plasticity, and efficiency of articulation appear to constrain the way in which motor equivalence is achieved in speech production. These are a major source of some aspects of micro-variability, and together make up what Lindblom (1987:15) has dubbed an articulatory 'strategy of adaptive variability'.

Economy in speech motor programming (Lindblom 1983, 1987) involves 'talker-oriented simplification' (Lindblom 1987:14) of articulation. Given a range of possible strategies for achieving a particular goal, speakers tend to opt for the most 'cost-effective' -- that is, the strategy which produces a satisfactory outcome in the most economical way. Lindblom (1983) identifies two different constraints which appear to underlie the basis on which performance may be considered to be economical or not, The first (labelled a 'synergy constraint') is that extreme displacements of articulators are avoided wherever possible. The second (labelled a 'rate constraint') is that whilst any given articulation could be made to occur at any point within the maximum and minimum possible velocities applicable to the vocal organs involved, normally, the extremes of that range are avoided (c.f the discussion above on the use of inertia as an explanation for micro-variability). Lindblom (1983) provides his own summary;

> .. languages tend to behave rather 'fastidiously' with respect to the total set of physical capabilities of the speech apparatus. In normal speech, the production system is rarely driven to its limits. Typically, we speak at a 'comfortable' volume or rate and we use a degree of articulatory precision that seems 'natural'. (1983:219)

Assuming that constraints such as these are applicable to modelling speech motor programming, how is it that economy of articulation gives rise to variability? If an articulatory goal can be considered to consist of an equivalence class of complex gestures, the computation of the optimum (i.e. most economical) means of attaining that goal is dependent on the context within which the gesture must be embedded, and on the amount of time available for performance of the gesture. This results in the use of different strategies from within the equivalence class (examples are given below).

The notion of plasticity of articulation (Lindblom 1987) interacts substantially with economy of articulation in accounting for phonetic variability. It is defined by Lindblom (1987:14) as 'listener-oriented reorganisation' of motor activity. Whilst on the whole, speakers use a 'comfortable' mid-range of the articulatory possibilities, extreme articulatory (such as bite-block speech -- Lindblom et al. 1979) or perceptual (such as loud background noise) circumstances are dealt with by speakers by the use of more 'extreme' gestures (i.e. a reorganisation of motor programming in order to meet the goals under the specific circumstances). Hence, variability can arise as a result of reorganisation (spatial or temporal) of articulatory gestures in order to ensure successful communication in a given set of circumstances.

Efficiency of motor organisation is not completely separable from the notion of economy of articulation, indeed it is perhaps best described as being one consequence of it. By efficiency, I am referring to the fact that articulatory gestures are overlapped, literally co-articulated, wherever possible. Given a notional set of sequential articulatory targets (corresponding for example to segments or syllables), the speech production mechanism does not run them off one at a time, but instead, anticipates and coproduces gestures wherever possible. This is efficient in the sense that it leads to a higher 'transmission rate' (Liberman et al. 1967)[8], and it makes use of the 'slack' in the system (for example if lip-rounding required for some future goal is not an impediment to achievement of the current and intervening goals, then lip-rounding can be anticipated). In other words, in computing a motor program for achieving the goals which have been set, motor programming does not merely take into account local (immediately adjacent) articulatory constraints, but also considers the wider context, in order to produce a maximally efficient implementation. Reviews of the strategies used in order to 'co-articulate' vocal gestures in this way are given in articles by Daniloff & Hammarberg (1973), Kent & Minifie (1977), Lubker (1981), and Kent (1983).

The way in which 'efficient' motor programming of this sort gives rise to micro-variability is relatively transparent. Depending on the context within which a particular goal is embedded, it is subject to different coarticulatory influences, which result in fine-grained differences in its configurational or temporal characteristics (examples are given below).

2.2.3 Characteristics of micro-variability at the level of motor programming

Many different types of variability in phonetic realisation seem to be attributable to processes (such as those described above) which take place at the motor programming stage of speech production. One example is the use of different trajectories to achieve the same target in different phonetic contexts. An example of this is given by Kent (1983:64) who illustrates the different combinations of tongue and jaw movements for [ai] in three different contexts (before [#sV], [#in], and [#ka]). Many aspects of 'coarticulation' seem to reflect efficiency of motor programming strategies: e.g. accommodation of place of articulation -- as found in the fronting and retracting of /k/ before [i] and [u], and the production of /t,n,l/ at a dental place of articulation before /θ, ð/ in English; anticipatory nasalisation or lip-rounding; temporal overlap of velar and alveolar stop closures in [kt] sequences (Hardcastle & Roach 1977).

These general characteristics of motor programming potentially go a long way to explaining many aspects of variability in phonetic realisation (only potentially, because a good deal more experimental data is required in order to fully evaluate their contribution). However, their explanatory power is limited in one critical way. As I have mentioned, these features of motor programming are part of the speech production mechanism which is common to all speakers, and as a result they give rise to certain universal types of variability adapted to meet the ends of efficient motor control and efficient communication. That, however, is the limit of their ability to give an account of micro-variability. They are universal processes driven by linguistic goals which are set elsewhere (i.e. outside the universal production mechanism). Therefore, what they do not give any account of is differences in the fine details of phonetic realisation found across different languages and accents. Furthermore, even without performing cross-language comparison, it is evident that these factors cannot be used to explain any aspect of fine-grained micro-variability which runs counter to expectations based what is known about strategies of motor programming.

In summary, the universal speech production mechanism (including the properties of utterance execution outlined above) automatically and consistently gives rise to certain types of micro-variability, but since the processes which operate at this stage are universal,[9] it does not determine the detailed differences in variability between languages. For example, this is why in learning a second language, it is not necessary to acquire the ability to coarticulate or to be economical with articulatory gestures (this happens automatically whenever speech is produced -- it is built-in to motor programming), but in order to sound like a native speaker, it is necessary to make sure that the detailed temporal and configurational features of articulation are appropriate (Port & Mitleb 1980, see section 3.2.4 below).[10]

2.2.4 Micro-variation and the phonetic representation

The discussion so far has suggested that it is possible to identify certain general principles which govern micro-variability at the execution and motor programming stages of speech production. I have argued that one important characteristic of accounts based on properties of execution and motor programming is that they can only explain universal processes, since they are based on factors which are themselves common to all languages (and, with regard to motor programming, possibly to all similar motor tasks). Clearly then, a different account is needed for aspects of micro-variability which are found not to be universal in nature (such as fine-grained temporal differences between languages, or patterns of variability within a language which are not explicable in terms of the sorts of general principles described above). It is here that the inadequacies of speech production models with regard to micro-variability are most evident.

In practice, most (translation) models adopt the hypothesis that the representation which drives the (universal) speech production mechanism is analogous to the output of the speaker's grammar (as formulated by linguistic analysis); i.e. a representation which results from the application of the phonological and phonetic rules of a language within a particular phonological framework. This representation has been labelled the 'systematic phonetic representation' (Chomsky & Halle 1968) 'phonetic representation' (Nolan 1982a), 'phonetic transcription' (Keating 1984a:287), and 'gestural score' (Browman & Goldstein 1986). It is the nature of this phonetic representation which is the source of the difficulty in accounting for non-universal aspects of micro-variability.

A fundamental problem is that, despite differing greatly in style and detail, the phonetic representations that have been proposed share the characteristic of lacking the resolution required to allow for representation of systematic fine-grained phonetic detail. In order to illustrate this point, let us consider the feature-matrix representations which emerged from work in generative phonology in the late 1960's, and which have commonly been imported into a model of speech production (Browman & Goldstein's 'gestural score' approach is considered in more detail later in this chapter).

Speech production models incorporating a feature-matrix representation are found quite commonly in the literature (although less so in recent years). Models which essentially have a basis of this sort have been proposed by Henke (1966), Moll & Daniloff (1971), Benguerel & Cowan (1974), Perkell (1980) and the overall modelling strategy is summarised by Kent (1983) and Keating (1984a, 1985). Within this framework, at a phonemic level, the plan for an utterance is considered to consist of a string of phoneme-sized units configured as a matrix of binary distinctive features. Whilst the inventory of features varies across different versions of this model, feature sets are usually designed to have two characteristics in common; (a) an ability to represent natural phonological classes; (b) they are articulatory or acoustic in nature (this is the means by which they interface with the speech production mechanism -- i.e. linguistic goals are represented in a form which can eventually be interpreted by the speech production mechanism -- the feature matrix is a 'bridge between abstract phonological entities and physical facts' (Lindau & Ladefoged 1986:464).

A binary feature representation of this sort effectively does no more than to minimally specify the contrasts which underlie the production of an utterance, without specifying in any detail how those contrasts are realised. If this representation is then to be converted into a more detailed (systematic) phonetic representation which could be used as input to the speech production mechanism, more detail has to be specified in order to capture the allophonic variation of a particular language. There are (at least) three ways in which this could be done within this sort of framework.

One possibility is the application of phonetic rules which have the effect of inserting or deleting whole segments, or of re-writing specific feature assignments. For example, stops could be specified appropriately as aspirated or unaspirated. /l/ could be re-written as [l] or [ɫ]. In accents of English spoken in USA, a rule could replace /t/ with [ɾ] in the appropriate context.

A second possibility, described by Henke (1966) and Benguerel & Cowan (1974), is that the unspecified cells of the matrix are rewritten as either '+' or '-' through the operation of a 'look-ahead' mechanism which anticipates features in the matrix providing that this is not incompatible with the segment being produced. This is another way of producing non-universal variability. i.e. a feature, which is unspecified in a particular language, may be assigned a '+' or '-', and hence realised differently, as a function of its context.

Thirdly, the binary values can be rewritten as scalar values, with different languages having the possibility of using different combinations of scalar values, possibly in the way envisaged by Chomsky & Halle (1968), Ladefoged (1971, 1980), and Keating (1984a). The result of this is to produce between-language variability in phonetic implementation of the same (segmental) phonological categories (Keating 1985:115).

The result of these processes is a phonetic representation in which a certain amount of allophonic variability is represented. However, since temporal specification is limited to the serial ordering of bundles of features, this representation offers no means of accounting for fine SUB-segmental variability. In particular, within this type of framework it is impossible to have allophonic rules which govern systematic fine-grained asynchronies of the phonetic features corresponding to a particular segment. Unless further elaborated, an approach of this sort suggests that the phonetic representation only specifies a subset of the surface realisation (basically that which is involved in phonological contrast, and some coarse-grained segmental aspects of language-specific allophonic variation), and it provides no means of specifying systematic micro-variability which is not capable of being explained in terms of universal phonetic processes at the level of motor programming and execution. Since this representation is then input to the speech production mechanism, it must be assumed that any systematic fine-grained variability is considered to be the result of processes at the motor programming stage or of the execution of the utterance (Keating 1985:116). In summary, in the feature matrix-based model of linguistic control commonly used in speech production models, micro-variability is predicted to be entirely attributable to processes external to the phonetic representation (motor programming and execution), and is therefore (for the reasons outlined earlier in this chapter) further predicted to be universal.

It is perhaps not too surprising that this situation has arisen. Recall from Section 2.1 that most work in speech production modelling assumes that the phonetic representation of an utterance is functionally equivalent to the output of the grammar as proposed by phonological theory. Given the particular concerns of phonological theory, it is arguably inevitable that systematic but fine-grained phonetic detail will not be well accounted for. However, the consequence of this is that detailed aspects of phonetic realisation which cannot reasonably be attributed to execution or motor programming have largely fallen outside a model of speech production.

Phoneticians, on the basis of auditory analysis, have always been keenly aware of fine-grained differences between languages, but it is only relatively recently that a significant number of instrumental studies have been carried out in this area. An increasing number of reports lend support to the idea that the output of the speaker's grammar (the phonetic representation) is rather different, and in particular is far more detailed, from that permitted by a segmental model such as that described above, and that the nature of the rules within the grammar which give rise to allophonic variation is likewise rather different to that envisaged within such models. As a result, a degree of consensus is emerging that there is a need to reformulate the nature of the linguistic control component of a speech production model. In summary, it seems that the role of the phonetic representation in determining surface realisation goes beyond the temporal and spatial constraints of a segment-based model. Some of the evidence is now briefly reviewed.

2.2.5 Non-universal aspects of micro-variability

There are numerous reports of patterns of micro-variability which cannot be accounted for entirely in terms of universal phonetic processes. The references shown in Table 2.1 represent a selection of these. In order to illustrate the points made above, two of these reports are now looked at in more detail.

Fourakis & Port (1986) set out to test two hypotheses concerning the occurrence of epenthetic stops in final sonorant-fricative clusters in English. One hypothesis was that this is the result of a 're-write' rule by which a stop is inserted in the appropriate context. The other was that the epenthesis was the result of a universal property of the temporal coordination of articulators involved in producing those sequences (as had been suggested by Ohala 1974). As the result of an acoustic study of sonorant-fricative and sonorant-stop-fricative clusters in American and South African accents of English, Fourakis & Port concluded that neither of these explanations were adequate.

Table 2.1: A selection of papers which report experimental evidence relating to non-universal aspects of micro-variability.

Author	Topic of Study
Bladon & Al-Bamerni (1976)	Coarticulation of /l/ and adjacent vowels
Chen (1970)	Contextual effects on vowel duration
Clumeck (1976)	Nasal coarticulation
Fourakis & Port (1986)	Stop epenthesis in /ns/ sequences
Keating (1985)	Contextual and 'intrinsic' effects on vowel duration/the timing of voicing
Kelly & Local (1986)	Long-domain secondary articulations
Lubker & Gay (1982)	Labial coarticulation
Lubker & Lindgren (1983)	Labial coarticulation
Mack (1982)	Contextual effects on vowel duration
Ní Chasaide (1979)	Coarticulation of /l/ and adjacent vowels
Port et al. (1980)	Timing of voicing
Port & Mitleb (1980)	Timing of voicing

The second of the two hypotheses could be rejected due to the fact that there were major differences in the occurrence of stop epenthesis in the two accents. The American subjects consistently produced an epenthetic stop in sonorant-VOICELESS fricative clusters. In clusters with VOICED fricatives there were frequent cases of the underlying stop being deleted (i.e. in sonorant-stop-fricative sequences), and occasional cases of stop epenthesis in sonorant-fricative cases. On the other hand the South African speakers maintained a consistent realisational difference between sonorant-fricative sequences, and sonorant-stop-fricative sequences.

Furthermore, Fourakis & Port argue that the former hypothesis is also unlikely, due to the fact that there are significant articulatory differences between the realisation of the inserted stop and the realisation of other underlying stops (the main difference is durational) -- 'if a phonological /t/ is what is inserted, there should be no way that the implementation rules which are responsible for timing could discriminate an underlying /t/ from a derived one. Yet our results do show a difference.' (1986:217). They use these results to argue for the existence of a type of language-specific rule which is able to manipulate relatively fine-grained temporal aspects of articulatory coordination. Their specific proposals are considered in Chapter 5.

The status of language-specific patterns of phonetic implementation is also open to being studied from the perspective of speakers' performance of non-native languages and accents. In an experiment to investigate the degree to which learners of a second language acquired the phonetic properties of that language, Port & Mitleb (1980) studied the realisation of VOICED and VOICELESS stops in English by native speakers of Jordanian Arabic. They looked in particular at the production of /p/ by the native Arabic speakers. It was found that whilst Arabic speakers were able to produce a VOICELESS bilabial stop (there is no /p/ in Arabic), they did not acquire a number of the fine-grained realisational strategies which are characteristic of the VOICED-VOICELESS distinction for native English speakers, such as a relatively long voice onset time for VOICELESS stops, and vowel lengthening before VOICED stops. The /p/ produced by the native Arabic speakers was produced with the same fine detail associated with /t/ in Arabic. Port & Mitleb speculated that it may be this inability to master the fine details of phonetic realisation which leads to the judgement that the native Arabic speakers were speaking English with a non-native accent.

The fact that the fine temporal patterns vary between languages suggests that they are not produced entirely as a result of motor programming or execution (i.e. by the universal speech production mechanism). Therefore the representation which drives the speech production mechanism is possibly a good deal richer than is permissible within a segmental model, including (to judge from these results) some detailed rules about interarticulator timing. It seems necessary to explore the possibility that the phonetic representation contains information relating to the fine-grained spatio-temporal control of articulation.

2.2.6 The nature of allophonic rules

If a phonetic representation is to be endowed with the richness which these findings suggest is required, it is clear that the nature of the phonetic rules which are applicable in the formulation of such a representation are also in need of some elaboration. As was pointed out above, the problem is that 'conventional' models do not provide a framework within which rules determining fine-detail of phonetic implementation (especially temporal aspects) can be incorporated. A number of strands of evidence have pointed out the inadequacies of this situation, and give some indication of what is required.

Some evidence suggests that the effect of segmental neutralisation or deletion rules may not be as complete as those labels suggest. Port & O'Dell (1984) found that in final stops in German which had been supposedly neutralised by a phonological rule, there was still a significant difference in the way in which the stops were realised depending on whether they were underlyingly

VOICED or VOICELESS. Beckman & Shoji (1984) made a similar discovery which appears to indicate 'partial deletion'. In an investigation of vowel devoicing following fricatives in Japanese, they found that even though a vowel had been deleted by phonological rule, the spectral features of the fricative were accommodated to the deleted vowel to such an extent that listeners were able to use them to correctly identify the vowels which had been deleted.

Further evidence which suggests that rules which can do no more than categorially manipulate discrete primes may not be sufficient is provided by Barry (1985). In an electropalatographic investigation of place assimilations in conversational speech in English, he discovered that in /tk/ clusters in which the /t/ assimilates to the place of articulation of the following velar, the resulting '[k]' gesture was often quite different from that corresponding to [k] gestures which were underlyingly /k/. In particular, Barry noted that in cases of assimilation, the velar constriction was often accompanied by a remnant of an alveolar gesture. This suggests (as Barry points out -- see also Nolan in press) that the assimilation which takes place cannot be accounted for by a discrete segmental assimilation rule (e.g. /t/ --> [k] /__[+velar]), since the assimilated velar which is produced as a result of this rule is significantly different from other velars (it appears to be 'partially assimilated'). Here too, a discrete allophonic rule is shown to be inadequate for describing what appears to be more of a continuous process.

Further debate on the nature of allophonic rules has come from a number of papers by Fujimura (1986, 1987). To take a specific example, Fujimura (1987) cites data produced by Laferrière (1982) regarding the so-called 'flapping' rule in American English by which an underlying /t/ is realised as a voiced tap in certain intervocalic contexts. Using an X-ray microbeam system (Abbs 1986, Fujimura 1987) jaw and tongue activity were recorded, and it was observed that the tongue blade gestures for the intervocalic [t] and [ɾ] were virtually identical in all but the time-course of the movement towards and away from the constriction.

Attempting to link this finding to a model of speech production, Fujimura notes that there are two possible interpretations; firstly that the observations correspond to the output of a discrete allophonic rule which replaces [t] with [ɾ] in particular environments, as would be the case within a segment-based model. The problem with this is that it does not capture the fact that the nature of the lingual gesture is not really very different, only the time course of the sub-parts of the gesture, a difference which is not expressed at all by a discrete rule of the sort mentioned; i.e. it seems that in describing the supralaryngeal component of this alternation, the temporal factors involved are at least as important as the configurational ones. The second explanation put forward by Fujimura is that the allophonic variability observed is not the result of replacing one segment with another quite different one, but rather is merely a fine tuning of the temporal structure of the VCV lingual gesture. This possibility is summed up by Fujimura (1987) in the following way:

> ..motor programming manifesting different syllable or foot structures has to be numerically different (perhaps only) in its timing configuration ... allophonic variation is a continuous phenomenon ... salient contrast evokes discretely or symbolically different perception or transcription, but depending on the context, particularly quantitatively specified phonetic parameters such as degree of emphasis or utterance speed, there may be intermediate cases from a phonetic point of view. (1987:20)

2.3 THE STATUS OF MICRO-VARIABILITY IN SPEECH PRODUCTION: SUMMARY

This discussion has suggested that in speech production modelling there is a discrepancy between models of a phonetic representation which do not predict the existence of significant non-universal micro-variability (since they do not have the means of representing it), and an increasing amount of data showing that it is an important feature of speech production. Of course this point has not escaped the attention of other investigators in the field, especially those who have particular interest in modelling temporal aspects of speech production (e.g. Lisker 1974, Löfqvist 1980, Port et al. 1980, Anderson 1981, Nolan 1982a, Liberman 1983, Keating 1984a, 1985, Port 1986, Harris et al. 1986, Fujimura 1986, 1987).

The diverse strands of evidence relating to this question have not yet led to the formulation of a model for accounting for fine-grained allophonic variation in speech production, but they do suggest certain features which such an account might have, two of which are particularly relevant within the context of the present study; the phonetic representation, which gives rise to the systematic aspects of phonetic realisation which are characteristic of a particular language or accent, seems to be more detailed than is allowed for in conventional models of speech production, and in particular, may govern some aspects of the fine-grained temporal implementation of speech production; if this is the case, the nature of phonetic rules must be rather different from how they have been envisaged up to the present -- they are not necessarily limited to being segment or feature 're-write' rules, and they may have to account for the fact that certain types of allophonic variation seem to be more gradient than discrete processes.

The strategy of investigation which work in this area is converging on is summarised by Fujimura (1986):

> As we become capable of obtaining abundant data with a quantitative accuracy ... we now discover that real phenomena are substantially different from what a simple coarticulatory model might predict based on the distinctive feature matrix representation of phonetic forms... there does not seem to be any justification for the so-called systematic phonetic level of speech description as the output of phonology. Unless we (1) consider the looseness of temporal relations between different articulatory dimensions; (2) appropriately construct a multi-dimensional model of temporal structures; and (3) relate such inherently continuous structures at the concrete level to abstract phonological representations of linguistic forms by a new organisation principle of speech, we will not be able to substantiate the validity of linguistically meaningful underlying representations in relation to physical observables. (1986:229)

The following is a summary of the discussion so far in this chapter. There is evidence that a full account of micro-variability of phonetic realisation involves making reference to three levels of a speech production model (execution, motor programming, linguistic representation). At the first two levels it is possible to establish some general principles which potentially[11] go a long way to explaining certain types of variability which occur. However, there are problems at the level of the phonetic representation, particularly with respect to accounting for fine-grained temporal aspects of phonetic realisation. Empirical evidence suggests that the phonetic representation which drives the speech production mechanism is possibly less abstract than is conventionally acknowledged.

2.4 MODELLING THE TIMING OF VOICING

In the fourth section of this chapter, in the light of the above discussion, I consider some proposals relating to the way in which the timing of voicing might be handled in a model of speech production. Before looking at specific proposals it is useful to recapitulate on what the main tasks are with regard to modelling the timing of voicing. There are three major characteristics which require an explanation: the systematic temporal asynchronies between supralaryngeal and laryngeal activity -- i.e. events at one level often do not coincide with events at the other; the fact that voicing timing is subject to considerable within-language variability as a function of structural and phonetic context (these characteristics are all evident in the data reviewed in Chapter 1); voicing timing patterns differ substantially between languages and accents (e.g. Keating et al. 1983).

There have been very few attempts to try and fit these observations into a model of speech production; i.e. to map out the relationship between patterns of voicing timing as observed in phonetic realisation and a phonetic representation. In the remainder of this Chapter I consider three such attempts. The first model to be discussed, that of Keating (1984a), is an attempt, within a strictly segmental framework, to show how languages differ in the detail of the way in which the underlying voicing categories are realised. The second and third models which I discuss (Browman & Goldstein (1986) and Kohler (1984) respectively) both advocate a significantly different conceptualisation of the utterance 'plan' incorporating into it aspects of the temporal structure and the 'articulatory phasing' of an utterance.

The scope of the three models varies a good deal. The proposal advanced by Keating focuses exclusively on patterns of voice onset time, Kohler's model considers a range of articulatory correlates of the voicing contrast, and the Browman & Goldstein model deals with interarticulator coordination in general, of which the timing of voicing is only one component.

The importance of these proposals lies in the fact that they are currently the most elaborated attempts to account for a mapping of phonological categories relating to the voicing contrast onto the level of the phonetic realisation of voicing timing. The limitation of these models is that whilst they acknowledge the problems associated with a simple segment- or feature-based model, they do not specify sufficient detail at the level of the output of a speaker's grammar to account for the fine-grained variability in the timing of voicing. Hence, despite their attempts to break away from some of the constraints of the models described above, they still have a number of shortcomings with respect to their ability to account for fine-grained variability of the timing of voicing.

2.4.1 Keating (1984a)

Keating's (1984a) proposals are essentially a modification of the way in which generative phonology deals with voicing, and concerns in particular the relationship between the phonological voicing categories [+/-voiced] and their realisation in different languages.

In criticising the conventional generative model of the timing of voicing (as represented by Chomsky & Halle 1968, and Halle & Stevens 1971[12]), Keating suggests that a major problem is the attempt to use 'physical features describing specific articulatory states, both to represent phonetic categories and to serve as the basis of phonological representation' (:288). After outlining some of the inadequacies of the conventional feature descriptions (chiefly that they are rather simplistic and occasionally phonetically inaccurate), Keating suggests that a better account could be achieved by making two changes to the generative framework: 'relax the constraint that phonological feature representations incorporate specific articulatory information', and 'consider how each level of representation' (phonological and phonetic -- GJD) ' can characterise some aspect of sound systems' (1984:289).

Her aim in the model described below is to 'modify SPE features so that within the general model of the relation between phonology and phonetics, we have only as many phonetic categories given by the phonetic features as there are contrasting phonetic types in languages' (1984:289). In doing this she outlines a possible means by which different patterns of voicing timing may be generated within a model of speech production.

Keating proposes a three-layered process for determining the timing of voicing in stops (see Figure 2.2). The topmost layer consists of a phonological representation of the voicing category of a segment. This takes the form of a non-redundant feature classification of the segments to be produced (non-redundant in the sense that the only features to be used would be those which are necessary to distinguish natural classes within a language). From the point of view of voicing, Keating envisages a binary [+/-voiced] distinction (her model is only applicable to languages with a 2-way contrast). Keating then proposes that the binary phonological categories are mapped (by language-specific rules) onto a *phonetic category* representation. With regard to the realisation of voicing in stops, Keating hypothesises that there would be three phonetic categories which would be available for a language to use; {voiced}, {voiceless unaspirated}, {voiceless aspirated}.

The final layer of the model involves implementation of these categories. This process is not dealt with in anything like as much detail as the previous two, but is described, in rather vague terms, as a 'pseudo-physical layer, continuous in time, and encompassing as many parameters as is necessary for phonetic description'(1984:291).

In order to support this framework, Keating first justifies the separation of the top two layers, mainly by pointing to the occurrence of allophonic variability (e.g. lengthening of vowels before stops which are [+voice]) which seems to depend on the underlying [+/-voice] category of a segment, and which does not seem to be affected by the fact that the underlying category may be realised by different phonetic categories in different languages.[13] Keating then backs up her claim that there is a universal set of phonetic categories for the realisation of voicing in different languages. This is based on reports in the literature concerning the fact that languages do not contrast more than three categories on the voice onset time continuum, and furthermore, that the three categories are realised fairly consistently in the same general areas of the voice onset time continuum. In addition, perceptual and auditory evidence is cited, suggesting that the three categories involved are perceptually salient and auditorily appropriate for carrying such important distinctions.

Figure 2.2: Summary of the model of the timing of voicing proposed by Keating (1984a)

Phonological Features

([+/- voice])

Phonetic Categories

({voiced}, {voiceless unaspirated}, {voiceless aspirated})

Phonetic Realisation

('polarisation' and 'specific quantitative rules')

Far less attention is given to the part of the model which attempts to bridge the gap between the phonetic category specification and the real-time implementation. Keating proposes that a universal phonetic principle of 'polarisation' can be imposed at the implementational level, and that this accounts for some of the between-language differences observed. The notion of 'polarisation' is similar in style to the dispersion theory of vowel systems first proposed by Liljencrants & Lindblom (1972).[14] Keating states it in the following way: 'within the limits of implementation chosen - the phonetic categories - there is a maximal separation of the distribution of values' (1984a:310). Hence the {voiceless unaspirated} category would be polarised to a low range voice onset time in a language which contrasted {voiceless unaspirated} with {voiceless aspirated}, and to a high range voice onset time in a language which contrasted {voiced} and {voiceless. unaspirated}. Beyond this, Keating is non-committal, acknowledging the possibility that grammars may contain another level of quantitative rules for accounting for micro-variability, but without being specific about these.

As far as it goes, Keating provides a model which has attractive aims, but which has a rather undefined way of dealing with the detail of the realisation of voicing timing (the level which I have claimed above to be in need of incorporation into a speech production model). There are one or two general problems; the model only deals with stops and is therefore very limited, the nature of the phonetic categories is rather ambiguous (they are 'abstract categories', 1984:290, but have 'a number of acoustic correlates and articulatory mechanisms', 1984:290), and there is over-emphasis on voice onset time as the carrier of the voicing contrast, with insufficient consideration given to general aspects of interarticulator coordination of which voice onset time is only one part. But the main problem from the point of view of the present study is that it does not deal very clearly with systematic surface variability in the timing of voicing.

There are two mechanisms established for this. Cross-language variability, and within-language context-sensitive variability are achieved by the choice of different phonetic categories for different contexts. For example, in English the phonological feature [+voiced] could be associated with the phonetic categories {voiced} or {voiceless unaspirated} depending on the context in which the stop marked [+ voiced] is embedded. The problem with this is that since the phonetic categories which are chosen are so abstract, rules of this sort give no account at all of the fine-grained aspects of between and within-language variation. Keating acknowledges this, saying that 'if differences in the way in which a given category appears are found across languages with identical phonological systems, then the grammars of those languages will have to contain rather specific quantitative rules.' (1984:310) i.e. yet another level of rules getting closer to the surface which Keating does not expand on in any detail. The concept of polarisation is put forward as a possible way of dispensing with the need to formulate language-specific, low-level, quantitative rules which give rise to the fine-grained but consistent between-language differences which can be observed. If polarisation fails to achieve empirical support (and Keating herself acknowledges that the evidence in its favour is not strong), it is clear that Keating's model will have to be expanded to include another layer of rules which will produce the low-level differences.

In summary, Keating concentrates on the level of categories and contrasts without really addressing the question of how to explain within-category variability which is not universal (e.g. micro-variability of voicing timing). It is stated that part of this may arise from a universal process of polarisation, and that part of it may well have to be a part of a speaker's grammar, but the model proposed does not elaborate on this latter area at all.

2.4.2 Browman & Goldstein (1986)

The second model of interarticulator sequencing to be considered in this section is that proposed by Browman & Goldstein (1986, 1991), and Goldstein & Browman (1986). This attempts to narrow the distance between the linguistic representation of an utterance and its articulatory realisation by redefining the nature of its phonological description, basing it on a tiered representation of relatively independent articulatory 'gestures'[15] and their abstract timing relations. This model attempts to marry a non-linear approach to phonology (very close to that proposed in autosegmental phonology and feature-geometry -- Clements 1985, Goldsmith 1990, Broe in press), and the approach to motor control represented by Action Theory and in particular by its implementation in Task Dynamics (e.g. Kelso et al. 1986, Hawkins in press). Browman & Goldstein claim that this approach dispenses with a large portion of the distance between the two types of representation which need to be reconciled (c.f. comments regarding 'translation' models of speech production in Section 2.1 above).

Their starting point is a claim that 'spatio-temporal descriptions of articulatory movements can provide the basis for stating phonological regularities' (1986:237). They see their work as an attempt to formalise this by proposing lexical descriptions based on articulatory gestures. In order to do this they organise gestures into what is called a **gestural score**.

The gestures which make up the gestural score are organised in a tiered structure in which the different tiers are defined on the basis of relative articulatory independence - i.e. each tier is an articulatory parameter which can be controlled relatively independently from the other tiers. For consonantal gestures, five main tiers are postulated, one specifying velic activity, one specifying glottal activity, and three specifying oral cavity activity. These are all dominated by vowel gestures, thus capturing the notion of consonant-vowel coproduction (Perkell 1969), one of the fundamental assumptions of the Task Dynamics approach to speech motor programming. In this way, coarticulatory accommodation between vowels and consonants is claimed to be generated automatically within this model. A simplified example of a gestural score is shown in Figure 2.3.

The temporal relationship between events on different articulatory tiers is not specified in real time, but in terms of the relative **phasing** of different events. Phase timing is based on the assumption of Task Dynamics that the production of vowels is essentially a cyclic, oscillatory activity. This basic vowel-to-vowel cycle is seen as the baseline for the specification of relative phase. The temporal relationships between events are captured in the gestural score as the relationship between the phasing of events on different articulatory tiers (see Figure 2.3).

The vowel-to-vowel gesture is split into four equal phase intervals, each representing a quarter cycle (90 degrees). The events on the consonantal tiers are all situated on one of the phase divisions and it is this which determines the relative timing of the events. For example, two events which are simultaneous are situated on the same phase division line. Browman & Goldstein claim that the advantage of this phasing approach to timing is that it allows timing relationships to be specified without relation to real time, and it provides a model within which differences attributable to rate and stress can be explained (e.g. at higher rates, the period of the cycle will be shorter, but the phasing relationships will remain unaltered).

Figure 2.3: Examples of 'gestural scores' for the words *cammer* and *camper*, adapted from Browman & Goldstein (1986). The vertical divisions represent 90° divisions of the vowel-to-vowel cycle (see text for explanations).

vowel tier	V	*	*	*	V	
	*	*	*	*	*	
supralaryngeal tier	*	*	β	*	*	
	*	*	*	*	*	'CAMMER'
laryngeal tier	*	*	*	*	*	
	*	*	*	*	*	
oral/nasal tier	+μ	*	*	*	-μ	
	*	*	*	*	*	

vowel tier	V	*	*	*	V	
	*	*	*	*	*	
supralaryngeal tier	*	*	β	*	*	
	*	*	*	*	*	'CAMPER'
laryngeal tier	*	*	*	γ	*	
	*	*	*	*	*	
oral/nasal tier	+μ	*	*	-μ	*	
	*	*	*	*	*	

Symbol	Gesture
β	bilabial opening-and closing
γ	glottal opening-and-closing
+μ	velic opening
-μ	velic closing
V	vowel

So, using a representation of this sort (as shown in Figure 2.4), VOICELESS stops are considered to be a combination of a gesture producing oral closure, and a glottal opening and closing gesture. Depending on the phase relationships between these two gestures, the stop could be aspirated or unaspirated. VOICED stops consist of a gesture producing oral occlusion, with no associated glottal activity (Goldstein & Browman 1986).

Figure 2.4: Gestural scores for (a) an intervocalic unaspirated stop, (b) an intervocalic aspirated stop, and (c) an intervocalic voiced stop.

(A)

vowel tier	V	*	*	*	V
	*	*	*	*	*
supralaryngeal tier	*	*	β	*	*
	*	*	*	*	*
laryngeal tier	*	*	γ	*	*
	*	*	*	*	*
oral/nasal tier	*	*	*	*	*
	*	*	*	*	*

(B)

vowel tier	V	*	*	*	V
	*	*	*	*	*
supralaryngeal tier	*	*	β	*	*
	*	*	*	*	*
laryngeal tier	*	*	*	γ	*
	*	*	*	*	*
oral/nasal tier	*	*	*	*	*
	*	*	*	*	*

(C)

vowel tier	V	*	*	*	V
	*	*	*	*	*
supralaryngeal tier	*	*	β	*	*
	*	*	*	*	*
laryngeal tier	*	*	*	*	*
	*	*	*	*	*
oral/nasal tier	*	*	*	*	*
	*	*	*	*	*

This model is certainly a challenging attempt to incorporate a temporal dimension into phonological representations, and to provide a transparent representation of the articulatory asynchronies which characterise speech production. It represents one of the very few attempts that have been made to overcome some of the temporal resolution problems characterising conventional approaches to phonetic representation, as described earlier in this chapter. However, as with Keating's model it essentially proposes an abstract representation, which is some distance removed from that necessary for specifying the systematic patterns of voicing timing that are characteristic of a language.[16] It may be that, at the level of a lexical description, a single glottal gesture is sufficient to express contrast, but it is clear that there would have to be another layer of 'rules' to account for the variability of glottal activity across and within languages. This situation is not dealt with by the authors. They view their model as being interfaced to an Task Dynamics model of motor programming, but one feature of this model of speech motor control (as has already been pointed out) is that it is effectively based on organisational principles common to all similar types of motor activity, and therefore does not independently generate language-specific phonetic variability. So this model offers no account of micro-variability other than that offered by Task Dynamics; i.e. micro-variability is considered to be 'universal'.

Even in the temporal domain (phase timing) the representation is rather abstract. Firstly, Browman & Goldstein are not specific about what they mean by two gestures being aligned; 'two gestures that are lined up on the same grid line are assumed to be relatively synchronous. For example, their onsets, or their maximum displacements might coincide in time' (Browman & Goldstein 1986:244). It is not clear how fixed points, such as the start, end, and peak, of **continuous** gestures are defined. Secondly, the temporal resolution is extremely coarse with respect to its potential. Presumably, within this model, temporal sequencing of gestures vis-a-vis the vowel-to-vowel cycle has the possibility of being specified by any phase angle within the range 0°-360°. However, Browman & Goldstein only use four points within this continuum (90, 180, 270, 360), and do not explore the available resolution of the phasing relationships, and the means by which they are assigned and varied in a given language.

So, within this model, as it stands, the question of micro-variability is attributed entirely to Task Dynamics. Without another set of language-specific implementation rules intervening between the gestural score (as envisaged by Browman & Goldstein) and the coordinative structures invoked to realise the utterance, it is difficult to see how non-universal micro-variability could arise (Nolan (1982b), in a discussion of the application of Action theory to speech production modelling, makes a similar point, noting that the inability of Action Theory to handle language-specific, arbitrary allophonic variability is a fundamental obstacle to its application to speech production modelling).

2.4.3 Kohler (1984)

The third approach to be considered in this section is that proposed by Kohler (1984). He dismisses the solution to the specification of voicing proposed by Keating (on the grounds that her proposals do not involve the integration of a temporal dimension into a phonological representation) and provides a provocative account of the timing of voicing, incorporating some of the assumptions of Action Theory. Kohler's starting points are (a) it is a mistake to view voicing as an 'atemporal distinction at a static point in the segment chain', and therefore (b) the 'time dimension should be incorporated into the phonology' (1984:152).

He rejects the traditional [+/-voice] category for describing the voicing contrast in languages, proposing that obstruents be specified using the abstract phonological category [+/-fortis]. In order to account for the wide variety of articulatory events that are correlated with the voicing (or [+/-fortis]) contrast in languages, Kohler invokes the idea of a coordinative structure. He outlines a coordinative structure composed of the three major 'valves' which are crucial for obstruent production -- the oral valve, the velopharyngeal valve, and the glottal valve. The coordinative structure has the task of controlling the degrees of freedom of the component muscles so that the abstract [+/-fortis] feature is appropriately realised (what is meant by 'appropriately' is discussed below). Kohler exemplifies this by pointing out that in fortis fricatives, all three valves would adopt appropriate configurations in order to produce high air flow through a narrow oral constriction, and that in stops, 'aspiration and voicing are glottal reinforcements of the fortis and lenis actions at the oral valve to produce the necessary intensity differences in the acoustic signal for a clear category separation in perception'. (1984:153).

According to Kohler's scheme then, obstruents are classified as fortis or lenis; this has a major effect on supralaryngeal activity. Fortis obstruents are characterised by 'more extensive movements and greater peak and average velocities of the articulators producing the stricture', leading to 'quick occlusion and slow release in fortis stops, and vice versa in lenis stops' (1984:154) -- i.e. a tendency towards constant VC duration. Kohler claims that these effects may well be universal. These features are combined with a set of glottal gestures which are language-specific; such as aspiration (glottal opening gesture timed appropriately), voicing, glottal tensing. The claim that the supralaryngeal effects may be universal seems to suggest that the manipulation of the coordinative structure takes place essentially at the glottal valve, resulting in particular types of glottal gesture, and in different timing of glottal gestures with respect to supralaryngeal gestures.

The timing of the events in the diverse systems dominated by [+/-fortis] is defined and modified in different contexts in order to maintain **sufficient perceptual separation** between categories. So, the contribution of the components of the coordinative structure are claimed to receive different weightings depending on the current auditory goal (as exemplified above for stops and fortis fricatives). This is where we find a definition of the term 'appropriately' used above -- in Kohler's model, auditory/perceptual criteria are major determinants of the variability which is observed in the realisation of the [+/-fortis] goals (note that this is quite different from the usual Action Theory approach in which articulatory goals are usually assumed to be the case).

Kohler's model is a valuable attempt to borrow some of the ideas emerging from an action-theoretical view of speech motor control and to use them in a concrete fashion, relating the concept of a coordinative structure both to the linguistic feature [+/- fortis] and to auditory/perceptual goals. However, it can be seen that this approach suffers from the same difficulty outlined for the proposals of Keating and Browman & Goldstein, namely no details are given of the rules/processes which give rise to fine-grained micro-variability. This omission is described by Kohler himself:

> (this) phonetic diversity [between and within languages -- GJD] has to be accounted for in an adequate phonological description over and above the specification as [+/- fortis]. The latter gives a general phonetic classification of elements within phonological obstruent systems by referring to greater/smaller power and tension. Thus the labels fortis/lenis are based on phonetic power relations which constitute the invariance in these phonological oppositions. The absolute values that enter into the relations represent the variability of obstruent production. (1984:169)

It seems then that 'an adequate phonological description' (one which could possibly be interfaced with the model of motor programming envisaged by Kohler) would have to contain those absolute values. Kohler does not elaborate at all on this part of the model.

2.4.4 General problems with the models

Evaluation of these models is not a simple task, given the relatively small amount of relevant data available against which to test their explanatory adequacy. However, even before the stage of matching model and data is reached, it is possible to argue that all three models share a feature which means that without further elaboration they have limited scope.

Whilst the models share the positive attribute of attempting to overcome some of the shortcomings of conventional segment- and feature-based models with regard to modelling temporal control, it is evident that, as they stand,[17] their primary aim is still only to provide a better account of **contrast** both within and between languages, rather than giving an account of the detail of the phonetic **implementation** of a particular language -- much of which may not have a crucial role to play in **contrasting** the sounds of a language, but which is nonetheless learned, and part of the phonetic control underlying the production of an utterance.

In Keating's model, the limit of speaker control is the choice of phonetic category -- i.e. still a fairly abstract level vis-a-vis the realisation of the categories. In Browman & Goldstein's model, a speaker can opt to choose the glottal gesture, and to elect an appropriate phase relationship with events on other tiers (0, 90, 180, or 270 degrees), but thereafter no active control is assumed to be necessary since the coordinative structures which are invoked by the gestural score are responsible for surface variability. In Kohler's model, speaker control is limited to choosing either [+fortis] or [-fortis]. From that point on, control is dependent on the coordinative structure which he describes and auditory/perceptual criteria.

Therefore, what these models do not provide is an explanation of systematic non-universal micro-variability in voicing timing. Unless they are further developed, these models predict that patterns of the timing of voicing are either a function of the relatively underspecified representations which they propose, or are a by-product of universal characteristics (motor, mechano-inertial) of the speech production mechanism. Despite the differences between these models of the voicing contrast, it seems that they all make essentially the same prediction: phonological voicing categories (whatever labels they are given and however they are formalised) will be produced with distinct general patterns of realisation, but the fine detail of those patterns will arise from factors inherent in the execution or motor programming of an utterance. One aim of the experimental sections of this study is to test that prediction, and to address the question of how best to account for non-universal micro-variability of the timing of voicing.

2.5 SUMMARY

This chapter has suggested that two types of explanation are required in order to account for fine-grained variability in speech production (of which the timing of voicing is but one aspect). On the one hand, motor programming and execution have a role to play in inter- and intra-segmental timing and coordination. The vocal organs, and the way in which they are organised in order to achieve particular goals, stamp their characteristics on the articulation of an utterance in a number of ways, and these factors must always have some place in an account of micro-variability in speech production, although the extent of their role, especially at the level of utterance execution, remains to be quantified. It was pointed out above that there has been a tendency in speech production modelling to attribute too much to peripheral, automatic effects, which do not reflect any aspect of the linguistic control exerted by a speaker on his/her vocal apparatus.

However, not every aspect of the fine-detail of phonetic realisation can be explained in this way, and an alternative account must be produced for fine-grained variability which is found to be language-specific, of differing spans and domains, sensitive to higher level structures, and generally not predictable from what is known of the physical properties of the vocal organs and of the ways in which they interact and are organised.

The second type of explanation required is that since some aspects of micro-variability are not explicable in terms of universal phonetic processes, they must therefore be part of the phonetic representation. However, on the whole, the phonetic representation which is assumed in most models only allows a limited specification of allophonic variation, and is too abstract to allow specification of non-universal, non-distinctive micro-variability. Without further elaboration, it fails to provide the means of accounting for the fine detail of phonetic realisation (i.e. systematic fine-grained variability which is characteristic of a particular language or accent).

This suggests that there is a particular type of phonetic variability which falls outside the range of phenomena which can conceivably be accounted for by current models of speech production; systematic, fine-grained (intra-segmental), non-distinctive, language-specific coarticulatory and temporal phenomena. Examples of this have been given earlier in this chapter. One aim of the experimental sections of this study is to shed a little more light on this question. The sort of evidence which it is important to find in order to evaluate this question is fine-grained systematic variability which is too subtle to be accommodated into the 'phonetic plan' as this is commonly considered to be in models of speech production, and which does not appear to be explicable in terms of the general principles pertaining to variability generated at the execution or motor programming phase.

In Section 2.4 it was pointed out that this criticism is fully applicable to the models of the timing of voicing which were reviewed. They are primarily designed to model a level of **contrast**, rather than **implementation**, and do not account for fine-grained aspects of voicing timing which do not arise from utterance execution or motor programming.

One of the aims of the experimentation described below is to study various aspects of the fine detail of the timing of voicing in VOICED and VOICELESS obstruents in SBE, and evaluate the status, vis-a-vis a model of speech production, of the patterns of voicing timing which are observed. The experiments focus on the following aspects of the timing of voicing in particular: (1) How does phonological voicing category affect the timing of intervals of voicing in stops and fricatives in SBE? It is of course, expected that there will be differences between VOICED and VOICELESS obstruents, but the focus of this experiment is predominantly on within-category variability; (2) In what ways are these patterns of voicing timing affected by adjacent phonetic context (specifically whether the adjacent context is voiced, voiceless, or a pause); (3) Does the type of boundary between two segments affect the timing of voicing in the transition between those two segments? This allows an assessment of the effects of the following factors on the timing of voicing in SBE obstruents: underlying voicing category, manner of articulation, place of articulation, nature of context, speaker identity, status of the boundary between two segments.

It is possible to conceive of three patterns of results which would have strong relevance for the points discussed in this chapter. Firstly, if it was found that there was a completely transparent relationship between underlying voicing category and the patterns of the timing of voicing in the surface realisation of those categories, this would suggest that there is not much more to the control of the timing of voicing than that which is represented in the plan for an utterance, as this is commonly perceived to be by speech production modellers. If it was found that there was no correspondence at all between patterns of voicing timing and underlying categories, this might suggest one of two conclusions; either that voicing timing is not a major exponent of the underlying distinction, or that the voicing timing which was programmed to take place was somehow altered or lost in the process of executing the utterance. The third possibility would be if it was found that the underlying voicing category had some effect on the patterns of voicing timing produced, but that this did not provide a complete account of the timing patterns observed. This would mean that the outstanding observations would require an alternative explanation. If, on balance, it seemed that execution or motor programming factors could not account for certain observations, this would necessitate consideration of the implications of the results for the nature of the phonetic representation in a model of speech production.

There are a number of ways in which an investigation of this type could be performed. In the experiments described in the following chapters, I have carried out an acoustic study of the timing of voicing. It could be argued that acoustic analysis is far from being an ideal method for investigation of interarticulator coordination, and that a study based on physiological instrumentation is more appropriate. It is true that there exist tried and tested instrumental techniques for the direct physiological investigation of laryngeal and supralaryngeal articulatory events (Hirano 1981, Baken 1987, and

Fujimura 1987, summarise the main techniques currently in use). Depending on the technique adopted, it is possible to obtain records of innervation patterns, glottal shape, tongue position, and a very large number of other articulatory parameters. However, these techniques almost all suffer from a number of practical difficulties which render them rather less than attractive propositions from the point of view of the present study.

In the first place, many of them (especially those intended for study of the larynx) are invasive techniques, a fact which normally has the effect of reducing the pool of potential subjects to one or two (there are a number of reports in the literature of electromyographic and fibre-optic laryngoscopic studies performed on, at most, two subjects, one of whom is usually the author of the paper). One of the aims of the experimentation reported here was to analyse the performance of a larger pool of subjects.

A second problem with many non-acoustic techniques is that it may be difficult to ensure cross-speaker consistency. The fact that a particular technique requires considerable manual intervention by the investigator (e.g. electrode placement; fibre-optic bundle positioning) means that it is difficult to ensure that observations obtained from different speakers were obtained under the same conditions.

A further feature of some forms of physiological instrumentation is that, whilst they may appear to give a very direct transduction of a particular physiological parameter, in fact, they produce data which are as difficult to analyse and interpret as acoustic data. Perhaps, the most extreme example of this is electromyography in which the raw signals detected by the sensor electrodes have to undergo a range of different transformations before they can be interpreted (Ladefoged & Fromkin 1967, Baken 1987). This means that the conclusions drawn on the basis of EMG data are based on signals which are a considerable abstraction away from the actual events which the investigator is attempting to observe.

An acoustic study of voicing timing has a number of points in its favour. It is possible to analyse the speech of a relatively large number of subjects since the techniques used are non-invasive, and the analysis can be performed on equipment which is available in most phonetics laboratories. A further advantage of an acoustic study is the quantity of data that can be gathered from each subject.

Whilst an acoustic study does not provide direct access to physiological and motor aspects of speech production, both voicing and the acoustic correlates of obstruents are relatively easy to identify on acoustic traces (a time-waveform or spectrogram), and these acoustic features are closely related to the articulatory characteristics of obstruents. This means that measurement of the relevant intervals is relatively unproblematic (once appropriate definitions have been provided of course). An added attraction of an acoustic study is that the acoustic studies of voicing which have been carried out in the past are highly limited in nature (see Chapter 1). Also, since the focus of the present experimentation is on the timing of voicing, rather than on the nature of glottal configuration during intervals of voicing/voicelessness, the fact that it is not possible to distinguish (for example) whispered voicelessness from open glottis voicelessness is not a crucial drawback; i.e. from the point of view of the aims of the present study it is possible that little would be gained by carrying out a physiologically-based experiment, and it is certain that a good deal would be lost, especially the size of the database.

NOTES

1. Other works which discuss the status of fine phonetic variability in a model of speech production, and which make a number of the same points made in this chapter, include MacNeilage (1972), Lisker (1974), Ladefoged (1980), Port et al. (1980), Anderson (1981), Hardcastle (1982), Nolan (1982a, 1982b), Tatham (1984), Keating (1985), and Fourakis & Port (1986).

2. Henceforth, the term 'micro-variability' is used to cover this class of variation in phonetic realisation. This term subsumes the category of phenomena often labelled 'coarticulation' (Daniloff & Hammarberg (1973), Kent & Minifie (1977), Fowler (1980). 'Coarticulation' (discussed in a little more detail below) is a sub-set of micro-variability since it refers to inter-segmental interactions, whereas micro-variability is concerned with both inter- and intra-segmental phenomena.

3. As pointed out by Laver (1980:28), it would be possible for laryngeal tension (and, as a result, fundamental frequency) to remain unaffected by larynx raising if 'compensatory adjustments' are carried out by the other laryngeal mechanisms involved in pitch control

4. One is tempted to speculate that the fact that accounts of this sort have persisted despite a lack of significant empirical verification may be partially due to the 'convenient' implications it has of a relatively transparent relationship between linguistic units and speech motor control.

5. 'Quasi' has been appended to 'universal' to reflect the fact that it would be very difficult to prove that a particular phenomenon is completely universal.

6. By 'target', I do not mean a fixed articulatory configuration. It is more likely to be an equivalence class of gestures (corresponding to an auditory goal), defined partially in spatial and partially in temporal terms (Fowler 1980, Abbs 1986, Fujimura 1987). In Chapter 5, I outline a proposal for a model of voicing timing which assumes that targets are as just described.

7. For an evaluation of these mechanisms within an Action Theory framework, see Fowler (1985). No evaluation is given here, because even though the mechanisms are different they all represent a possible means by which micro-variability could be generated at the level of motor programming.

8. 'Speech can be produced rapidly because the phonemes are produced in parallel. They are taken apart into their constituent features, and the features belonging to successive phonemes are overlapped in time.' (Liberman et al. 1967:454).

9. Not only are the above-mentioned phenomena common to all languages, it is possible that they are a reflection of principles of motor organisation for the achievement of complex tasks in general, as suggested by the parallels which have been drawn between motor organisation in speech, and motor organisation in other types of serial goal-directed motor activity, such as sign language (Bellugi & Studdert-Kennedy 1980) and typewriting (Sternberg et al. 1978). The notion of a coordinative structure in speech motor control (and much of the evidence in support of it) has been borrowed directly from work in other (decidedly less complex) areas of human motor activity.

10. The position outlined here also suggests that the distinction occasionally drawn between **intrinsic** allophones (defined as those which reflect the properties of the speech production mechanism) and **extrinsic** allophones (defined as variability characteristic of a particular language or accent) -- a distinction originally devised by Wang & Fillmore (1964) -- may not be as clear cut as suggested; i.e. it may be the case that no systematic aspect of phonetic realisation is entirely intrinsic other than those which arise from the organic characteristics of a speaker's vocal apparatus (Laver 1976:57).

11. This statement is qualified due to the fact that these processes have not been fully quantified.

12. Halle & Stevens' (1971) rather controversial attempt to define a small but powerful set of distinctive features for the laryngeal tiers of a feature matrix have been subject to a good deal of critical comment (e.g. Catford 1977, Ladefoged 1980, Keating 1984a), chiefly on the grounds of phonetic inaccuracy.

13. Other evidence (briefly) cited by Keating in support of this separation of levels relates to voicing assimilation in clusters, and F0 perturbation at the margins of stop consonants.

14. It is actually slightly different, as Keating points out. Liljencrants & Lindblom viewed vowel dispersion occurring over the whole vowel space. In Keating's model, since the space consists of three discrete categories, dispersion only occurs within the particular categories

15. Browman & Goldstein define a gesture as 'the movement of articulators through space over time that constitutes an organised, repeatable, linguistically relevant pattern.' (:224), i.e. fairly abstract archetypal gestures, devised primarily as a result of analysis of x-ray microbeam data

16. Indeed, the only occasion in which the proposers of this model deal with the timing of voicing in any detail at all is in Goldstein & Browman (1986).

17. Whilst both Keating and Kohler leave the door open to the possibility of lower-level phonetic-detail 'rules', the nature of these is not specified, and they do not form part of the frameworks which they propose.

CHAPTER 3
Experiment 1

3.1 INTRODUCTION

This experiment set out to investigate the effect of underlying phonological category and phonetic context on certain aspects of the timing of voicing in single stops and fricatives, and in sequences in which stops and fricatives are combined with other consonants. One of the chief motivations for this experiment (as well as providing acoustic data on the timing of voicing in SBE) was to investigate the adequacy of the models of voicing timing described in Chapter 2, in particular to identify patterns of voicing timing that are not explicable either as a function of the phonological voicing category of an obstruent, or as a function of phonetic processes originating in the motor programming or execution stages of speech production. The voicing timing parameters studied were: (a) voice onset time; (b) the duration of intervals of voicing occurring during the medial phase of VOICED and VOICELESS obstruents. These two parameters were studied in conjunction with the following variables:

(i) factors relating to the identity of the consonant or consonant sequence, i.e. its place and manner of articulation, and whether it is VOICED or VOICELESS;

(ii) factors relating to the context and positioning of the criterial consonant or sequence: whether the adjacent environment is voiced or voiceless; word-initial vs word-final position; the quality of the vowel in the same syllable as the obstruent.

3.2 EXPERIMENTAL METHOD

3.2.1 Linguistic material

A list of 207 words was prepared. The words were almost all (C)CVC(C) words[1], in which the initial consonantal portion was either a single stop or fricative or one of a set of permissible English initial consonant sequences. The final consonantal portion was either a single stop or fricative or one of a set of permissible final consonant sequences. Table 3.1 shows the inventory of the single stops and fricatives, and of the sequences containing stops and fricatives that were used in this study.

Table 3.1: Inventory of single consonants and consonant sequences investigated in experiment 1.

Single Stops	Single Fricatives
/p t k b d g/	/s ʃ f θ ð z v/

Initial stop sequences	Initial fricative sequences
/pr pl tr tw kr kl kw br bl dr dw gr gl/	/sp st sk sm sn fr fl sl θr θw/

Final nasal-obstruent sequences	Final lateral-obstruent sequences
/mp mz nz ns nθ nt nd ŋk/	/lb lp lt ld lz ls lf lθ lʃ/

A range of vowels occurred as the syllable nucleus, but a high front vowel (/ɪ/) and a low front vowel (/a/) were used most frequently (145/207 words) as syllabic nuclei (this was done to allow a comparison of the findings as a function of vowel height). With only a few exceptions the words were all real English words, and all of the exceptions conformed to the phonotactic constraints of English (the full list of words is given in Appendix B). It was necessary for some of the words to be nonsense words given the low frequency of some of the obstruents being studied (e.g. initial and final [ð]).

Table 3.2 shows the number of tokens of initial and final consonants and consonant sequences which were contained within the word list. In designing the word list, the following guide-lines were applied; it was decided that a list of around 200 words (i.e. 600 utterances per subject) represented a reasonable length of task (around 30 minutes of reading time); within this constraint (and others such as the vowel quality and syllable structure of the words), an attempt was made to obtain as close to 10 tokens of each single consonant and 5 tokens of each sequence as possible. There were fewer cases of the single consonants and sequences which only occur rarely in a given position in English (e.g. initial /dw/, final /nθ/ and /ð/).

3.2.2 Subjects

Five subjects took part in the experiment. They were all male speakers of Southern British English, aged between 18 and 21. They were all undergraduate students at Edinburgh University, and were educated and brought up in the South-East of England. None had a marked regional accent, and there was no evidence of any systemic difference between them. They will be referred to by their initials; RT, PB, TC, BD, FD.

Table 3.2: The number of tokens of each consonant or sequence contained within the word list.

Initial Single Consonants

p - 8	b - 11	t - 7	d - 9	k - 9	g - 6
s - 8	z - 5	ʃ - 9	f - 7	v - 8	θ - 3	ð - 3

Final Single Consonants

p - 9	b - 9	t - 11	d - 11	k - 8	g - 8
s - 10	z - 13	ʃ - 7	f - 8	v - 8	θ - 4	ð - 2

Initial Consonant Sequences

pr - 5   pl - 6   tr - 5   tw - 4   kr - 5   kl - 5   kw - 6   br - 5   bl - 4   dr - 6   dw - 2
gr - 5   gl - 5   sm - 6   sn - 5   sl - 4   fl - 5   fr - 5   θw - 1   θr - 3   sp - 5   st - 5
sk - 5

Final Consonant Sequences

mp - 6   mz - 5   ns - 4   nz - 8   nt - 5   nd - 5   ŋk - 8   nθ - 2   lp - 5   lb - 1   lt - 4
ld - 5   ls - 2   lz - 6   lf - 1   lʃ - 1   lθ - 2

3.2.3 Reading task

Each word in the list was read under three different experimental conditions (henceforth referred to as environment conditions 1, 2, and 3 respectively);

[1] in isolation; this allowed assessment of the timing of voicing adjacent to pause, and the comparison of words produced in the phrase conditions (2) and (3) with the same words produced in isolation.

[2] in a carrier phrase providing a voiced context for both the initial and final consonant(s): Say_____instead;

[3] in one of four carrier phrases providing a voiceless context for both the initial and the final consonants:

Wash_____Sally   Wash_____Tammy
Tough_____Sally   Tough_____Tammy

In environment condition 3, a range of different carrier phrases was used in order to aid segmentation and measurement. Both sibilant and non-sibilant fricatives are characterised by a noisy signal, but it is possible to distinguish them by the fact that sibilant fricatives are normally considerably more intense than the non-sibilants (see Figure 3.4 for an illustration of this). Therefore, it was decided that segmentation would be facilitated if sequences of adjacent sibilant fricatives, and sequences of non-sibilant fricatives were avoided (details of segmentation procedures are given below).

It can be appreciated that whilst the individual test-words are real words, almost all of the phrases which are formed are nonsensical (especially those in environment condition 3). Therefore the use of these carrier phrases means that the circumstances of the subjects' performance were some distance removed from those found in normal speech communication (clearly one factor which has to be borne in mind in the interpretation of the experimental results -- Lindblom 1987:13). However, the use of carrier phrases did provide a somewhat more natural task for the subjects, than (for example) reading a list of isolated nonsense words, and it enabled controls to be made on some important sources of variation which could not have been made in a more natural task, such as conversation or passage reading, without a large increase in the amount of data gathered.

The words were randomised and read three times in a row, once under each experimental condition.[2] This made for (207*3) 621 items which were read in seven blocks (the first containing 66 utterances, followed by five of 90, and one of 105). One subject (RT) omitted the first block of the data. This lead to a total of [(4*207)+(1*185)*3] 3039 utterances to be analysed across all five subjects.

The following procedure was used to attempt to control for intra- and inter-subject tempo variation. A small flashing light was placed within the subject's visual field. A flash of 1.2 secs duration occurred at intervals of 2.5 secs (the duration of the flash was established by trial and error at a value which allowed for a moderate rate of speech). The timing of the light was controlled by the programmable clock in a BBC microcomputer. The subject was asked to commence each utterance when he saw the light come on, and to complete it *as* the light went out. In this way an attempt was made to regulate the duration of the utterance in accordance with the duration of the flash.

3.2.4 Recording and analysis

Recordings were made in a recording studio, using a SENNHEISSER MKH815T RF Condenser Microphone. The speech waveform was recorded on channel 1 of a REVOX A77 tape recorder, and the output of a throat microphone (FJ ELECTRONICS), attached to the subject at the level of the thyroid cartilage, was recorded on channel 2. A short tone burst was mixed onto both channels following each utterance in order to facilitate alignment of the two signals. After low pass filtering, both signals were digitised on a PDP11/40, the speech waveform at a sampling rate of 20Khz (in order to preserve the high frequency detail of fricatives), the throat waveform at a sampling rate of 10Khz. The digitised signals were transferred to a VAX11/750, and stored on disk for analysis using the ILS (Interactive Laboratory System) signal processing package.

The analysis procedure involved displaying the two aligned signals on separate portions of the screen, and using a manually controlled cursor for segmentation and durational measurements. By adjusting the number of points per frame of the display (the ILS **CTX** command), it is possible to achieve a measurement resolution of +/- 1 ms. An interactive VMS command procedure, written by the author, controlled the alignment and display of the waveforms. Examples of the aligned display are shown in Figure 3.1.

Figure 3.1: Example of the aligned speech waveform and throat microphone waveform display as used in the data analysis. The utterance shown is the middle portion of *'say thick instead'*.

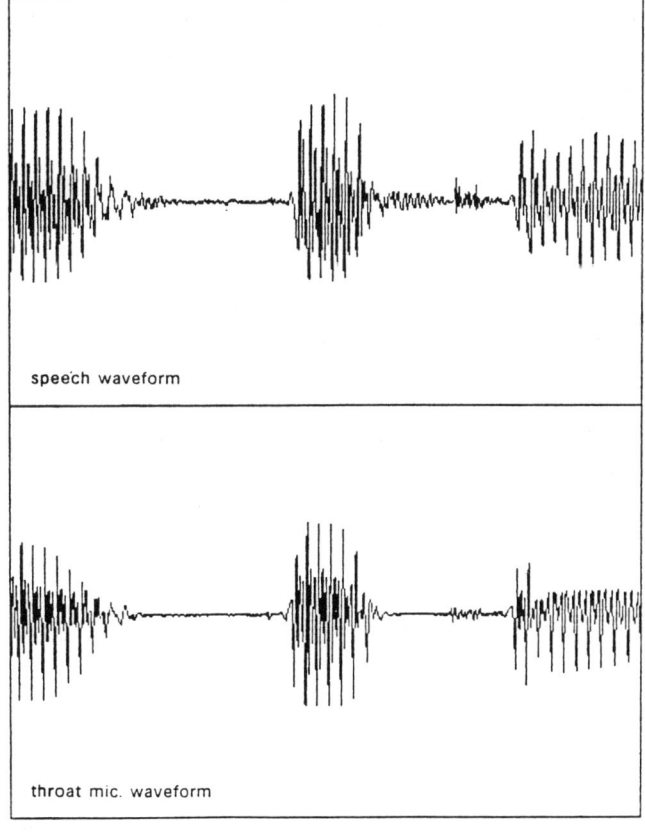

3.2.5. Voicing detection

As was pointed out in Chapter 1, a key procedural issue to be addressed in measuring intervals of voicing is the nature of the threshold which is adopted for separating voiced and unvoiced intervals of speech. A major influence on the threshold adopted in acoustic studies is the technique used for representing intervals of voicing.

There are a number of techniques available for automatically detecting whether a portion of a speech signal is voiced or not (Hess (1982) provides a detailed review of these). They include algorithms based on tracking time-domain parameters in a speech waveform (such as average zero crossings and energy), inverse filtering (such as the SIFT algorithm, Markel 1972), and cepstral analysis (Noll 1967). On the whole, these algorithms are not suitable for the present task, due to the fact that they offer rather poor time resolution (e.g. cepstral analysis requires analysis windows of the order of 30-40 ms in order to obtain reliable detection of periodicity -- Rabiner & Schafer 1978:359, 377)[3]. Furthermore, the fact that voicing in obstruents has low energy, compared to that in adjacent vowels, means that the voicing detection threshold would have to be set at a particularly low level, thus increasing the possibility of an erroneous voiced/unvoiced decision.

The method which until recently has been most frequently used to identify voiced portions of a speech signal is not dependent on processing the signal with a computer. It involves visual inspection by the experimenter of either a time-domain (time waveform, laryngograph or throat microphone waveform) or frequency-domain (e.g. spectrogram) representation of the speech signal. The procedure which is usually adopted is to identify areas of the waveform or spectrogram which are clearly voiced (as evidenced by strong periodicity, or regular vertical striations), and then based on this 'island' of certainty to look backwards and forwards in time in order to determine when the interval of voicing started and ended. It is relatively easy to identify overall areas of periodicity, but more difficult to identify its precise start- and end-point. This, of course, is because voicing does not normally begin or end instantaneously. This means that the investigator is forced to state in advance where on the continuum between 'no voicing' and 'unambiguous voicing', he will conclude that voicing begins (see the discussion, in Chapter 1, of the paper by Fischer-Jorgensen & Hutters (1981) in which candidate thresholds are discussed).

In the present experiment (and in experiment 2), this visual method was used. A throat microphone was used to provide an indication of the presence or absence of voicing. The microphone functions in the following way: 'Vibration of the larynx causes the body wall to vibrate. The microphone picks up this vibration whose temporal structure is closely related to that of the excitation signal.' (Hess 1982:112). The advantage of this method is that it requires no extra filtering of, or computation on, the original speech signal, it provides good temporal resolution, and gives a clear representation of when the vocal folds are vibrating. The criterion used to establish the threshold between voiced and unvoiced stretches of speech is given below. An alternative would have been to use a laryngograph, and indeed the results obtained using that technique would have been quite similar (Lindsey et al. 1986). Askenfelt et al. (1980) compared the laryngograph and an accelerometer[4] as a means of monitoring glottal vibration for computation of fundamental frequency. The laryngograph, which provides a transduced analog representation of the degree of approximation of the vocal folds, was found to give the best results during modal phonation, and when used with subjects without large accumulations of neck tissue. The accelerometer was found to provide good results for all the subjects investigated, and provided a good record of glottal vibration during non-modal phonation.

3.2.6 Segmentation and measurements

The following are the measurements that were made on the digitised tokens, together with an account of the segmentation procedure that was used.

In all cases measurements were taken of the onset, offset and duration of intervals of voicing in relation to the medial phase of stops and fricatives occurring singly, and in sequences with other consonants. Two measures of the duration of intervals of medial voicing were used: an absolute measure (in ms) of the duration of the voiced interval, and the percentage of the obstruent medial phase accompanied by voicing. This approach was adopted because absolute values do not necessarily say anything about 'how voiced' an obstruent is, since they do not take into account variations in obstruent duration; a percentage figure gives an index of how much voicing there is in an obstruent which takes varying duration into account.

Of course, the drawback of using a percentage indicator of medial voicing such as this is that any observed differences could be a result of changes in obstruent duration rather than of differences in the duration of intervals of voicing (i.e. the same absolute duration of medial voicing could be given a high or low percentage value depending on the duration of the medial phase). This was controlled for, firstly by comparing the absolute and percentage values of intervals of medial voicing and noting any discrepancy between them (for example, cases where there is a significant percentage-based difference which is not matched by a significant difference between the corresponding absolute results; some cases of this are described later in this chapter), and secondly, by checking for any statistical correlation between the percentage figures and the duration of the corresponding obstruent medial phases. If the percentage-based results were significantly reflecting variation in closure duration, there should be a negative correlation between closure duration and the percentage-based measure of medial voicing. The results of this analysis are shown in Table 3.3. No significant correlation was obtained. The following sections describe in more detail the segmentation criteria used.

Table 3.3: Pearson's r correlation coefficients of consonant duration and duration of intervals of medial voicing expressed as a percentage of medial phase.

	Pearson's r
Initial VOICELESS stops	.5009
Initial VOICED stops	.4642
Final VOICELESS stops	-.2868
Final VOICED stops	-.0681
Initial VOICELESS fricatives	.2890
Initial VOICED fricatives	-.0099
Final VOICELESS fricatives	-.2626
Final VOICED fricatives	-.3626

Stop medial phase: The moment of release of a stop is normally clearly visible in the speech waveform as a noise burst of varying duration and frequency according to the identity of the stop (see Figure 3.2). The onset of this noise was used to identify the end of the stop medial phase. The beginning of stop closure was marked when there was a sudden drop in amplitude in both the audio and throat traces, coinciding with a clear modification in the nature of the speech waveform from being a complex wave with regular sharp peaks, to taking on a more sinusoidal shape, with more rounded peaks. The identification of the moment of oral closure on a speech waveform representation is problematic, given that it has no single clear acoustic correlate. The criteria adopted here, the coincidence of amplitude drop and waveform alteration, have been used in the past by Keating et al. (1983:281), and Westbury (1979) (see Figure 3.3). The lowering of amplitude is caused by the progressive closure of the oral cavity, and the alteration in the waveform is the result of the attenuation of higher formant resonances (Klatt 1975:699).[5]

Figure 3.2: An example of the application of the criterion used to determine stop release. The figure shows part of time waveform display for the utterance *'say quids instead'*. The cursor is positioned at the point of release of the [k] in *'quids'*.

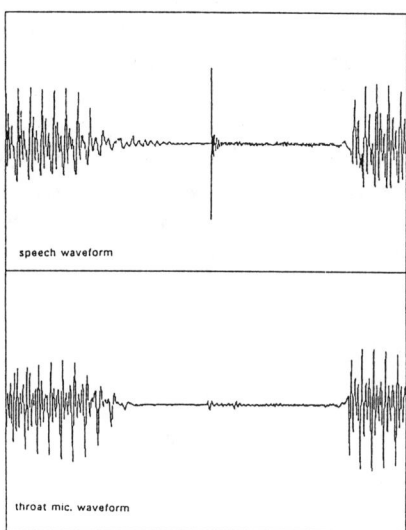

Figure 3.3: An example of the application of the criteria used to determine stop closure. The figure shows a portion of the time waveform display for the utterance *'say prince instead'*. The cursor is positioned at the onset of the closure for the initial [p] in *'prince'*, based on the criteria defined in the text.

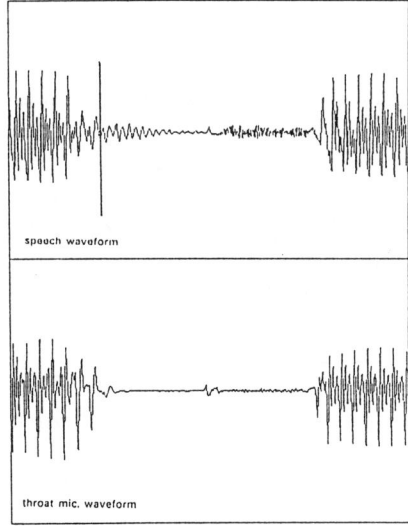

Fricative medial phase: The acoustic correlate of the close approximation which identifies the medial phase of a fricative, is a noise component in the speech waveform.[6] This is clearly visible in the speech waveform, and its onset and offset were used to mark the boundaries of the fricative medial phase. In order to separate sibilant and non-sibilant fricatives as was required in some of the phrases listed in Section 3.2.3, it was decided to mark the boundary between the two segments in the following ways (examples are shown in Figure 3.4), based on the different noise amplitudes associated with these different types of fricatives. In weak (/f,θ,v,ð/) - strong (/s,ʃ,z/) sequences, the boundary was marked at the point at which the amplitude of noise began to rise sharply for the sibilant. In strong-weak sequences, the boundary was marked at the end of the sharp drop in amplitude between the sibilant and the non-sibilant.

Sequences of consonants: The measurements taken from the consonant sequences varied according to the type of sequence. In /sp,st,sk/ sequences, measurements were taken of the duration of the noise component corresponding to /s/, the duration of oral closure for the VOICELESS stop, and the delay in voice onset after the release of the stop. In stop-sonorant sequences, measurements were taken of the displacement of voice onset from the moment of release of the stop. In /s/-nasal sequences, measurements were taken of the duration of the noise component corresponding to /s/, and the duration of any transitional unvoiced interval occurring between the fricative, and the onset of voicing for the nasal. In the fricative-sonorant sequences, the only measurement taken was of the total duration of the noise component, which included both the fricative, and any 'devoicing' of the following sonorant which might have occurred.

In nasal-fricative and lateral-fricative sequences, the measurements taken were the same as for single fricatives (i.e. the duration of any intervals of voicing co-occurring with the fricative noise in the signal). In nasal-stop and lateral-stop sequences, a somewhat different measurement procedure was used. Since nasals and laterals themselves give rise to a significant drop in the amplitude of the speech waveform (compared to an adjacent vowel), it was impossible to confidently use amplitude attenuation as an indicator of the start of stop closure (and of course in nasal-stop sequences this would not have made sense, since an oral closure is required throughout such sequences). Therefore in order to give some indication of the duration of medial voicing in such sequences, measurements were taken of the duration of any interval of voicelessness which occurred between the nasal and the release of the following stop (i.e. a fully voiced stop would have a value of zero, and longer measurements would indicate longer intervals of voicelessness). Hence, the information gained for these stops is somewhat different from that obtained for single stops.

Figure 3.4: Examples of the application of the criterion used to determine the boundary between a sibilant and a non-sibilant fricative. (a) shows the aligned display for the sequence [ʃ f] from subject PB. The cursor is positioned at the onset of the non-sibilant fricative, based on the criteria defined in the text. (b) shows the aligned display for the sequence [f s] from the same subject. The cursor is positioned at the onset of the sibilant fricative medial phase, based on the criteria defined in the text.

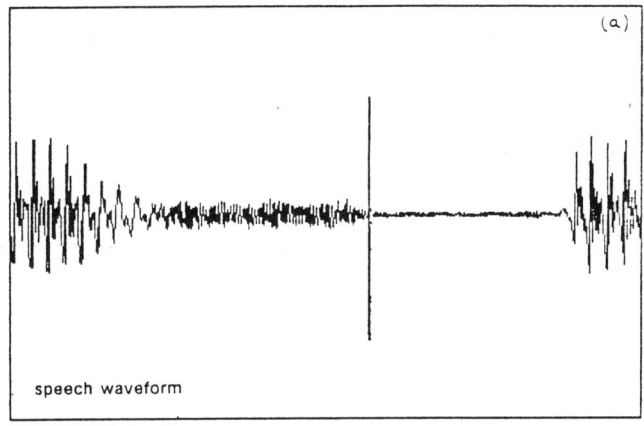

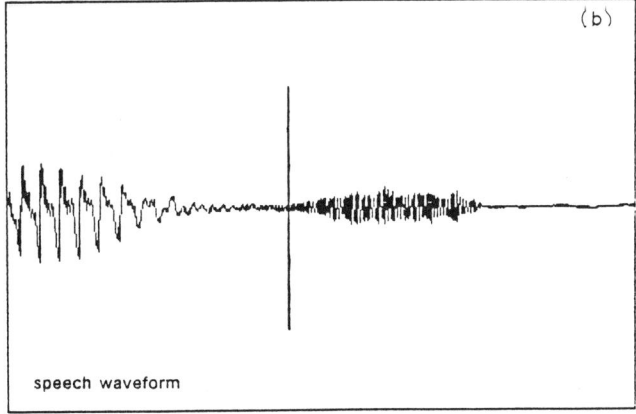

Voicing: The technique used in this experiment to record intervals of voicing has been described above. The beginning and end of intervals of voicing were marked respectively at the first and last peaks of the periodic signal in the throat microphone waveform (see Figure 3.5).

Figure 3.5: Examples of the application of the criterion used to determine the beginning and end of intervals of voicing. (a) shows a portion of the aligned display for the utterance *'say thick instead'*. The cursor is positioned at the end of voicing for the [I] of *'thick'*, and the onset of voicing for the [I] of *'instead'*, based on the criteria defined in the text. (b) shows a portion of the aligned display for the utterance *'tough zag Sally'* [V g s a]. The cursor is positioned at the end of voicing for the vowel of *'zag'*, and the onset of voicing for the following vowel, based on the criteria defined in the text.

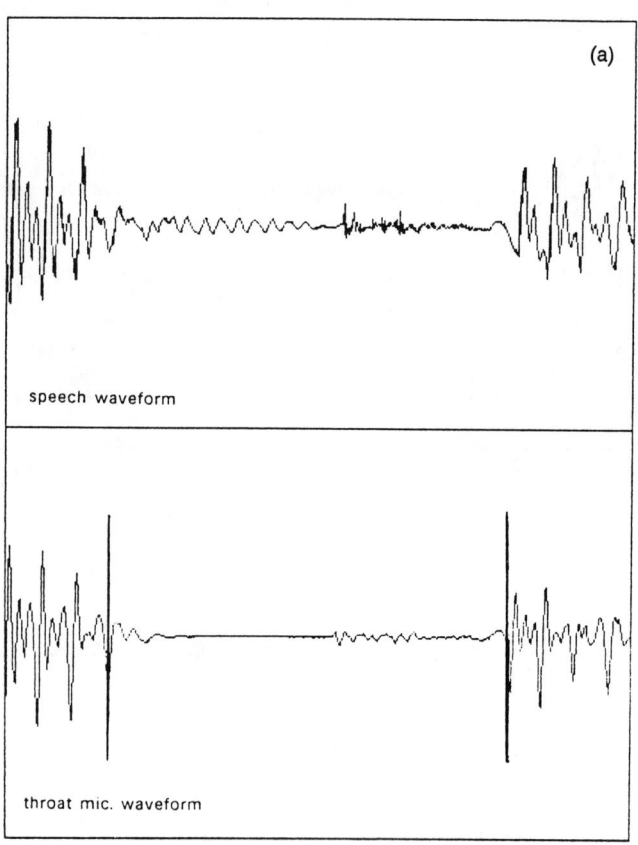

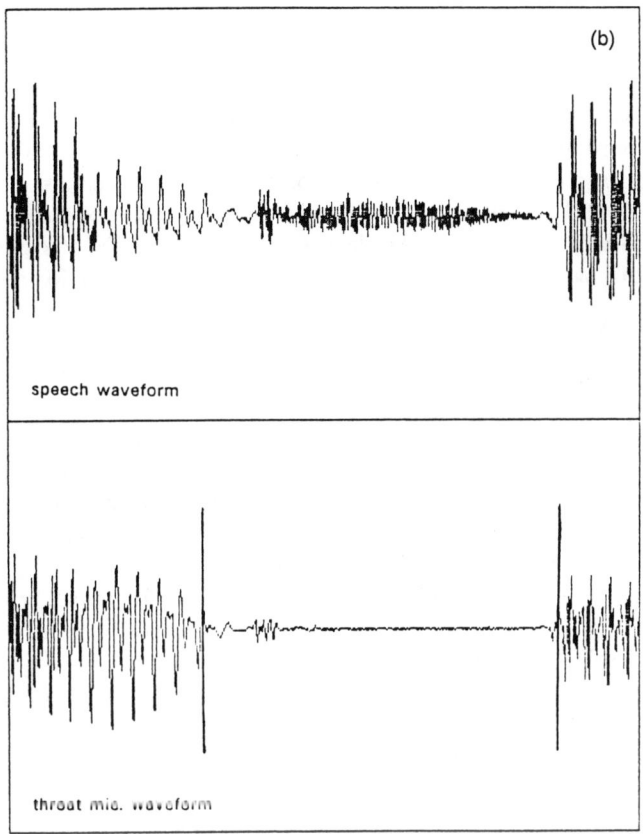

3.2.7 Consistency of measurements

In order to gauge the consistency with which these measurement criteria were applied, 54 utterances were remeasured 6 months after the original analysis. The Pearson's r correlation coefficient between the original and the repeated measures was $r = .9602$ ($p < 0.001$). This suggests that there was a good degree of consistency in the application of the segmentation and measurement criteria described above.

3.2.8 Database Description

The database produced by the five subjects' performance of the reading task contained a total of 5553 tokens of the single consonants and sequences under investigation. Prior to performing the statistical analysis of the measurements carried out on the data, 632 (11%) of the tokens were discarded, leaving a database of 4921 tokens. Table 3.4 provides a comparison of the number of cases potentially usable from the database, and the number of cases which were actually analysed. There were a number of motivations for discarding data.

1. Glottal reinforcement: It is well known that in many accents of English, syllable-final stops occurring in a range of environments may be subject to glottal reinforcement, or in some accents complete replacement by a glottal stop. This is dealt with in some detail by Roach (1973) and Wells (1982). The latter lists the environments as being after a vowel, liquid or nasal, and before an obstruent, lateral, nasal, semi-vowel, vowel (with or without an intervening word boundary), or pause. The nature of the glottal reinforcement (or pre-glottalisation, Wells 1982:260) is that a glottal closure is formed prior to, or simultaneously with the primary oral closure for the stop (Wells 1982:260, Gimson 1980:159). It is not the case that this always occurs in an appropriate environment. Wells points out that in some speakers it may not occur at all, whereas in other speakers it may occur only in a subset of the potential environments. In two of the environments studied in this experiment glottal reinforcement could potentially arise: final VOICELESS stops occurring in environment conditions 1 and 3 (it is unlikely that glottal reinforcement would occur in environment condition 2 due to the fact that the following vowel is unstressed: Brown 1977:27). Furthermore, it can be seen that from the point of view of the measurements taken in this experiment, glottal reinforcement could represent a source of error, in that claims could be made about vowel-oral stop sequences (especially in comparisons with other VC sequences), when in fact some portion of the measurements are from vowel-glottalised oral stop sequences.

Table 3.4: Summary of experimental database: (i):(ii):(iii). (i) - total number of single consonants and consonant sequences contained in the word list. (ii) number contained in the database analysed (iii) difference between (i) and (ii).

Initial Single Consonants

p 120:114: -6	b 162:157: -5	s 117:109: -8	z 69: 62: -7
t 102: 95: -7	d 135:129: -6	ʃ 132:128: -4	
k 132:130: -2	g 90: 86: -4	f 99: 92: -7	v 117:105: -12
		θ 42: 36: -6	ð 36: 32: -4

Final Single Consonants

p 132:107:-25	b 135:102: -33	s 147:151:*+4	z 192:172: -20
t 162:127:-35	d 162:121: -41	ʃ 105:102: -3	
k 114:104:-10	g 114: 81: -33	f 120:107:-13	v 117:101: -16
		θ 51: 35: -16	ð 30: 27: -3

Initial Consonant Sequences   **Final Consonant Sequences**

pr 75: 69: -6	fr 75: 62: -13	mp	87: 65: -22
pl 87: 81: -6	θw 15: 13: -2	mz	75: 68: -7
tr 75: 73: -2	θr 39: 35: -4	ns	60: 45: -15
tw 60: 58: -2	sp 75: 69: -6	nz	120:114: -6
kr 75: 75: 0	st 75: 65: -10	nt	75: 66: -9
kl 75: 73: -2	sk 75: 72: -3	nd	75: 56: -19
kw 90: 88: -2		ŋk	120:107: -13
br 72: 67: -5		nθ	27: 14: -13
bl 60: 53: -7		lp	75: 68: -7
dr 90: 82: -8		lb	15: 13: -2
dw 24: 24: 0		lt	60: 37: -23
gr 75: 71: -4		ld	72: 47: -25
gl 75: 73: -2		ls	30: 18: -12
sn 75: 70: -5		lz	90 76: -14
sm 90: 88: -2		lf	12: 8: -4
sl 57: 42: -15		lʃ	12: 12: 0
fl 75: 66: -9		lθ	30: 26: -4

* the increase in the number of final /s/ observations was due to some subjects performing the word spas /spɑz/ as [spas], presumably thinking it was a nonsense word.

In order to eliminate this source of error, I attempted to discard all cases of glottal reinforcement encountered in the performance of the five subjects.

Since glottal reinforcement is difficult to detect in a time-domain speech signal, I relied on auditory judgement. Tokens were discarded when there was any doubt that they were not exclusively oral stops. Of course, auditory analysis is far from being absolutely foolproof, and it is not possible to be 100% certain that the judgements made were always correct. There is therefore the possibility that a number of glottally reinforced stops were not detected, and consequently were analysed as if they were simple oral stops. This possibility must be borne in mind in the interpretation of the findings regarding final stops in environment conditions 1 and 3 (a relatively small portion of the database). However, some evidence that the detection procedure *was* largely successful is available in the experimental results (described in detail below, but anticipated here). In the majority of post-vocalic VOICELESS stops in final position, it was found that voicing continued into the early part of the stop medial phase. This observation could not have been made if these stops had been pre-glottalised, due to the fact that voicing is incompatible with a glottal stop (i.e. the presence of glottal reinforcement would make it impossible for any medial voicing to take place).

2. Incomplete stop closure: a less well-documented, but arguably just as frequent, characteristic of British English is that many speakers frequently produce 'stops' without complete articulatory closure, especially before unstressed vowels (Brown 1977:74). A number of cases in which this happened in the present data corpus were excluded from the subsequent analysis. Acoustically, lack of complete articulatory closure can be identified by an absence of a release burst, in VOICELESS 'stops' the presence of noise in the place of the expected silence, and in VOICED 'stops' relatively high (compared to closure voicing) intensity periodicity throughout.

3. Lack of noise in fricatives: Not only are stops in SBE occasionally lenited to fricatives, but VOICED fricatives are occasionally produced without any detectable noise in the acoustic signal. This means that it is not possible to identify their start- and end-point (i.e. their medial phase).

4. Epenthetic stops: Sequences of nasal-VOICELESS fricative produced with epenthetic stops (identified by an interval of silence between the end of the nasal and the beginning of the noise characterising the fricative) were discarded.

5. General performance problems: a number of tokens were discarded due to general performance problems encountered in the running of the recording sessions; e.g. noise on the signal, hesitation, mispronunciation, slip of the tongue, etc.

3.2.9 Data analysis

Data analysis consisted of testing for significant effects of the independent variables (consonant identity, environment class, quality of the vowel in the test word), using analysis of variance (ANOVA) followed by post hoc pairwise comparisons between categories (Scheffé's procedure, c.f. Hinkle et al. 1979, Snedecor & Cochrane 1980). All the calculations were carried out for each subject separately, and for the pooled data.

3.3 RESULTS

For reasons of space, only that part of the database most directly relevant to the issues considered in Chapter 2 is discussed in this account of experiment 1. In particular, the results pertaining to lateral-obstruent and nasal-obstruent sequences are not dealt with. However, the results obtained for these sequences are listed in Appendix D.

3.3.1 Effect of phonological voicing category on voice onset time and medial voicing

Voice onset time: stops

Histograms showing the distribution of positive voice onset times in the data pooled across subjects are shown in Figure 3.6.[7] Observed voice onset times in single stops ranged from 143 ms before the release of the stop to 127 ms following the release of the stop. Table 3.5 shows mean voice onset times in the pooled data as a function of stop identity and environment condition.

The results of an ANOVA (in which cases of prevoicing were excluded) show that underlying phonological voicing category is a significant factor in relation to the voice onset time of stops ($p < 0.001$), and post hoc comparison shows that the category of VOICED stops has significantly shorter voice onset times than the category of VOICELESS stops ($p < 0.005$).[8] This is found in the pooled data and in the data from each of the subjects.

Figure 3.6: Histograms showing the distribution of positive voice onset times observed in VOICELESS and VOICED stops in the pooled data.

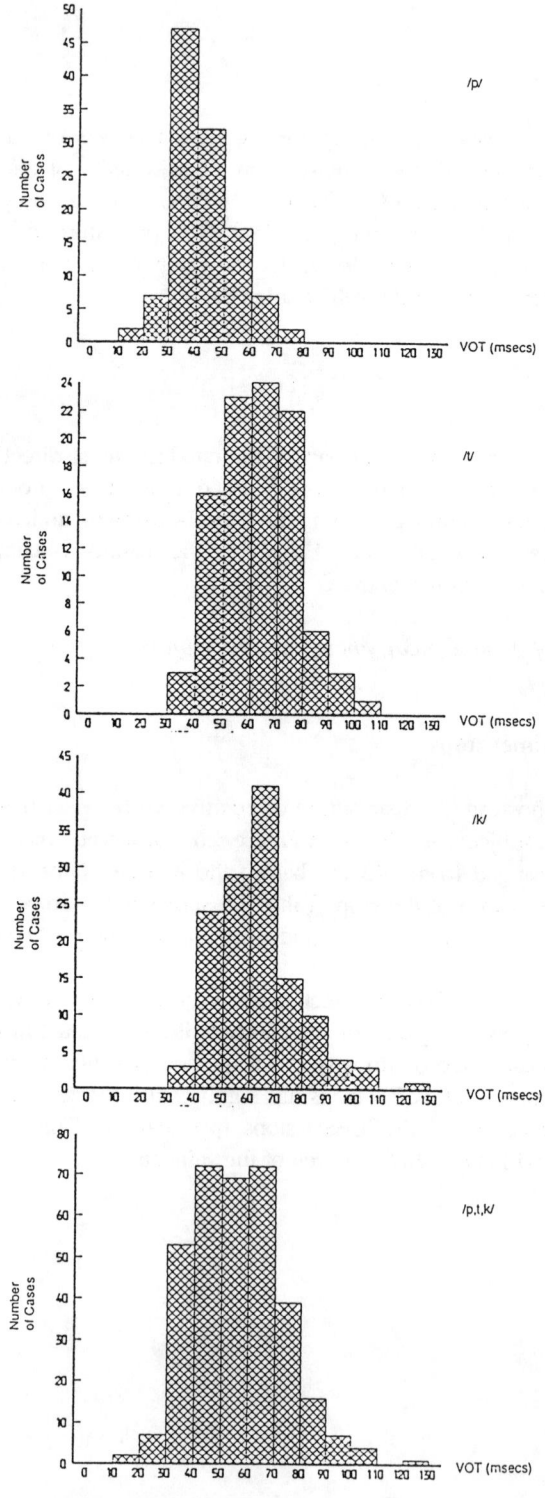

Figure 3.6 (continued):

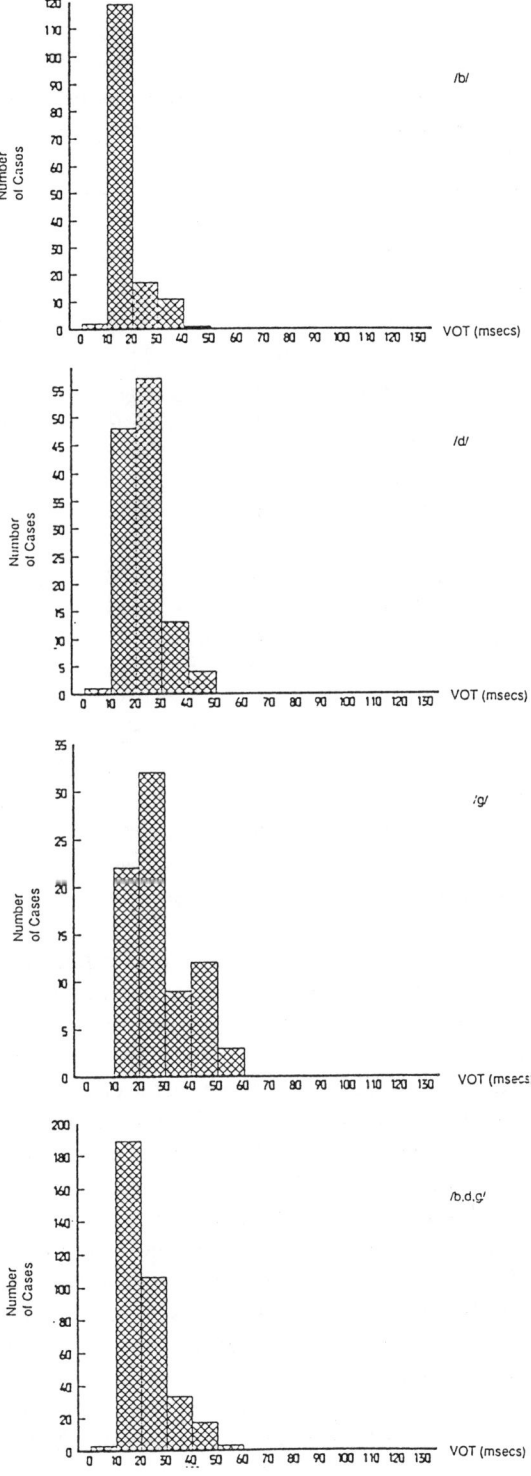

Table 3.5: Mean voice onset times (ms) in single stops in the pooled data as a function of environment condition (excluding cases of prevoicing which would have artificially lowered the mean voice onset time.

		Environment Condition			
		1	2	3	Mean
/p/	X	45.74	41.54	38.68	42.01
	s.d.	10.44	12.22	10.85	11.48
	n	38	39	37	114
/t/	X	66.45	64.54	58.45	63.19
	s.d.	15.11	13.49	11.26	13.71
	n	33	31	31	95
/k/	X	66.09	62.18	60.19	62.86
	s.d.	17.15	13.56	16.19	15.77
	n	44	44	42	130
/b/	X	25.00	15.24	15.15	18.25
	s.d.	8.26	5.84	5.07	6.54
	n	44	51	53	148
/d/	X	32.84	20.63	23.30	25.64
	s.d.	7.48	5.92	7.05	6.86
	n	38	43	40	121
/g/	X	39.96	26.81	26.14	30.50
	s.d.	11.09	9.46	10.57	10.73
	n	22	26	29	77

These patterns of variation of voice onset time as a function of underlying voicing category support previous instrumental and impressionistic accounts of the timing of voice onset in English stops (see Chapter 1). An essentially tri-modal distribution of voice onset times is found across the two phonological classes. VOICELESS stops are characterised by a relatively long delay in voice onset (ranging from 18 to 127 ms) compared to their VOICED counterparts. For VOICED stops there is a bi-modal distribution, reflecting the fact that there are two patterns of voicing timing used by speakers of this accent of English in realising VOICED stops; one which involves commencing voicing prior to the stop release (within the range ⁻19 ms to ⁻143 ms), and one in which voicing commences at about the same time as, or relatively shortly after the release of the stop (as reflected by voice onset times in the range from 3 ms to 52 ms). The second of these timing patterns is used in the vast majority, 346/372, of cases (see section 3.3.5 below for further discussion of the effect of speaker identity on voice onset time). The interpretation of the VOICED stop voice onset time distribution as being two distinct patterns (as opposed to a single widely varying pattern) is supported in the literature by the finding that there is normally a gap in the middle of the distribution such that voicing rarely begins just before the stop release (between approximately 0 and ⁻30 ms in Flege 1982). A similar finding emerges from the present data. With the exception of a single case of a voice onset time of ⁻19 ms, there is a gap in the distribution between 3 ms and ⁻52 ms.

Table 3.6 summarises the major characteristics of the voice onset time distributions for the five subjects (with data pooled across environment conditions as in the above histograms). Each subject shows some overlap in the overall voice onset time distributions for VOICED and VOICELESS stops. Four out of the five subjects show a degree of overlap of the distributions for homorganic cognates (TC is the exception to this, and in other subjects, the cognate overlap tends to be slight).

Table 3.6: Summary of voice onset time distributions for each subject: (i) no distribution overlap of any sort (ii) VOICED/VOICELESS distributions overlap (iii) some distribution overlap between homorganic cognates (iv) all homorganic cognates overlap.

	\multicolumn{5}{c}{SUBJECT}				
	RT	PB	TC	BD	FD
(i)	-	-	-	-	-
(ii)	+	+	+	+	+
(iii)	+	+	-	+	+
(iv)	-	-	-	-	+

A similar pattern of events is found in stop-sonorant sequences (see Table 3.7). As in single stop-vowel sequences, there is a tri-modal distribution, with VOICED and VOICELESS cognates occupying different areas of the voice onset time continuum (although with some overlap). The voicing category of the stop is a significant factor with respect to the voice onset time observed ($p < 0.001$), with voice onset times consistently and significantly shorter in VOICED stop-sonorant sequences than in the VOICELESS stop-sonorant sequences.

Table 3.7: Mean voice onset times (ms) in stop-sonorant sequences in the pooled data as a function of environment condition.

		Environment Condition			
		1	2	3	mean
/pr/	X	60.78	58.61	55.04	58.14
	(n)s.d.	(23)15.77	(23)18.06	(23)14.17	(69)16.02
/pl/	X	55.64	58.70	51.54	55.35
	(n)s.d.	(28)17.91	(27)13.45	(26)14.72	(81)15.60
/tr/	X	88.08	90.50	78.33	85.67
	(n)s.d.	(25)14.67	(24)14.16	(24)10.75	(73)14.16
/tw/	X	83.70	90.58	83.11	85.76
	(n)s.d.	(20)16.57	(19)12.45	(19)11.86	(58)14.02
/kr/	X	83.44	88.28	74.64	82.12
	(n)s.d.	(25)13.64	(25)16.21	(25)15.84	(75)16.10
/kl/	X	79.68	78.80	67.43	75.72
	(n)s.d.	(25)16.31	(25)19.28	(23)11.45	(73)16.8
/kw/	X	78.04	84.48	70.03	77.01
	(n)s.d.	(28)11.79	(29)15.93	(31)16.10	(88)15.68
/br/	X	29.67	21.05	21.13	23.58
	(n)s.d.	(18)14.41	(20)5.92	(24)7.99	(62)10.04
/bl/	X	23.87	15.63	18.12	19.08
	(n)s.d.	(15)12.87	(16)4.65	(17)7.94	(48)9.46
/dr/	X	50.19	49.92	43.64	47.63
	(n)s.d.	(21)17.76	(25)12.56	(28)10.56	(74)13.76
/dw/	X	31.14	28.00	28.75	29.27
	(n)s.d.	(7)13.27	(7)10.95	(8)9.97	(22)10.93
/gr/	X	45.57	36.85	37.88	40.05
	(n)s.d.	(21)10.92	(20)13.37	(24)13.36	(65)12.66
/gl/	X	36.48	32.50	33.75	34.21
	(n)s.d.	(23)15.26	(24)10.49	(24)11.49	(71)12.47

Voice onset time: fricatives

There are no cases of a delay in onset of voicing in the transition from a VOICED or VOICELESS fricative to a following vowel (although see Section 3.3.3 on the timing of voicing in /s/-sonorant and /s/-nasal sequences). The general pattern of events is that towards the end of a fricative, the level of fricative noise gradually attenuates, and the noise stops as voicing begins. The noise attenuation is probably due to adduction of the vocal folds in readiness for voicing causing a gradual reduction in the airflow through the oral cavity.

Another factor which could lead to a reduction in fricative noise level is a gradual widening of the consonant constriction as the active articulator begins to move towards the configuration required for a following vowel (Hardcastle & Clark 1981, Fraser & Docherty 1990).

Given that it is physically possible to produce both stops and fricatives with or without a delay in voice onset for a following vowel, it does not seem necessary to search for an explanation of the fact that delayed voice onset occurs in English stops but not fricatives in terms of properties inherent in the production of the two types of sounds -- degree of stricture, articulator velocities, oral cavity sizes, etc. The observations reflect a systematic (rule-governed) characteristic of English, that in fricatives there is no delay in voice onset for a following vowel, whereas in stops there is, with the duration of the delay being dependent on, amongst other factors, the phonological voicing category of the stop. This conclusion, however, does set one requirement for the speech production modeller, namely to explain how this difference in the way in which the voicing contrast is realised can be represented in the phonetic 'plan' for an utterance. This matter is discussed further below.

Medial voicing

Initial stops: Table 3.8 shows the frequency of occurrence of zero medial voicing (A), complete medial voicing (B), and interrupted medial voicing (C) in initial stops. Out of a total of 238 word-initial VOICED and VOICELESS stops occurring in a post-vocalic environment (environment condition 2), there are only 11 cases (4.6%) where there is no incursion of voicing into the stop medial phase. These are mainly VOICELESS stops (although there is one case each of /b/, /d/ and /g/ in which there is no voicing incursion), and six of the cases come from one speaker (FD). There are only 7 cases (2.9%) in which voicing continues uninterrupted throughout the stop medial phase. These are all VOICED stops, and six of these come from one subject (BD).

The VOICELESS stop results support Suomi's (1980) findings (one of the few studies with comparable data) that VOICELESS stops, with a preceding VOICED environment normally have a short interval of voicing at the start of their medial phase. The VOICED stop data reveals that voicing is normally interrupted during the medial phase of intervocalic word-initial VOICED stops. The only report in the literature which deals with VOICED stops in the same type of environment is Suomi (1980). The present results show a far higher incidence of interrupted voicing in word-initial VOICED stops in intervocalic position than that reported by Suomi (97% of all cases in this experiment compared to 68% in Suomi's data).

Table 3.8: Frequency of occurrence (no. of cases) of main patterns of voicing timing (A/B/C) in initial stops in the pooled data as a function of environment condition (1/2/3). Timing pattern A = no medial voicing; B = voicing throughout medial phase; C = voicing only during part of medial phase

		/p/	/t/	/k/	/b/	/d/	/g/	total
Environment								
A	1	38	33	34	52	45	29	241
	2	2	3	3	1	1	1	11
	3	37	30	42	53	40	29	231
B	1	-	-	-	-	-	-	0
	2	-	-	-	3	1	3	7
	3	-	-	-	-	-	-	0
C	1	-	-	-	-	-	-	0
	2	37	28	41	48	42	24	220
	3	-	1	-	-	-	-	1
		114	95	130	157	129	86	711

The duration of the portion of VOICED and VOICELESS stop closure phase that is accompanied by voicing in the pooled data is shown in Table 3.9. There are no significant between-subject differences at the $p < 0.005$ level. The duration of the interval of voicing which occurs during initial stops is dependent on whether the stop is VOICED or VOICELESS. Intervals of voicing during the medial phase of VOICED stops are significantly longer than those observed in VOICELESS stops ($p < 0.001$).[9]

Table 3.9: Mean duration (in percentage-of-medial phase and absolute terms) of intervals of medial voicing in initial stops in the pooled data (for all cases when the percentage of medial phase accompanied by voicing is greater than zero).

	/p/	/t/	/k/	/b/	/d/	/g/
%	13.95	17.59	17.88	51.9	58.9	66.48
ms	13.78	15.28	15.73	40.04	50.53	55.52
n	37	29	41	51	43	27

These results are slightly different to those reported by Suomi (1980:66). In the case of VOICELESS stops the absolute duration of medial voicing is similar in the two studies, but when this duration is compared as a percentage of the stop closure duration, in the present data the mean percentage of stop closures accompanied by voicing is higher (less than 10% in Suomi's data, and between 10% and 20% in the present data). The converse applies to VOICED stops. Approximately the same percentage of closure is voiced in the two studies, but the actual duration of closure voicing is somewhat longer in Suomi's data than in the present data.

Similar timing patterns are found in initial stop-sonorant sequences. If the percentage of voicing during the stop medial phase in VOICED stop-sonorant sequences is compared with that which takes place in VOICELESS stop-sonorant sequences (results shown in Appendix D), the voicing category of the stop proves to be a significant factor. In VOICED stop-sonorant sequences, the percentage of the stop medial phase which is voiced is considerably and significantly longer than that which is observed in VOICELESS stop-sonorant sequences ($p < 0.001$).

Final Stops: Out of a total of 642 word-final stops in the three environment classes, 56 (8.7%) have voicing throughout their medial phase (see Table 3.10). Of these 56, only 2 are VOICELESS stops, only 6 occur in pre-pausal position, only 13 in stops with a following VOICELESS environment, and the rest occur in stops in intervocalic position. In 81/642 (12.6%) cases, there is no incursion of voicing into the medial phase of the stops. Of these 81, 8 correspond to VOICED stops, and 14 correspond to stops occurring word-finally in intervocalic position.

These figures show that in most of the word-final stops in the database, both VOICED and VOICELESS, voicing continues into the medial phase from a preceding VOICED environment, and it stops at some point during the medial phase. Voicing throughout the medial phase can generally only be expected to occur with VOICED stops. Totally unvoiced medial phases occur most frequently with VOICELESS stops, but can also be observed with final VOICED stops. As was the case with initial stops, the only data which is strictly comparable to this is that described by Suomi (1980:71), in which 36% of the word-final intervocalic VOICED stops were not voiced throughout the duration of their closure. In the present data a rather higher proportion (31/68: 46%) of the intervocalic final VOICED stops are produced without voicing throughout their medial phase.

Table 3.10: Frequency of occurrence (no. of cases) of main patterns of voicing timing (A/B/C) in final stops in the pooled data as a function of environment condition (1/2/3). Timing pattern A = no medial voicing; B = voicing throughout medial phase; C = voicing only during part of medial phase

	Environment	/p/	/t/	/k/	/b/	/d/	/g/	total
A	1	5	14	13	1	3	0	36
	2	1	6	5	1	-	1	14
	3	10	13	6	-	2	-	31
B	1	-	-	-	3	2	1	6
	2	-	-	-	9	19	9	37
	3	-	1	1	4	4	3	13
C	1	23	27	22	30	39	27	168
	2	35	33	31	15	4	10	128
	3	33	33	26	39	48	30	209
		107	127	104	102	121	81	642

Table 3.11 shows the duration of the portion of final VOICED and VOICELESS stop medial phases that are accompanied by voicing. Subjects TC and PB are significantly different from each other ($p < 0.005$ -- TC has significantly higher percentages of stop closures accompanied by voicing), but both subjects show the same significant effects and tendencies as the other subjects. The voicing category of the stop has a significant effect on the duration of voicing that occurs during its medial phase ($p < 0.001$). Post-hoc comparison of the identity independent variable showed that VOICED stops have significantly longer intervals of closure voicing than VOICELESS stops.

<u>Initial Fricatives:</u> Out of a total of 564 initial fricatives, there are 89 cases (16%) in which voicing continues throughout the entire duration of the fricative medial phase (see Table 3.12). These correspond to VOICED fricatives occurring post-pausally (36 cases), intervocalically (49 cases), or with a preceding voiceless environment (4 cases). In 338 cases (60%) out of the total number of fricatives, there is no incursion of voicing into the consonant medial phase. Of this figure, 71 of the fricatives are VOICED consonants occurring across all the environments, and the remainder (267) are VOICELESS.

Table 3.11: Mean duration (in percentage-of-medial phase and absolute terms) of intervals of medial voicing in final stops in the pooled data as a function of environment condition (for all cases when the percentage of medial phase accompanied by voicing is greater than zero).

Environment		/p/	/t/	/k/	/b/	/d/	/g/
1	%	16.25	22.48	19.91	55.47	56.24	49.66
	ms	21.09	21.37	25.05	35.36	25.67	27.41
	n	23	27	22	33	41	28
2	%	12.62	29.54	21.35	79.92	90.38	84.38
	ms	9.63	15.47	15.48	42.03	34.71	37.64
	n	35	33	31	24	23	19
3	%	16.18	27.44	29.56	51.75	58.38	55.83
	ms	13.12	16.68	19.77	29.05	32.35	33.45
	n	33	34	27	43	52	33
Mean	%	14.80	26.87	23.68	61.96	67.02	63.16
	ms	13.79	17.62	19.56	34.62	30.67	32.59
	n	91	94	80	100	116	80

These figures suggest that there are three main patterns of voicing in initial fricatives in the environments which have been studied.[10] The first is that the entire duration of the fricative may be completely voiced. This does not occur very frequently, and when it does, only with VOICED fricatives and rarely when a VOICED fricative is preceded by a VOICELESS sound (but more frequently when a VOICED fricative occurs word-initially after a pause). The second pattern is for the fricative to be completely voiceless. This occurs very frequently, especially in VOICELESS fricatives, but also with VOICED fricatives. The third type is when there is a portion of the medial phase which is voiced, and a portion which is voiceless, with the size of the voiced portion depending on whether the fricative is VOICED or VOICELESS, and on the environment in which it occurs. This is the pattern of timing most frequently observed in post-vocalic VOICELESS fricatives (although as is discussed immediately below, the interval of medial voicing in these cases is of very short duration, averaging less than 10 ms).

Table 3.12: Frequency of occurrence (no. of cases) of main patterns of voicing timing (A/B/C) in initial fricatives in the pooled data as a function of environment condition (1/2/3). Timing pattern A = no medial voicing; B = voicing throughout medial phase; C = voicing only during part of medial phase.

	Environment	/s/	/ʃ/	/f/	/θ/	/z/	/ð/	/v/	total
A	1	37	41	29	14	3	4	13	141
	2	4	5	11	6	-	-	1	27
	3	35	43	31	11	15	11	24	170
B	1	-	-	-	-	14	6	16	36
	2	-	-	-	-	16	11	22	49
	3	-	-	-	-	2	-	2	4
C	1	-	-	-	-	4	-	6	10
	2	32	39	21	5	4	-	10	111
	3	1	-	-	-	4	-	11	16
		109	128	92	36	62	32	105	564

Table 3.13 shows the mean percentage of VOICED and VOICELESS fricative medial phases accompanied by voicing for the pooled data and for each of the subjects. Post-hoc comparison revealed no significant between-speaker difference at the $p < 0.005$ level. Both the identity of the fricative, and the environment class are significant factors with respect to the duration of intervals of medial voicing. Within the identity variable, the voicing category of the fricative is significant ($p < 0.005$), with VOICED fricatives having longer intervals of medial voicing than their VOICELESS counterparts. This is a significant effect in the data from all the subjects.

Table 3.13: Mean duration (in percentage-of-medial phase and absolute terms) of intervals of medial voicing in initial fricatives in the pooled data as a function of environment condition (for all cases when the percentage of medial phase accompanied by voicing is greater than zero).

Environment		/s/	/ʃ/	/f/	/θ/	/z/	/ð/	/v/
1	%	-	-	-	-	84.83	100.0	89.32
	ms	-	-	-	-	93.5	68.33	91.55
	n					18	68	22
2	%	6.34	6.41	5.86	7.0	89.7	100.0	80.66
	ms	9.94	9.97	9.24	10.0	84.25	56.55	63.56
	n	32	39	21	5	20	11	32
3	%	6.0	-	-	-	61.67	-	49.69
	ms	9.0	-	-	-	83.0	-	42.08
	n	1				6		13
Mean	%	6.33	6.417	5.918	7.0	84.37	100.0	78.0
	ms	9.91	9.97	9.24	10.0	87.86	60.71	68.58
	n	33	39	21	5	44	17	67

There is an interaction between environment condition and consonant identity. In VOICELESS fricatives a potential for voicing only exists in environment condition 2 (when they occur with a preceding voiced environment), whereas in VOICED fricatives, medial voicing can occur in any of the environment conditions, but more frequently in post-pausal and intervocalic position than when they follow a VOICELESS environment.

Final Fricatives: Three patterns of voicing timing in final fricatives can be observed (see Table 3.14). Voicing throughout the fricative medial phase occurs in only 56/695 (8%) cases, all except one of these in VOICED fricatives, and all except (a different) one in environment condition 2. In 226/695 (33%) cases there is no voicing during the fricative medial phase. This includes both VOICED and VOICELESS fricatives, but is more common in the latter than in the former. The most common voicing timing pattern observed is for there to be some incursion of voicing into the medial phase of the fricative with this dying out during the medial phase. This is found in 413/695 (59%) cases, in both VOICED and VOICELESS fricatives, and in all the environment conditions.

Table 3.14: Frequency of occurrence (no. of cases) of main patterns of voicing timing (A/B/C) in final fricatives in the pooled data as a function of environment condition (1/2/3). Timing pattern A = no medial voicing; B = voicing throughout medial phase; C = voicing only during part of medial phase

		/s/	/ʃ/	/f/	/θ/	/z/	/ð/	/v/	total
	Environment								
A	1	28	26	23	4	15	5	10	111
	2	13	17	12	6	2	-	2	52
	3	13	15	19	4	1	3	8	63
B	1	-	-	-	-	-	1	-	1
	2	-	-	-	1	28	6	20	55
	3	-	-	-	-	-	-	-	0
C	1	21	8	8	5	43	5	23	113
	2	39	18	26	7	25	1	10	126
	3	37	18	19	8	58	6	28	174
		151	102	107	35	172	27	101	695

The identity of the fricative and the environment condition under which it is produced (see Table 3.15) have a significant effect on the duration of intervals of voicing during the fricative medial phase ($p < 0.001$). The mean duration of medial voicing in VOICED fricatives is consistently greater than that for VOICELESS fricatives. However, the two categories are not completely different statistically. Post-hoc analysis has shown that /ð/ has significantly greater voicing during its medial phase than all the VOICELESS fricatives, and that /z/ has significantly greater voicing than /s/, /ʃ/, and /f/, but not /θ/ ($p < 0.005$ in both cases). The effect of environment class is discussed in further detail below (section 5.2.4.3).

Table 3.15: Mean duration (in percentage-of-medial phase and absolute terms) of intervals of medial voicing in final fricatives in the pooled data as a function of environment condition (for all cases when the percentage of medial phase accompanied by voicing is greater than zero).

Environment		/s/	/ʃ/	/f/	/θ/	/z/	/ð/	/v/
1	%	5.0	3.5	5.67	9.08	14.02	33.17	14.57
	ms	10.48	7.38	8.13	14.60	17.84	36.17	20.86
	n	21	8	8	5	43	6	23
2	%	8.87	8.0	7.08	22.50	61.75	86.57	76.63
	ms	11.00	10.06	8.50	20.13	43.81	51.86	47.80
	n	39	18	26	8	53	71	30
3	%	11.16	8.56	8.37	14.63	19.38	15.17	24.96
	ms	9.35	9.06	7.63	13.13	13.71	12.17	15.57
	n	37	18	19	8	58	6	28
Mean	%	8.91	7.41	7.3	16.48	32.47	47.16	41.15
	ms	10.26	9.16	8.13	16.14	25.22	34.37	29.22
	n	97	44	53	21	154	19	81

3.3.2 Discussion of the effect of phonological category

These results show that, in accord with previous studies of SBE and other accents of English, different mean voice onset times are found for VOICED and VOICELESS stops, and when the voice onset time measurements are pooled across the three different environment conditions, homorganic cognates tend to have non-overlapping distributions (in section 3.3.3 the consistency of this finding across the different environment conditions is considered). However, a description of the timing of voicing in the transition from stop closures to a following voiced context, based entirely on mean voice onset time measurements, hides another important result of this experiment (especially given the particular aims of this study), namely that there is a large amount of within-category variability. In VOICELESS stops, voice onset times range over 109 ms (18 ms - 127 ms). In VOICED stops the voice onset time distribution is narrower in the positive voice onset time area (maximum = 52 ms), but if cases of prevoicing are included, the distribution for VOICED stops can be considered to be even wider than that for VOICELESS stops.

The effect of underlying voicing category on voice onset time seems to be best described as one of homorganic stop separation (although even this is not achieved completely). However, within each voicing category, there is a good deal of variability, and there are large overlaps between the voice onset time distributions of stops belonging to the same voicing category. There is also, in all of the five speakers, some overlap in the voice onset time distributions for VOICED and VOICELESS stops.[11]

These findings contrast with the claim made by Stevens & Klatt (1974:653) that 'voice onset times for the two classes of consonants [VOICED and VOICELESS labial and apical stops] in pre-stressed position are clustered around 0-20 ms and around 50 ms or more, and intermediate voice onset times are rarely found.' Furthermore, the results illustrate a problem associated with the use of the terms 'aspirated/unaspirated' as labels relating to the timing of voicing in the post-release phase of stops. Whilst English VOICED and VOICELESS stops are often said to be unaspirated and aspirated respectively, voice onset time distributions in the present data do not correspond to the simple binary pattern that use of these terms implies.

With regard to the medial voicing parameter, the results show that there are significantly longer intervals of medial voicing during VOICED obstruents than during VOICELESS obstruents. However, it is not the case that all VOICED obstruents are produced with medial voicing, or that all VOICELESS obstruents are completely voiceless. VOICED stops and fricatives produced in environment conditions 1 and 3 are frequently completely or partially 'devoiced'. On the other hand, VOICELESS stops occurring in a post-vocalic environments tend to begin with an interval of voicing being carried over from the preceding context.

Hence, the overall effect of the phonological voicing category with regard to medial voicing appears to be to impart a potential for being voiced. VOICELESS obstruents only have a potential for voicing when they occur after vowels or sonorants, whereas VOICED obstruents have a potential for being voiced in all of the environments studied. Of course, having a potential for voicing does not mean that voicing always occurs, and the actual occurrence of medial voicing appears to be a function of a number of contextual and structural factors. In none of the environments studied are VOICED obstruents always VOICED throughout their medial phase (intervocalic /ð/ is an exception to this), and in many instances there is a good deal of, apparently free, variation with regard to whether medial voicing occurs or not (e.g. initial /v/ in post-pausal position, or word-final pre-pausal /z/). In the instances in which medial voicing does occur in both VOICED and VOICELESS obstruents, there tend to be relatively longer intervals of voicing in the VOICED obstruents, but the actual duration of the voiced interval varies as a function of a range of factors to be described below.

These findings regarding medial voicing underline some of the points made in Chapter 1 about the inadequacies of the conventional descriptive phonetic terms applied to the timing of voicing. The frequency with which VOICED obstruents are 'devoiced' means that there is a good deal of overlap in voicing timing patterns (at least at the acoustic level) between sounds which would typically be labelled differently as 'voiced' or 'voiceless'. The results also highlight the ambiguity inherent in the term 'partially devoiced', since in order to describe the detail of voicing timing in the present data, it would be necessary to be able to identify degrees of partial 'devoicing', for example in order to compare the duration of medial voicing in VOICED fricatives occurring intervocalically and pre-pausally.

In summary, phonological voicing category has an important influence on both of the voicing timing parameters studied. It is associated with differences in the general level of voice onset time, differences in the overall percentage of an obstruent medial phase which is accompanied by voicing, and the potential for medial voicing in different environments. There is, therefore, clearly a relationship between voicing category and surface patterns of voicing timing (as reflected in measurements of voice onset time and medial voicing), but it is not a transparent one. Many aspects of the realisation of voicing timing are not predictable from the nature of the voicing category. This appears to govern no more than relatively coarse-grained cognate separation along the two dimensions being studied. Within these general patterns corresponding to each category there is a good deal of additional variability.

Much of the within-category micro-variability which is observed appears to be systematically determined by a number of factors. In the rest of this account of experiment 1, I examine these in some detail. From the point of view of refining our understanding of the control of the timing of voicing in speech production, it is necessary to determine their status: i.e. are they a reflection of general properties of speech production (properties of the vocal organs or motor programming strategies), or is there any evidence that they might be to a certain extent a reflection of implementation strategies originating in the phonetic representation? This forms the general focus of the discussion in the remainder of this chapter.

Our inadequate knowledge of the acoustic, aerodynamic, and mechanical factors involved in the production of VOICED and VOICELESS obstruents means that some of the following discussion is of a rather tentative nature, and all of the conclusions are subject to further verification by future research. Of course, in this respect, the present study is no worse off than previous studies of the timing of voicing (such as those carried out by Klatt 1975, Weismer 1980, and Suomi 1980), to which the same reservations must apply.

3.3.3 Other factors affecting voice onset time

Place of articulation

Within each voicing category (excluding cases of prevoicing), labial stops have shorter mean delays in voice onset than stops produced at other places of articulation ($p < 0.005$ in both cases -- see Table 3.5). There is no significant difference between the alveolar and the velar stops. This is the case in the pooled data and in the results of all the subjects (the data suggest that on the whole, there is a slight tendency for VOICELESS alveolars to have longer mean voice onset times than VOICELESS velar stops). Table 3.16 shows the mean percentage increase in voice onset times at different places of articulation, for comparison with Table 1.2 in Chapter 1.

Table 3.16: Percentage difference in mean voice onset times in VOICELESS stops in the pooled data as a function of stop place of articulation.

/p/	--->	/t/	50.41 %
/p/	--->	/k/	49.63 %
/t/	--->	/k/	-0.52 %

The place of articulation effect found here is different to that which has been reported in a number of studies of English, and of certain other languages (e.g. Lisker & Abramson 1964). With few exceptions, the reports in the literature note that there is a gradual increase in voice onset time the more retracted the place of articulation of the stops in question (one exception, with comparable data, is Suomi (1980) who reports similar, but less consistent, results to those found in the present experiment in his study of voice onset time in British English).

The place of articulation effect found in stop-vowel sequences also applies to stop-sonorant-vowel sequences. The identity of the stop in VOICELESS stop-sonorant sequences is a highly significant factor with respect to voice onset time (Table 3.7). Sequences with labial, alveolar, and velar stops are all significantly different from each other ($p < 0.005$). Labials have the shortest voice onset times, alveolars the longest, and velars fall between these two. Likewise, in VOICED stop-sonorant sequences (also shown in Table 3.7), the identity of the stop has a significant effect on the duration of voice onset time.

/b/-sonorant sequences have significantly shorter delays in voice onset than both /d/-sonorant and /g/-sonorant sequences (p < 0.005). There is no significant difference between these latter two classes, although there is a tendency for the average voice onset time in /d/-sonorant sequences to be longer than in /g/-sonorant sequences.

Stop place of articulation also influences the duration of voice onset time in /s/-stop-V sequences (see Table 3.17). /sp/ sequences have significantly (p < 0.001) shorter voice onset times than /st/ and /sk/ sequences (although the actual differences between the means are relatively small). This result is consistent with the place of articulation effect observed for voice onset time in stops preceding vowels, described above. The preceding environment of the sequence did not prove to be a significant variable, and no strong tendency could be observed either in the pooled data or in the data from each subject. Further discussion of these sequences is given in Section 3.3.4.

Table 3.17: Mean voice onset times (ms) of stops in word-initial /s-stop-V/ sequences in the pooled data as a function of environment condition.

		Environment Condition			
		1	2	3	Mean
/sp/	X	18.52	15.39	19.04	17.65
	s.d.	6.5	4.7	6.3	6.0
	n	23	23	23	69
/st/	X	23.70	22.78	24.82	23.75
	s.d.	4.8	6.8	6.2	6.0
	n	20	23	22	65
/sk/	X	27.92	26.28	27.48	27.21
	s.d.	7.6	6.9	6.9	7.0
	n	24	25	23	72

In summary, stop place of articulation is a source of systematic micro-variability of voice onset time, but the place effect found in this data is rather different to that observed in many other studies of English. The fact that voice onset time is significantly affected by the place of articulation of a stop was established in the earliest studies of voice onset time (Lisker & Abramson 1964), and has been replicated a number of times since. However, despite the frequency with which this effect has been noted, it is rather surprising that no generally accepted explanation for this has been formulated (indeed, most authors note the presence of the effect without attempting an explanation).

As outlined by Fischer-Jorgensen (1980), there are a number of candidate explanations, but the problem with all of these with regard to the present data is that they are designed to account for progressively greater voice onset times the more retracted the place of articulation of the stop, whereas the results of this experiment suggest that the main difference to be accounted for is that between labial stops and alveolar/velar stops.[12] Most of the 'explanations' proposed in the literature claim that different durations of voice onset time are produced automatically, either by the aerodynamic conditions or by the mechanical factors associated with stops produced at different places of articulation.

One hypothesis (Weismer 1980) is that since, all else being equal, more retracted stops have relatively higher intra-oral air pressure at the moment at which the stop is released, it takes longer for the trans-glottal pressure difference to reach the level at which voicing might commence. This explanation is one which could be tested using an articulatory synthesiser; i.e. given a model of the vocal apparatus, it would be possible to hold constant other articulatory parameters, whilst investigating whether place-related differences in voice onset time are produced 'automatically' as a result of the aerodynamic effects of producing stops at different places of articulation. Whilst a lot of work on modelling the interaction of laryngeal and supralaryngeal aspects of the vocal apparatus has been carried out (Keating 1984b, Scully 1987, 1990, Bickley & Stevens 1987) there are no reports in the literature of this test being performed.

Another hypothesis claims that velars have longer voice onset times because of the relatively slow movement of the tongue body compared to the tongue tip/blade and the lips (Klatt 1975, Fischer-Jorgensen 1980). Since labial release is relatively quick, the aerodynamic conditions for the onset of voicing (i.e. a sufficient trans-glottal pressure drop) can be achieved relatively quickly.

In fact, Klatt's (1975) account of the place effect on voice onset time is based on two different explanations. He suggests that the increasing voice onset times observed in /b/, /d/, and /g/ are the result of physiological factors (described in the previous paragraph), but that in the case of /p/, /t/, and /k/ the progressively higher voice onset times are the result of a strategy designed to ensure a voiceless percept:

> A longer VOT is needed in a voiceless plosive with slower formant transitions such as /k/ to prevent listeners from hearing the low frequency

> energy that would indicate a /g/. There is probably a rule of English phonology that delays glottal closure in /k/ relative to /p, t/ which share the same laryngeal feature assignment. (1975:702)

These are all plausible, if unverified[13], possible explanations for a place of articulation effect which produces progressively longer voice onset times the more retracted the place of articulation of the stop. However, none of them provide an immediate account of the present results, especially of the finding that alveolars and velars are not significantly different, and that there is a tendency for alveolars to have slightly longer mean voice onset times than velars.

One possibility is that the velar/alveolar ordering could be an artefact of an interaction between adjacent vowel environment and voice onset time (this is the suggestion put forward by Hawkins (1979:256) in relation to the findings of Peterson and Lehiste (1960) that front allophones of /k/, which occur before high front vowels, have longer voice onset times than back allophones). Since (as is discussed in more detail below) high vowels tend to be associated with slightly longer voice onset times than low vowels, it is conceivable that the alveolar - velar ordering could arise if in the present data, there were more cases of /t/ and /d/ before high vowels than /k/ or /g/. However, this is not a possible explanation for the present findings; firstly because it is not the case that there are many more tokens of alveolars occurring before high vowels than velars (52 and 59 respectively in the case of VOICELESS stops, 54 and 38 respectively in the case of VOICED stops), and secondly because of the fact that the same place effect is found in stops occurring before all types of vowels (i.e. there is no interaction between place of articulation and vowel environment with respect to voice onset time).

Suomi (1980) puts forward a different explanation. In attempting to account for the effect of place of articulation in his study of voice onset time in British English (labials consistently had the shortest durations, the ordering of alveolars and velars was different in the data from different subjects), he concluded that:

> there is an invariant glottal gesture indiscriminately employed in the production of /voiceless/ stops, and that the acoustic variation observed with regard to VOT is simply an automatic inevitable concomitant of differences in the duration of the supraglottal constrictory articulations (conditioned by /place of articulation/ specifications). (1980:75)

Suomi reached this conclusion[14] on the basis of a comparison of mean values for stop closure duration and the duration of the 'abduction gesture' which he took to correspond to the interval of voicelessness between the offset of voicing from a preceding voiced context until the moment of voice onset for a following vowel. He found that within the data from each speaker the mean duration of the 'abduction gesture' was relatively constant across the three places of articulation, and that there was a reciprocal relationship between mean stop closure duration and mean voice onset time. This suggests that in accounting for variability in voice onset time, it is essential to take into consideration not just the voice onset time measurements themselves, but also how these relate to the closure duration for the stop.

There are some obvious procedural problems involved in claiming that the duration of a laryngeal abduction gesture is equal to the duration of the interval of voicelessness in a VCV sequence. Given the gradual nature of glottal abduction (described in Chapter 1) voicing only ceases some time after the abduction gesture has been initiated. Equally problematic is that the end of the interval of voicelessness would vary as a function of the criteria used to indicate that voicing has recommenced (the range of possible criteria was discussed earlier in this chapter). In order to be absolutely certain what the voiceless interval actually corresponds to, it would be necessary to compare measures of the voiceless interval with fibreoptic recordings of laryngeal activity (which, to the best of my knowledge, has not been done). Therefore, any conclusions drawn on the basis of this measure are clearly subject to confirmation by more direct observation (although as has already been noted, direct observation itself is far from being trouble-free). However, if we assume, along with Suomi, that the voiceless interval **does** provide a reasonable indication of the duration of the glottal gesture in obstruent production, an analysis of the sort carried out by Suomi appears to be a fruitful line to follow in accounting for the place of articulation effects on voice onset time.[15] Although as is shown below, the facts are not as straightforward as suggested by Suomi.

If exactly the same analysis is performed with the data from the present experiment, it is possible to evaluate the extent to which Suomi's explanation accounts for the findings. Table 3.18 shows for VOICELESS stops the mean duration of voice onset time, stop closure, and 'abduction gesture' (calculated as in Suomi's method: 'abduction gesture' = [stop duration + voice onset time] - duration of closure voicing) for each of the speakers. The figures discussed in the rest of this section are for environment condition 2 only, since this is the only condition in which the start and finish of the 'abduction gesture' can be reliably determined.

Table 3.18: Mean duration (ms) of stop closure, voice onset time, and 'abduction gesture' in initial VOICELESS stops in environment condition 2 for each subject (arrows show direction of difference).

Subject	stop duration			VOT			'abduction' duration		
	/p/	/t/	/k/	/p/	/t/	/k/	/p/	/t/	/k/
RT	77	<79	>72	39	<53	>52	101	<120	>111
s.d.	9	12	15	6	8	11	6	17	17
PB	90	>68	<79	38	<68	>59	116	<127	>122
s.d.	14	18	11	19	13	7	21	23	14
TC	113	>105	>101	46	<70	>62	139	>138	=138
s.d.	13	32	12	11	6	11	10	28	17
BD	105	>94	<97	40	<61	<68	132	<143	<151
s.d.	9	16	19	13	14	11	16	23	23
FD	82	>65	>58	45	<67	<69	122	<124	>122
s.d.	11	12	9	7	19	20	10	19	20
Pool	94	>81	<82	42	<64	>62	123	<130	>129
s.d.	16	23	21	12	14	14	18	22	23

In VOICELESS stops, on the whole, there appears to be a reciprocal relationship between labial closure duration and labial voice onset time. In every case, labials have the shortest voice onset time measures and the longest mean durations (except in the data from RT). The situation is not so clear with alveolars and velars. Suomi's hypothesis predicts that a shorter stop should have a longer voice onset time. Table 3.18 shows that this is only found in the non-labial stops of subjects PB and FD, as well as in the overall means.

It is also apparent from the relatively large standard deviations shown in Table 3.18 that the duration of the 'abduction gesture' is not as constant as claimed by Suomi for his data. Some speakers show more variability than others. More importantly, the overall **pattern** of variability of the 'abduction gesture' duration within each speaker (as indicated by the arrows) is at least as good a predictor of the **direction** of the observed place effects on voice onset time as the duration of the stop closure. In the light of this evidence, Suomi's explanation may require some elaboration. This point is underlined if we pursue this line of analysis.

Suomi reached his conclusions on the basis of a comparison of means, without any consideration of the fact that underlying those means were rather wide distributions (the standard deviations for Suomi's voice onset time measurements are rather higher than those observed in the present data). A stronger test of his hypothesis that there is an inverse relationship between voice onset time and closure duration is to perform correlation analyses on the data rather than just visually inspect mean results such as those in Table 3.18. Suomi's hypothesis predicts that there should be a negative correlation between closure duration and voice onset time, and that even though there might be some random variability in the duration of a speaker's 'abduction gesture', this would not be expected to correlate positively with voice onset time. The results presented above in Table 3.18 suggest, however, that there is also likely to be a degree of positive correlation between duration of the 'abduction gesture' and voice onset time.

Table 3.19 shows the results of a correlation analysis of voice onset time with closure duration and duration of the 'abduction gesture' in VOICELESS stops. There is a tendency for there to be a negative correlation between closure duration and voice onset time, but it is only significant in the data from a single speaker (FD), and correlation coefficients are extremely low in some of the other speakers (e.g. BD). There is however a considerably stronger positive correlation between duration of the 'abduction gesture' and voice onset time. Pooling across stops, this is significant in the pooled data and in 4 out of 5 subjects.

Suomi's account of place differences in voice onset time is therefore not wholly appropriate for the present data. It would be inaccurate to claim that the figures shown in Table 3.18 suggest that speakers use an invariant glottal 'abduction gesture' across different places of articulation, and that the difference in stop duration as a function of place of articulation is the unique correlate of differences in voice onset times. At least as strong a correlate seems to be the duration of the glottal 'abduction gesture' which on the whole is longer in stops with longer voice onset times.

Table 3.19: Pearson's *r* coefficients (all data from environment condition 2): * = significant at p < 0.001. The figures on the top of each cell are coefficients for the voice onset time/abduction correlation, the figures on the bottom of each cell are coefficients for the voice onset time/closure duration correlation.

	RT	PB	Subject TC	BD	FD	Pool
/p/	.48	*.96	.47	.57	.21	*.61
	-.56	-.67	-.50	-.29	-.45	-.02
/t/	.96	.82	-.17	.63	.88	*.57
	-.92	.27	-.39	-.08	-.53	-.05
/k/	.83	.80	-.54	.78	.84	*.70
	.15	.01	-.29	-.51	-.32	-.04
Mean	*.82	*.76	.21	*.69	*.67	*.59
	-.09	-.28	-.39	-.11	-.63*	-.19

As for the place effect on voice onset time in VOICED stops, Suomi proposes an aerodynamic explanation along the lines of those used by other investigators, as outlined above (e.g. Klatt 1975). It is evident that the notion of an 'abduction gesture' as used in the analysis of VOICELESS stops is not really appropriate for VOICED stops in which, if there is any interruption of voicing, glottal abduction does not take place (Catford (1977:112) describes the glottal configuration for VOICED obstruents which are not accompanied by voicing as a 'whisper-like narrowing of the glottis'). However, if we consider the relationship between the duration of VOICED stops, their voice onset time, and the duration of the 'voiceless interval' (without making any assumptions about the nature of the glottal gesture that this corresponds to[16]), results emerge which are similar to those for VOICELESS stops (see Table 3.20).

As is the case with VOICELESS stops, there is a reciprocal relationship between voice onset time and stop duration. The relationship between the mean voice onset time and duration of the 'voiceless interval' is less consistent across speakers. The correlation coefficients for voice onset time and stop duration, and voice onset time and 'voiceless interval' duration are shown in Table 3.21. Pooling across all speakers, both correlations are significant (p < 0.001), with the higher of the two being between voice onset time and 'voiceless interval' duration.

Table 3.20: Mean duration (ms) of stop closure, voice onset time, and 'voiceless interval' in initial VOICED stops in environment condition 2 for each subject (arrows show direction of difference).

Subject	stop duration			VOT			'abduction' duration		
	/b/	/d/	/g/	/b/	/d/	/g/	/b/	/d/	/g/
RT	75	>63	<71	13	<17	<23	49	>39	<52
s.d.	8	11	7	1	1	4	3	11	9
PB	85	>74	<76	16	<22	>24	62	>55	>53
s.d.	11	14	12	5	5	5	22	17	6
TC	113	>105	>98	13	<25	>19	65	<71	>55
s.d.	15	18	7	2	5	2	15	34	10
BD	100	>94	<90	13	<18	<28	33	<42	>35
s.d.	16	14	6	4	5	2	16	9	6
FD	76	<78	>60	21	<22	<40	77	>73	>72
s.d.	8	12	15	8	8	10	15	19	10
Pool	90	>84	>79	15	<21	<27	58	>56	>55
s.d.	19	19	17	6	6	10	20	24	14

In summary, the differences in voice onset time in stops as a function of their place of articulation correlate to a certain extent with variability in stop duration, but also with differences in the duration of the interval of voicelessness caused by glottal abduction (or a whisper configuration in VOICED obstruents). These results do not support the hypothesis espoused by Suomi (1980) that the differences in voice onset time observed as a function of stop place of articulation are exclusively the result of differences in stop closure duration. They also cast doubt on the idea (Weismer 1980, Suomi 1980) that a uniform abduction gesture is used in VOICELESS stops regardless of their place of articulation.

Table 3.21: Pearson's *r* coefficients (all data from environment condition 2): * = significant at $p < 0.001$. The figures on the top of each cell are coefficients for the voice onset time/abduction correlation, the figures on the bottom of each cell are coefficients for the voice onset time/closure duration correlation.

			Subject			
	RT	PB	TC	BD	FD	Pool
/b/	.13	.41	.25	.26	.75	*.58
	-.47	-.09	.52	-.62	-.27	-.38
/d/	.28	.71	.82	.33	.82	*.72
	-.10	.53	-.40	-.09	-.01	.18
/g/	.92	-.21	.43	-.11	.84	*.59
	-.47	-.67	-.48	.87	-.03	*-.62
Mean	.27	.19	.43	22	.47	*.46
	-.27	-.16	-.39	-.38	-.44	*-.33

This opens the question of why (at least in VOICELESS stops) is there a tendency for the 'abduction gesture' to be longer in non-labial than in labial stops? As was pointed out above, a 'post-occlusion cavity size' hypothesis (Weismer 1980) is not appropriate here since it predicts that **all else being equal** voicing should commence later in velars than in alveolars, which is not found to be the case in the present data. It is possible that there is some other physiological factor which is the source of this finding. However, if this were the case, the same findings regarding place effects on voice onset time would be expected to be found across a number of languages. But, as has already been mentioned, the effect which has been found across a number of languages is rather different.

The failure to find an explanation for the place of articulation differences observed in which they emerge as a by-product of some other process points towards an alternative interpretation; that these findings reflect an aspect of the systematic language-specific micro-variability of this accent of English. If it is the case that a progressive increase in voice onset time resulting from greater retraction of stop place of articulation (found most commonly in the literature) is, in fact, explicable in terms of aerodynamic and/or myodynamic terms, then one interpretation of the present findings is that in this accent of English, there is a 'rule' which has the effect of partially overriding this property of stop production, resulting in similar voice onset times for non-labial stops. If this is the correct interpretation, it would support the position outlined above that a phonetic representation can potentially specify some fine-grained subsegmental aspects of phonetic realisation.

Utterance type (isolated words vs sentences)

Analysis of the effect of the different environment conditions on voice onset time shows that there are no significant differences between conditions at the p < 0.005 level. However, there does appear to be a tendency in both the pooled and individual subject data for voice onset times in VOICED and VOICELESS stops to be longest under the post-pausal / isolated-word condition (see Table 3.5). This conforms to what has been reported in the literature (Lisker & Abramson 1964, 1967, Baran et al. 1977[17]) although the effect is not as strong as that which has been found by these other investigators.[18]

In VOICELESS stop-sonorant sequences, the mean voice onset time in sequences occurring in environment condition 1 is not significantly different from either of the other two environments. However, there are a number of between-speaker differences in this regard. The effect is found to be significant in the data from subject TC. In two other subjects the same effect occurs but is not significant, whereas in two other subjects it is not observed at all. In VOICED stop-sonorant sequences, there is no significant difference in voice onset times as a function of environment condition, although there is a tendency for voice onset times to be longer in the post-pausal/isolated word condition than in the other two environments.

It is interesting to consider the effect of the isolated word vs phrase condition in the light of the overall distributions of voice onset times in single stops, described in 3.3.1 above. Lisker & Abramson (1967) and Baran et al. (1977) suggest that there is greater overlap of voice onset times for VOICED and VOICELESS stops in sentence conditions than in isolated word conditions. In the present data (see Table 3.22) the occurrence of cognate overlap is higher in the sentence than in the isolated word condition (in this latter case no cognate overlap is found in any of the subjects.). In the data from subject FD, there is overlap between all the cognate pairs. RT shows a small degree of overlap between /t/ and /d/, and PB shows a similarly small degree of overlap between the labial stops. If, as was claimed above, the relationship between underlying voicing category and voice onset time is reflected as a separation of cognates on the voice onset time continuum, these results suggest that this is not achieved absolutely consistently across speakers when stops are embedded in sentence contexts. This supports the point made above that, in the present data, there is a less-than-transparent relationship between phonological voicing categories and voice onset time.

In discussing their similar, although rather more significant effect, Lisker & Abramson (1967:9) made two proposals. Firstly, they pointed out that the greater amount of overlap observed in the sentence conditions could be part of a 'general blurring of distinctiveness at higher articulation rates' (1967:11). Secondly, they suggest that the poorer discriminatory power of voice onset times in the sentence conditions could be evidence in favour of the existence of 'other acoustic features whose contribution may be redundant for deliberate speech but indispensable at higher transmission rates' (1967:11). Lisker & Abramson consider these to be two possible, but 'rather different' (1967:11) types of explanation. However, it seems appropriate to fit these two proposals together, in the light of more recent proposals concerning general principles of motor programming such as plasticity of articulation (Lindblom 1983, 1987, 1990).

Table 3.22: Summary of voice onset time distributions for each subject as a function of environment condition: (i) no distribution overlap of any sort (ii) VOICED/VOICELESS distributions overlap (iii) some distribution overlap between homorganic cognates (iv) all homorganic cognates overlap.

Environment Condition 1

	SUBJECT				
	RT	PB	TC	BD	FD
(i)	-	-	+	-	-
(ii)	+	+	-	+	+
(iii)	-	-	-	-	-
(iv)	-	-	-	-	-

Environment Condition 2

	SUBJECT				
	RT	PB	TC	BD	FD
(i)	-	-	-	-	-
(ii)	+	+	+	+	+
(iii)	+	+	-	+	+
(iv)	-	-	-	-	+

Lisker & Abramson may be correct to point out that the slight differences observed between these two conditions, and the consequent 'blurring of distinctiveness', may be the result of the different types of articulatory organisation required for isolated words as opposed to sentences (in the latter case, global factors such as tempo, and rhythmic constraints create a macro-temporal framework within which finer-grained variability must be accommodated -- these are factors which are not present in the same way in the production of a word in isolation). However, the fact that in the sentence conditions there is a greater amount of contextual information of all sorts (phonetic, phonological, syntactic, pragmatic, semantic) means that the 'blurring' can take place without jeopardising the intended communication; i.e. whilst there may be a tendency to produce less contrastive voice onset times in sentence conditions, it is not inevitable, as witnessed by the fact that it is quite simple to produce 'unusually' long voice onset times in sentences when circumstances demand it (e.g. for reasons of emphasis). Hence, the underlying reason for the 'blurring' may be related to articulatory organisation in sentences as opposed to isolated words, but plasticity ('listener-oriented reorganisation', Lindblom 1987) of motor programming may permit this to be overridden if circumstances should demand it.

In order to investigate further the relationship (if any) between the isolated word vs. sentence effect on voice onset time, and plasticity in motor programming, it would be interesting to look at voice onset time in isolated words, and words in sentences which are contextually appropriate and anomalous. The prediction of the interpretation offered for the present findings is that stops in words which are contextually anomalous should show less compression of voice onset times in the sentence conditions than stops in words which are contextually harmonious. If this prediction were confirmed, the fact that the present results show less 'blurring' than is reported by Lisker & Abramson could then be rationalised by reference to the fact that the sentences produced by the present speakers were 'nonsense' sentences.[19]

If the interpretation offered here is the correct one, it therefore seems unlikely that the observed slight compression of voice onset times in the sentence condition (or slight lengthening in the isolated word condition) is the result of a 'phonetic rule' of English. Rather, it is possibly a reflection of the flexibility and economy of motor organisation as a result of varying perceptual constraints and phrase level temporal organisation.

Vowel quality

Despite the small differences involved (see Table 3.23), vowel quality is a significant factor with respect to voice onset time ($p < 0.001$), with longer voice onset times occurring before high front vowels than before low front vowels (the two types of vowel which were used in the vast majority of the utterance analysed). Vowel quality is a significant factor for all of the subjects (with the exception of FD), and for both VOICED and VOICELESS stops.

Table 3.23: Mean voice onset time (ms) for VOICED and VOICELESS stops (pooled data) in different vowel contexts.

	/p/	/t/	/k/	/b/	/d/	/g/	Mean
High V	42.38	65.52	67.12	16.75	24.07	30.61	41.96
n	58	52	59	53	54	38	314
Low V	41.05	60.37	59.63	15.47	20.74	26.44	37.72
n	41	43	59	47	54	39	283

These results back up the findings of Klatt (1975) and Ohala (1981) that stops before high vowels tend to have longer voice onset times than stops occurring before low vowels. Since the majority of the high vowels used were /I/, and the majority of the low vowels /a/ (i.e. both 'lax' vowels -- as was pointed out in Chapter 1, there is considerable uncertainty concerning the application of the terms tense/lax to vowels), these results do not provide a direct test of the claims that the tenseness/laxness of a vowel has an effect on voice onset time (as claimed by Weismer 1979, and Port & Rotunno 1979). However, the fact that there is a strong significant effect of vowel height does suggest that, if there *is* a difference in voice onset time as a function of vowel tenseness, it does not exclude the possibility of there also being a vowel height effect. These findings also argue against claims that vowel quality has no significant effect on voice onset time (Lisker & Abramson 1967).[20]

Klatt (1975) puts forward two explanations for this effect of vowel quality on voice onset time. Firstly, he suggests that voice onset time increases when F1 of the following segment is low (1975:691). It is not made clear what the rationale for this might be, although it is possible that Klatt had a perceptual motive in mind, similar to that used for accounting for the place differences in voice onset time in VOICELESS stops (i.e. in order to avoid the stop being erroneously perceived as being VOICED, voice onset time is delayed in segments in which F1 is low, as in high vowels). However, this does not seem to be compatible with Klatt's account of the effect of place of articulation on VOICELESS stop voice onset time. Since voice onset time in /t/ and /k/ is already relatively long (in order to guarantee a voiceless percept), there should be no motivation for any additional delay. Furthermore, accounting for the vowel quality effect in VOICELESS stops in this way, suggests that a different explanation is needed for the vowel quality induced voice onset time differences in VOICED stops, which are equally significant.

The second explanation proposed by Klatt (1975:694) is that high vowels have a mechanical influence on the larynx which results in it being 'harder' for voicing to commence (and in higher F0 when voicing does begin). Presumably the mechanical influence would reside in the fact that fronting and raising of the tongue body can result in a slight upward pull on the larynx (via the hyoid bone), which in turn may slightly increase the longitudinal tension of the vocal folds making it slightly 'more difficult' for phonation to start (i.e. a slightly higher sub-glottal pressure would be required to initiate phonation).[21] One way of investigating this hypothesis (Isard, personal communication) would be to investigate F0 as a source of variance in voice onset time. If greater longitudinal tension is a source of longer intervals of voice onset time, all other things being equal one might predict a correlation between fundamental frequency and voice onset time, given that one of the major correlates of raising of F0 is an increase in the longitudinal tension of the vocal folds.

Another possible aerodynamic factor which could go some way to explaining these findings (pointed out by Summerfield 1975, and Ohala 1981, 1983) is that the rate of decrease of intra-oral air pressure in the immediate post-release stage will be slower when stops precede a high vowel than when stops precede a low vowel, since in the low vowel case there will be a faster and greater increase in the vocal tract cross-sectional area. Therefore, in low vowels, the trans-glottal pressure drop necessary for the onset of voicing should be achieved more quickly.

The results of the present experiment show only a very slight difference in mean voice onset time across the different vowel qualities. Klatt's perception-based explanation can, at best, only give a partial account (i.e. for VOICELESS stops). The second of Klatt's hypotheses seems to be a stronger possibility. However, the assumptions on which it is based (in particular, the nature of the mechanical linkage between the tongue and larynx, and the effect of different tongue configuration on the tension and positioning of intrinsic laryngeal muscles and structures) are far from being well documented and tested. Similar difficulties apply to the explanation put forward by Summerfield and Ohala. Whilst their account is doubtless a plausible one, it is in need of further evaluation, possibly by using an articulatory synthesiser to replicate the aerodynamic factors that are involved, and observing whether the lingual configuration associated with different vowels does give rise to the claimed aerodynamic effects and voice onset time differences.

Hence, it is not possible to fully confirm or reject these mechanical and aerodynamic explanations without a good deal of additional experimentation. However, if it could be shown that they provided a full account of the observed effect of vowel quality on voice onset time, this would suggest that the differences observed are not an aspect of the phonetic control of speech production.

The nature of the post-stop environment

From Table 3.7, it is evident that many of the findings concerning voice onset time in stop-sonorant sequences are similar to those found in stop-vowel sequences. Comparisons were carried out between each stop-sonorant class and its corresponding stop-vowel class in order to assess the effect of the manner of articulation of the following segment (see Table 3.24). With the exception of /b/, voice onset time in stop-sonorant sequences is consistently significantly higher than in stop-vowel sequences (p < 0.001). This raises the question of whether the delay in voice onset following the release of a stop in stop-sonorant sequences is a result of the same process as the delay in voice onset in stop-vowel sequences, with the differences being attributable to some characteristic of the following environment. This matter is dealt with below.

Table 3.24: Comparison of mean voice onset times (ms) in stop-vowel and stop-sonorant sequences (pooled data).

	Stop Identity					
	/p/	/t/	/k/	/b/	/d/	/g/
stop-vowel	42.01	63.19	62.86	18.25	25.64	30.56
stop-sonorant	56.74	85.72	78.22	21.33	38.44	37.13

Not only does the presence of a sonorant rather than a vowel have an effect on voice onset time, but the place of articulation of that sonorant also influences the distribution of observed voice onset time measures, although this effect is not significant. In /p/-sonorant sequences, /pr/ tends to have a longer voice onset time than /pl/ across all the subjects with the exception of RT. In /t/-sonorant sequences, there is no clear tendency resulting from the identity of the sonorant. In /k/-sonorant sequences, there is a non-significant tendency in all subjects for voice onset time in /kr/ to be slightly longer than /kw/ or /kl/ (these results are shown in Table 3.7).

As is the case with VOICELESS stop-sonorant sequences, the identity of the sonorant in VOICED stop-sonorant sequences is not a significant variable with respect to voice onset time, with the exception of /d/-sonorant sequences (p < 0.005). In /dr/ sequences, mean voice onset time is around 20 ms longer than in /dw/ sequences, in all environments. This is found not only in the pooled data, but for all the subjects (with the exception of RT who did not produce any /dw/ sequences, since they were all contained in the part of the word-list not read by that subject).

These results are similar to those which have been found for other accents of English, and in other studies of the same accent (described in Chapter 1). The same general patterns of voicing timing are observed in stop-sonorant as in stop-vowel sequences, but the systematically longer voice onset times observed in the former case are, in the light of the focus of this study, in need of explanation. There are virtually no attempts in the literature to account for these differences.

Hoole (1987:34) claims that in stop-sonorant clusters a uniform glottal gesture is 'superimposed on reorganised oral gestures'. This is similar in style to the explanation proposed by Suomi (1980) for place of articulation effects on voice onset time. Klatt (1975:691) suggests that the increase in voice onset time in VOICELESS stop-sonorant sequences is a reflection of a general realisation strategy whereby voice onset times are longer if F1 of the following segment is low, so that the low frequency formant cannot be taken as a cue for a VOICED segment (the same argument as is used to account for longer voice onset times in stops preceding high vowels and velar stops). This, however, does not explain why there is an increase in voice onset time in VOICED stop-sonorant sequences. To the best of my knowledge, there are no other attempts in the literature to provide an explanation for these observations.

It is fruitful to pursue the line of analysis used in attempting to account for the effect of place of articulation on stop voice onset times (subject to the same qualifications, of course). Hoole's claim suggests that explanation for the stop-sonorant findings is that the longer voice onset times which are observed (compared to stop-vowel sequences) are the result of the 'same' laryngeal gesture being coordinated with stops which are shorter due to the fact that they occur in a cluster (Haggard 1973, Hawkins 1979, Klatt 1973); i.e. the stop closure is released relatively sooner than in stop-vowel sequences, at an earlier stage in the glottal abduction gesture, with the result that measured voice onset times are slightly longer.

This possibility would be supported by data which showed that the increase in voice onset times from stop-vowel to stop-sonorant sequences could largely be attributed to compression of the stop durations in the clusters. If this were the correct explanation, it should also be the case that the interval of voicelessness caused by the glottal abduction gesture should be relatively similar in stop-vowel and stop-sonorant sequences. Table 3.25 shows the mean durations of stop closure, voice onset time and 'abduction gesture' (*à la* Suomi 1980) in stop-vowel and stop-sonorant sequences (environment condition 2 only), and the differences in these parameters as a function of the post stop environment.

Table 3.25: Comparison of mean closure duration (DUR), voice onset time (VOT), and 'abduction' duration (ABD) in stop-vowel and stop-sonorant sequences in the pooled data (all values in ms).

	Stop-V			Stop-son.			Difference		
	DUR	VOT	ABD	DUR	VOT	ABD	DUR	VOT	ABD
/p/	94	42	123	90	59	131	-4	+17	+8
/t/	8	64	130	65	91	141	-16	+27	+11
/k/	82	62	129	73	84	151	-9	+22	+22
/b/	90	15	58	86	18	50	-4	+3	-8
/d/	84	21	56	66	39	58	-18	+18	+2
/g/	79	27	55	74	35	68	-5	+7	+13

Whilst all the stops are, as expected, consistently shorter in stop-sonorant than in stop-vowel sequences, in some cases the degree of shortening is rather small in comparison to the increase in voice onset time. Alveolars contract the most, and this correlates with the fact that they tend to have relatively large increases in voice onset time,[22] but the small degree of shortening for the velars and labials does not match up with the voice onset time data which shows fairly large increases (the exception is VOICED labials, which also show the smallest amount of cluster shortening).

As was the case with the effect of stop place of articulation on voice onset time, a more powerful account emerges if we take into consideration the duration of the interval of voicelessness caused by the laryngeal gesture. Table 3.25 shows that this is longer in stop-sonorant than in stop-vowel sequences (VOICED labials are the exception). It seems, then, that the increase in voice onset time from stop-vowel to stop-sonorant sequences is correlated with two factors; compression of the stop closure durations in consonant clusters; slight increase of the duration of the voiceless interval caused by laryngeal abduction (or tensing in the VOICED stops). This explanation receives further support in the correlation coefficients of voice onset time and closure duration, and of voice onset time and the duration of 'abduction', shown in Table 3.26.

In VOICELESS stop sequences there is a consistent significant positive correlation between voice onset time and duration of the 'abduction gesture', but no significant correlation, or even non-significant trends between voice onset time and consonant duration. In VOICED stop sequences, pooling across the different places of articulation and sonorant types, both correlations are significant.

148   CHAPTER 3

Table 3.26: Pearson's *r* correlation coefficients of voice onset time (VOT) and stop closure duration (DUR), and voice onset time and duration the 'abduction gesture' (ABD) in VOICED and VOICELESS stop-sonorant sequences occurring in environment condition 2 in the pooled data (* = significant at p < 0.001).

	VOT/ABD	VOT/DUR		VOT/ABD	VOT/DUR
/pr/	*.70	-.08	/br/	.15	-.35
/pl/	*.65	-.07	/bl/	.07	-.63
/tr/	*.66	.46	/dr/	.53	.23
/tw/	*.74	.32	/dw/	.86	.28
/kr/	*.83	.51	/gr/	.56	-.46
/kl/	*.81	.24	/gl/	.41	-.42
/kw/	*.74	.53			
Mean	*.67	-.14		*.52	*-.39

In summary, with the reservation that more direct articulatory data are needed on laryngeal-supralaryngeal coordination in these sequences, it is possible that the difference in voice onset time between stop-vowel and stop-sonorant sequences can partially be explained by reference to (a) compression of the duration of stop occlusions and (b) the possibility of a longer laryngeal gesture for velars and VOICELESS labials in stop-sonorant sequences than in stop-vowel sequences. It is interesting to note that in stop-sonorant sequences, the supralaryngeal gestures for the stop are compressed vis-a-vis stop-vowel contexts, but the laryngeal gestures tend to be slightly lengthened. It therefore does not seem to be the case that a uniform glottal gesture is coproduced with reorganised supralaryngeal gestures, as has been claimed. The results also suggest that any attempt to model the temporal effects of clustering on consonants may have to consider laryngeal and supralaryngeal components separately.

It is conceivable that this variation in duration of the laryngeal gestures arises aerodynamically. Compared to stop-vowel sequences, in stop-sonorant-vowel sequences, there is a high degree of oral constriction in the immediate post-release phase (especially in stop-/l/ and stop-/w/ clusters). This may increase the time required to re-establish the trans-glottal pressure drop necessary for the initiation of voicing, and thereby lead to the observations that the interval of voicelessness corresponding to the laryngeal gesture is longer than in simple stop-vowel sequences. This account could apply to sequences with both VOICELESS and VOICED stops (except of course where the latter are voiced throughout). This is similar to the account given for the effect of vowel quality on voice onset time. However, the differences observed as a result of the presence of a following sonorant are considerably greater, and as a result this aerodynamic factor may only give a partial account. In order to reach firmer conclusions on this matter, further data is needed for English and other languages which have aspirated stops occurring before vowels and sonorants.

Nature of post-fricative environment

It is not only in stops that the manner of articulation of the following environment affects the timing of voicing. It was pointed out above that in fricatives, voicing timing is usually well synchronised with the close articulatory approximation for the fricatives. However, when the following environment consists of a nasal consonant or another sonorant, delays in voice onset are observed.

In sequences of /s/ and either /m/ or /n/, between the period of random noise corresponding to the medial phase of the fricative and the onset of voicing for the nasal consonant, there is consistently an interval during which there is no periodicity, and no evidence of high frequency noise such as that observed during the preceding fricative. The mean duration of this 'voiceless transition' (labelled 'VOT') for the pooled data is shown in Table 3.27. Two of the subjects (RT and TC) are particularly consistent in the durations of the voiceless transition (with standard deviations of 6.4 ms and 6.3 ms respectively), but subject PB produces voiceless transitions which are significantly longer than those of all the other subjects. In addition the voiceless transitions in subjects BD and TC are significantly different, being the longest and the shortest respectively ($p < 0.005$ in both cases). Statistical analysis has shown that neither the identity of the nasal consonant, nor the environment preceding the /s/-nasal sequence has a significant effect on the duration of the voiceless transition, either in the pooled data, or in the data corresponding to each subject.

At first glance these findings seem to suggest that in this environment the timing of voicing in fricatives is rather different to that observed in the other environments investigated. At an acoustic level, of course, this is quite true; there is a relatively long delay in voicing onset after fricatives in these clusters, which is not found in fricative-vowel sequences.

However, at the articulatory level, the facts seem to be rather more complex. As well as showing the mean duration of the 'voice onset time' observed in these sequences, Table 3.27 also shows the mean duration of fricatives in /s/-nasal sequences and in /s/-vowel sequences. Since in /s/-vowel sequences there is no delay in voice onset, it can be seen that the duration of voicelessness in

/s/-nasal sequences (/s/ duration plus the duration of the voiceless transition) is slightly longer than the duration of voicelessness in /s/-vowel sequences. In addition the duration of /s/ is considerably shorter in /s/-nasal sequences than in /s/-vowel sequences. So, what appears in the acoustic trace to be a simple matter of a delay in voice onset following /s/ in /s/-nasal sequences, in articulatory terms appears to be a result of a lengthening of the interval during which the vocal folds are not vibrating, in conjunction with some compression of the supralaryngeal gesture corresponding to the fricative.

Table 3.27: Mean duration (ms) of /s/, the voiceless transition (VOT) in /s/-nasal sequences and of /s/ in /s/-vowel sequences as a function of environment condition in the pooled data. 'dur. diff.' indicates the difference between /s/ duration in /s/-vowel sequences, and /s/ duration in the /s/-nasal sequences.

		Environment Condition		
		1	2	3
/sn/	/s/ dur.	104.86	120.32	115.42
	'VOT'	43.86	35.64	38.54
	dur. diff.	24.57	23.54	31.66
	n	21	25	24
/sm/	/s/ dur.	106.29	112.17	115.23
	'VOT'	38.29	39.47	39.77
	dur. diff.	23.14	31.69	31.85
	n	28	30	30
/s/	/s/ dur.	129.43	143.86	147.08

This latter difference is likely to be the result of compression of segment duration in consonant sequences. Haggard (1973) found that /s/ was around 20 ms shorter in clusters than when it occurred singly. The difference of /s/ duration in /s/-nasal and /s/-vowel sequences in the present data is also similar to that reported for American English by Umeda (1977:852) in her analysis of the reading of a passage by a single speaker.

The lengthening of the interval of voicelessness requires a different explanation. One reason for this might be found in the complexity of the articulatory transition from /s/ to a nasal. The fricative requires velic closure, glottal abduction, high intra-oral air pressure, and a finely balanced stricture of close approximation between the tongue and the alveolar ridge, whereas the nasal consonant requires differences at each of these levels; velic opening, glottal vibration, and complete closure in the oral cavity. Given that each of these changes requires a finite, and different, amount of time to be achieved[23], it is not surprising that there is some articulatory asynchrony in the transition from the fricative to the nasal. Table 3.28 illustrates the set of transition sequences which could potentially arise.

Evidence from an airflow study of these sequences (Barry & Kunzel 1978) suggests that in English, the components of this transition progress in a consistent pattern with respect to each other, and that the interval between the end of the fricative noise in the acoustic signal and the onset of voicing for the nasal corresponds to a period of 'devoiced' nasal, or of voiceless nasalised fricative, or a sequence of both these (Barry & Kunzel 1978, Barry 1981); i.e. from the range of possibilities shown in Figure 3.28, English speakers tend to use option (C).

Table 3.28: Six possible means of achieving the articulatory transition from /s/ to a nasal consonant. The articulatory processes involved are numbered as follows: (1) voiceless-to-voiced (2) fricative-to-stop (3) oral-to-nasal.

Option			Symbolic Representation				
A	s	---->	s̃ (3)	---->	z̃ (1)	---->	n (2)
B	s	---->	z (1)	---->	z̃ (3)	---->	n (2)
C	s	---->	s̃ (3)	---->	n̥ (2)	---->	n (1)
D	s	---->	z (1)	---->	d (2)	---->	n (3)
E	s	---->	t (2)	---->	n̥ (3)	---->	n (1)
F	s	---->	t (2)	---->	d (1)	---->	n (3)

The first part of the transition normally involves lowering of the velum. This is probably due to the fact that in speech the velum tends to be moved relatively slowly, and therefore begins to lower some time in advance of the beginning of the nasal stop (Kent et al (1974) illustrate this with X-ray data of tongue and soft palate movement in vowel-nasal-stop sequences). The second part of the transition is normally the formation of the complete closure for the nasal stop. Finally voicing is initiated. It seems then, that given the almost complete impossibility for the /s/ and the nasal to be coproduced (since their articulatory requirements are largely incompatible), the transitions between the fricative and nasal are produced in a very constrained way, with one aspect of this temporal constraint being that onset of voicing is the last part of the transition to take place. The temporal coordination in the transition between /s/ and following nasals in English appears to be constrained in order to prevent the occurrence of intrusive stops, or an intrusive voiced fricative (see options (A), (B), (D), (E) and (F) in Table 3.28).

If voicing onset is slightly delayed in these sequences due to a temporal constraint such as that just described, then two further questions arise. Firstly, why does the transition from /s/ to the nasal proceed in this precise way? Early velic lowering, as explained above, is probably due to the rate at which the position of the velum is altered, but why is voicing normally the last part of the transition? It is not a universal aspect of the realisation of these sequences; e.g. in Spanish (Canellada & Madsen 1987), systematically different articulatory asynchronies are observed -- rather than there being a delay in voice onset, voicing tends to begin during the fricative in /s/-nasal sequences (option (A) or (B) in Table 3.28).[24] One could begin to answer this question by studying /s/-nasal sequences across a number of languages, in order to observe which of the possibilities shown in Table 3.28 actually occur. Secondly, if these findings do reflect a temporal constraint of English, what is the nature of the phonetic representation which can specify both very precise temporal control such as this, and the less rigid constraints governing (for example) medial voicing in fricatives? This is discussed further in the following chapter.

In summary, it is possible that the timing of voicing in /s/-nasal sequences could be attributed to the existence of a very tight (as evidenced by the fact that little within- and between-subject variation is observed) temporal constraint applicable in the production of those sequences, such that voicing is delayed until other components of the /s/-to-nasal transition have passed certain thresholds. It is possible that this is quite a different type of 'rule' from that which delays voice onset time in initial VOICELESS stops, given the different amounts of variability of observed, and the fact that it only occurs in a limited set of circumstances (i.e. unlike stops, there is no delay in voice onset after /s/ in /s/-vowel sequences). It seems reasonable to conclude that the experimental findings do reflect a rule-governed aspect of the phonetic realisation of /s/-nasal clusters in SBE, given the fact that other means of going from an /s/ to a nasal configuration do exist, and are observed to occur in other languages.

Claims in the literature (Bladon & Al-Bamerni 1976, Dent 1984) about delayed voice onset in sonorants following VOICELESS fricatives were harder to test using the techniques adopted in this experiment, due to the difficulty in separating out on a time-waveform the noise corresponding to the close approximation for the fricative, and the noise corresponding to the 'devoiced' sonorant. However, it was possible to estimate whether, and to what extent, delayed voice onset was taking place by examining the durations of intervals of noise in the signal corresponding to fricative-vowel sequences and to fricative-sonorant sequences.

A comparison of the mean durations of the noise intervals corresponding to /s/ occurring singly and in clusters with laterals is given in Table 3.29. These figures show that the duration of the noise portion in /s/ clusters is longer than in single consonants. This is significant at the $p < 0.001$ level. The same comparison has been carried out for /f/ and /θ/ (the results are shown also in Table 3.29). In the case of /f/, the mean duration of the noise interval is slightly longer in a cluster than in a single consonant, but the difference is not significant. In /θ/-sonorant sequences the duration of the noise interval is significantly longer than in /θ/-vowel sequences ($p < 0.001$).

Table 3.29: Comparison of mean duration (ms) of fricative 'noise' corresponding to /fricative-V/ sequences and /fricative-sonorant-V/ sequences as a function of environment condition in the pooled data.

Environment Condition	single /s/	single /f/	single /θ/
1	129.43	88.69	97.86
n	37	29	14
2	143.86	130.69	117.82
n	36	32	11
3	147.08	79.87	85.91
n	36	31	11
	/s/-sonorant	/f/-sonorant	/θ/-sonorant
1	146.07	93.11	110.56
n	15	44	16
2	165.43	134.59	155.29
n	14	46	17
3	163.08	84.58	114.73
n	13	38	15

Thus, in fricative-sonorant sequences, the noise interval in the signal is normally longer than when the fricative occurs singly. There are two possible explanations for this. The first, which is the least likely, is that the fricatives are lengthened when they occur in a cluster. This is unlikely, because it is well attested in the literature (e.g. Haggard 1973, Klatt 1973, Hawkins 1979, Umeda 1977) that consonant durations are substantially reduced when they occur in clusters. The second possibility is that the noise portion which has been measured consists of two separate components; noise corresponding to the fricative, and noise corresponding to a delay in voice onset at the start of the sonorant. In the speech waveform there is no clear marker to indicate when the fricative ends and the 'devoiced' sonorant begins, but the increased length of the noise portion is an indication (in the light of what is known about shortening of /s/ in clusters) that a delay in onset of voicing for the sonorant is taking place.

Using other techniques (electropalatography would be a particularly suitable means of confirming or otherwise inferences made on the basis of this acoustic data; see Dent 1984), it would be possible to establish what proportion of the 'noise' in the signal corresponds to the fricative, and what proportion corresponds to the 'devoiced' sonorant. However, even without performing this additional experimentation, it can be seen that the pattern of voicing timing observable with acoustic analysis is of some interest given the focus of the present study. Whilst it is likely (given other reports in the literature) that the lingual gesture for the fricative is actually being shortened in these sequences, it appears that the laryngeal gesture (as indexed by the duration of the 'voiceless interval' in the signal) is being lengthened, resulting in some 'devoicing' of the sonorant (i.e. the same pattern of events observed above in stop-sonorant sequences).

There do not appear to be any aerodynamic or mechanical reasons why these differences between single /s/-vowel and /s/-sonorant-vowel sequences should take place. One possible explanation is that the difference is the result of a temporal constraint similar to that observed in /s/-nasal sequences. The transition from /s/ to /l/ involves complex changes in lingual configuration, and it is not the case that the fricative and lateral can be coproduced to a great extent since the configurations are incompatible. Hence, one might hypothesise the existence of a temporal constraint delaying voicing onset until the lateral gesture is complete. If this is the case it may explain the differences between /s/-sonorant and /f/-sonorant sequences; in the latter there is potentially greater coproduction of the fricative and sonorant gestures, and as a result a far smaller increase in the duration of voicelessness.[25]

Effect of /s/ preceding the stop

Table 3.30 shows the mean voice onset times for stops in /# s stop V/ sequences. Post-hoc comparison shows a significant difference between subjects TC and FD, who have the lowest and highest mean voice onset times respectively. For the purposes of comparison, Table 3.30 also shows the mean voice onset times in single VOICED and VOICELESS stops. There is no significant difference between the onset times for single VOICED stops and VOICELESS stops occurring in the /#s_V/ frame.

There is also a tendency for voice onset times to be shorter in word-initial stops which have /s/ as the preceding context than when the preceding context is voiced (i.e. environment condition 3 produces shorter voice onset times than environment condition 2 -- the figures showing this effect are shown in Table 3.5). This is in agreement with the claim made by Gimson (1980) that there is a slight reduction in the duration of aspiration under these circumstances (discussed in Chapter 1).

Table 3.30: Mean voice onset time (ms) in stops in /s/-stop-vowel and VOICED and VOICELESS stop-vowel sequences in the pooled data.

Stop Identity	VOICELESS Stop-V	VOICED Stop-V	/s/-stop-V
bilabial	42.01	18.25	17.65
n	114	148	69
alveolar	62.84	25.56	23.75
n	95	121	65
velar	62.86	30.50	27.21
n	130	77	72

The nature of the preceding environment is not a significant variable in VOICELESS labial stop-sonorant sequences, but it is significant in /t/-sonorant and /k/-sonorant sequences ($p < 0.002$ and $p < 0.001$ respectively (see Table 3.7). In /t/-sonorant sequences, post-hoc comparison showed that voice onset time in sequences with a preceding vowel context is significantly longer than in sequences with a preceding voiceless or pause context ($p < 0.005$). Post-hoc comparison showed that voice onset times in /k/-sonorant sequences with a preceding VOICELESS context are shorter than in the same sequences occurring in the two other environments tested. However, in both the /t/- and /k/-sonorant sequences, a certain amount of caution is advised in interpreting these findings, since these differences are only present in three of the five subjects, and are only significant in two of them.

The reduction of voice onset time for /p,t,k/ in a /#s_V/ environment is in accord with other studies of these sequences reported in the literature. Yoshioka et al. (1979) have shown that this is caused by the fact that a single glottal abduction gesture is used in the production of an initial sequence. However, the timing of this gesture is very different from that found in a single VOICELESS fricative-vowel, or VOICELESS stop-vowel sequence. In a single fricative-vowel sequence, the timing is such that lingual and laryngeal gestures coincide (fricatives in SBE are not aspirated and have very little voicing incursion from a preceding voiced context). In a single stop-vowel sequence, laryngeal and supralaryngeal gestures are coordinated such that the glottis is still open at the moment of release of the stop, and voicing does not begin until some time into the following vowel. In /#-s-stop-V/ sequences, a third different pattern of timing occurs, with the glottal gesture coinciding with the supralaryngeal events for both the fricative and stop, *and* carrying over into the following vowel, but to a significantly smaller extent than in the /stop-V/ sequence. This is facilitated by adjustments to the durations of the stops and fricatives which are both at their shortest in these environments.

The tendency for some shortening of voice onset time in word-initial stops preceded by a voiceless context compared to stops preceded by a voiced context (i.e. environment condition 2 vs. environment condition 3), may reflect the overall plasticity of laryngeal-supralaryngeal coordination. Löfqvist (1990) reports the findings of a transillumination study of the glottal activity in /s-#-t/ sequences in English as a function of different rates of articulation. He found that at slow rates, two separate glottal abduction gestures took place (observable in the transillumination trace as two peaks with a profound medial dip). At higher rates of speech, the gestures became blended together (two peaks, of slightly lower amplitude, were still visible on the transillumination trace, but the medial dip became less noticeable -- it was as if the two gestures were moving towards each each other due to being compressed into a smaller time span). At the highest rates studied, Löfqvist observed that the two gestures became completely fused, resulting in a single peak in the transillumination trace. This shows that the timing of glottal gestures can be reorganised as a result of overall rate constraints. The fact that the subjects in the present experiment spoke at a comfortable rate (neither extremely slow or fast), means that it is possible that the laryngeal abduction gestures in /s-#-stop-V/ sequences were subject to a certain degree of 'merging' in the way described by Löfqvist, which in turn gave rise to some shortening of mean voice onset times in that environment.

A further feature of the present data is that at least in the utterances investigated, resyllabification (i.e. /s-$-stop/ --> /$-s-stop/) does not take place. This conclusion is based on the fact that if it had taken place, we might have expected the reduction in voice onset times in environment condition 3 to be far greater, resulting in mean voice onset times similar to those obtained in /$-s-stop-V/ sequences. Shockey (personal communication) suggests that resyllabification would be expected to occur to a significant extent in conversational speech (and not necessarily just in fast speech). In the light of Löfqvist's findings, it would interesting to obtain samples where 'resyllabification' had taken place (although this would not be a simple matter to prove -- see discussion in Chapter 4), and ascertain whether the laryngeal gesture is timed as in the canonical /$-s-stop-V/ sequences, or whether it appears to be the result of the 'merger' of two separate laryngeal gestures (possibly showing a slight dip between two peaks of glottal aperture corresponding to two underlying gestures).

In summary, the differences in the timing of voicing between /#-VOICELESS stop-V/ sequences and /#-s-VOICELESS stop-V/ sequences is very likely part of the linguistic control exerted on articulatory coordination characteristic of speakers of English.[26] On the other hand, the slight reduction in voice onset time observed in environment condition 3, is probably not a feature of the timing of voicing which is governed by the phonetic representation. It is more likely to be due to the plasticity of motor organisation in the face of macro-temporal constraints.

3.3.4 *Other factors affecting the occurrence of medial voicing*

Manner of articulation

There are two particular manner-based differences in medial voicing that arise from the results. Firstly, there are environments in which medial voicing occurs relatively more frequently in stops than in fricatives (e.g. there are relatively fewer cases of zero medial voicing in final VOICELESS and VOICED stops than in final VOICELESS and VOICED fricatives -- see Tables 3.10 and 3.14). Secondly, as shown in Table 3.31, in the cases where medial voicing takes place in both stops and fricatives, there is a tendency for the duration of the voiced interval in stops (expressed as a percentage of stop duration) to be longer than that observed in fricatives, within each of the phonological categories (with the exception of initial VOICED fricatives). On the whole, stops appear to be 'more voiced' than fricatives. If the duration of medial voicing (expressed in absolute terms) is compared across the two manner categories, the manner-based differences are less evident. VOICELESS stops have longer intervals of medial voicing than VOICELESS fricatives. In initial VOICED obstruents there are longer intervals of medial voicing in fricatives than in stops, but in final VOICED obstruents no trend emerges due to an interaction with the environment condition variable (discussed further in this section).

These results suggest that, on the whole, there is somewhat greater resistance to medial voicing in VOICELESS fricatives than in VOICELESS stops. In VOICED obstruents any differences are less apparent, but in initial VOICED fricatives there are longer mean intervals of medial voicing than in initial VOICED stops. It is important to bear in mind that in many instances, stops and fricatives (both VOICED and VOICELESS) are produced without any medial voicing (see Tables 3.8, 3.10, 3.12, and 3.14). The discussion in this section is based only on the cases when medial voicing was observed to occur.

Table 3.31: Duration of intervals of medial voicing (in percentage-of-medial-phase and absolute terms) as a function of obstruent manner of articulation and position in word in the pooled data (for all cases when percentage of medial accompanied by voicing is greater then zero).

	VOICELESS			
	initial stops	initial fricatives	final stops	final fricatives
all environments	16.50% 14.93ms	6.30% 9.78ms	21.77% 16.99ms	8.96% 10.92ms
environment condition 2	16.64% 15.10ms	6.30% 9.78ms	21.16% 13.53ms	9.37% 12.42ms
	VOICED			
	initial stops	initial fricatives	final stops	final fricatives
all environments	57.63% 51.70ms	82.97% 73.09ms	64.26% 32.63ms	38.95% 29.60ms
environment condition 2	57.63% 51.70ms	86.69% 68.12ms	85.02% 38.13ms	72.33% 47.82ms

In interpreting these findings from the point of view of understanding the control of the timing of voicing in speech production, it is necessary to ascertain whether there is any factor inherent in the production of stops and fricatives which could be the source of the differences in voicing timing which are observed. One hypothesis in this regard is that the differences might be due to the aerodynamic factors associated with the different manners of articulation involved in the production of stops and fricatives. As was described in Chapter 1, the production of voicing requires adequate flow of air across the glottis, which in turn is dependent on the presence of a continuous and adequate trans-glottal pressure drop. The greater the constriction in the oral cavity, the more difficult it is to maintain that aerodynamic requirement due to equalisation of the pressure above and below the glottis.[27] On this basis, then, one might conclude that under the aerodynamic conditions existing during the production of a fricative, it is 'easier' for voicing to occur than under the aerodynamic conditions imposed by the production of a stop. In other words, the different degrees of stricture of stops and fricatives should affect their propensity to be accompanied by voicing.

In the results from this experiment, the only findings which are compatible with this hypothesis, are those which show that initial VOICED fricatives are relatively more voiced than initial VOICED stops, and the fact that on the whole there is a higher incidence of complete (i.e. 100%) medial voicing in fricatives than in stops (but this finding is probably not independent of the fact that complete voicing frequently occurs on fricatives which have relatively short durations: e.g. [ð]). The other findings (the majority), however, are contrary to those which would be predicted from this aerodynamic hypothesis, with longer intervals of medial voicing observed in stops than in fricatives.

However, a closer look at the physiological literature suggests that the aerodynamic conditions caused by the production of different degrees of oral stricture are not as simple as just stated. The consensus of a number of physiological studies of intra-oral air pressure during obstruent production (Subtelny et al. 1966, Arkebauer et al. 1967, Brown & McGlone 1969, Prosek & House 1975) is that peak intra-oral air pressure is higher in VOICELESS stops than in VOICELESS fricatives. However, in the case of VOICED obstruents, the situation is less certain (VOICED obstruents have not been studied as much as VOICELESS ones), but there does seem to be a tendency for intra-oral air pressure to be LOWER in VOICED stops than in VOICED fricatives (Arkebauer et al. 1967, Prosek & House 1975).

The first of these findings corresponds to what would be expected given the different degrees of stricture involved in stop and fricative production (the reasoning behind this expectation is given above). This supports the claim made above that the fact that VOICELESS fricatives are apparently more resistant to incursion of voicing from preceding voiced contexts does not seem to correspond to predictions based on knowledge of the aerodynamic properties of stop and fricative constrictions.

The findings regarding intra-oral pressure in VOICED obstruents are more difficult to interpret. On the one hand, it is true that if fricatives are characterised by higher intra-oral air pressure, this could well explain why in final VOICED fricatives there are overall shorter intervals of medial voicing in fricatives than in stops (a separate account would then be needed for the fact that initial VOICED fricatives appear to be 'more voiced' than initial VOICED stops). However, the results of the physiological studies which have been referred to must be treated with some caution.

The investigators who report these findings make no mention of whether the VOICED fricatives and stops which they measured were produced with voicing throughout, or whether there were cases of only partial voicing. The presence or absence of phonation is clearly not an independent variable with respect to intra-oral air pressure, yet the only mention of voicing in these reports is of the underlying phonological voicing category of the segments being investigated. If it was the case that the subjects in these experiments were frequently, or even just occasionally, producing their VOICED obstruents as partially voiced (which would not be too surprising in the light of the present results), this would have a major effect on measurements of peak intra-oral air pressure, with higher pressures being produced during unvoiced intervals than during intervals of voicing. If, after further study, it is confirmed that intra-oral air pressure is higher in VOICED fricatives than in VOICED stops, then this is a factor which has to be taken into consideration in accounting for the apparently greater resistance to medial voicing in final VOICED fricatives than in VOICED stops. For the moment, the evidence is rather weak.

A more likely explanation of the differences in medial voicing between stops and fricatives is that they are the result of timing constraints on laryngeal/supralaryngeal coordination in the two different types of sound, in order to optimally achieve the auditory goals with which they are associated.

In VOICELESS stops occurring before stressed vowels the glottal abduction gesture is timed to peak at or around the moment of stop release in order for aspiration to take place (Löfqvist & Yoshioka 1984). In fricatives the abduction gesture has to be timed to terminate at the same time as the interval of close approximation. Hence, longer intervals of medial voicing in post-vocalic VOICELESS stops may reflect a relatively later abduction gesture than that which is found in fricatives. Some evidence in support of this is provided by Löfqvist & McGarr (1986). They found that the onset of ADDuction (i.e. peak glottal opening) occurs closer to the onset of oral constriction in fricatives than in stops. Since they also found that the duration of the entire abduction gesture was about the same across stop and fricatives, this suggests that the gesture begins earlier in fricatives than in stops (they also found that fricatives were characterised by a wider and faster glottal opening).

This is a reasonably plausible hypothesis for explaining the differences between VOICELESS stops and fricatives, but it is difficult to extend it to their VOICED counterparts. Since VOICED stops are unaspirated, there is no reason for there to be a delayed glottal abduction gesture, therefore the hypothesised motivation for the greater resistance in fricatives is non-existent.

However, with a slight modification of the hypothesis (to take into account the different nature of the auditory goals in VOICED fricatives), it is possible to capture how at least some of the differences between VOICED stops and fricatives may arise. As has been pointed out by Ohala (1983:201), the simultaneous production of voicing at the glottis and turbulent airflow through a narrow oral constriction are in conflict to a certain extent; vocal fold vibration has the effect of reducing intra-oral air pressure, but the production of turbulent noise for the fricative requires high intra-oral pressure: 'to the extent that the segment retains voicing it may be less of a fricative, and if it is a good fricative it runs the risk of being devoiced' (1983:201). A similar point had been made in an earlier study by Lisker et al. (1969): 'a well formed fricative requires audible turbulence, and that airflow needed for this is easily supplied when the glottis is at least partially open' (1969:1546).

There is a possibility, then, that voicing is less compatible with fricatives than with stops (Ohala 1983:202). This may explain why, in certain cases in the present data, there is more frequent and greater 'devoicing' of VOICED fricatives than in stops in the same environment.[28] However, the situation is not quite as straightforward as this. If resolving the friction/voicing conflict is a major influence in determining voicing timing in VOICED fricatives, the present data suggest that the way in which it is resolved depends on a number of factors, including the identity of the fricative, its position in a word and its environment.

Where VOICED fricatives appear to be particularly resistant to medial voicing compared to VOICED stops, this may reflect articulatory organisation geared towards ensuring a high enough intra-oral air pressure for noise generation at the place of constriction. However, as is shown below, both VOICED stops and fricatives are frequently fully or partially 'devoiced' when they occur with an adjacent voiceless context, suggesting that 'devoicing' is sensitive to context, as well as being a function of auditory and aerodynamic factors. Medial voicing in fricatives occurs with greatest regularity in intervocalic position. It could be hypothesised that this arises because the 'cost' of rapidly switching vocal fold vibration on and off may be higher than losing clarity of frication in those particular instances.[29]

This auditory-based explanation is complementary to the explanation given for the differences between VOICELESS obstruents. In VOICELESS fricatives, in the interest of achieving the goal of noise in the signal, it is necessary for the glottal abduction gesture to begin as soon as possible, thus precluding the possibility of significant intervals of voicing incursion. A certain amount of voicing incursion into VOICELESS stops does not threaten their principal auditory goal of a noisy release burst followed by a period of aspiration.

In summary, manner of articulation does affect the frequency with which stops and fricatives in SBE are accompanied by voicing, and the relative duration of intervals of medial voicing. On the whole, it appears that VOICELESS fricatives have greater resistance to the occurrence of medial voicing than VOICELESS stops. In VOICED fricatives the duration of medial voicing varies as a function of the environment condition and place of articulation of the fricative, and it is not consistently less than that found in VOICED stops. Final VOICED fricatives tend to have shorter intervals of voicing than final VOICED stops, but in initial position, VOICED fricatives tend to have longer intervals of voicing than VOICED stops. The fact that stops and fricatives are produced with different degrees of oral constriction, and thereby have dissimilar aerodynamic properties, does not appear to explain the observed differences. In fact, such knowledge as is available regarding intra-oral air pressure in obstruents predicts, in most cases, the opposite to what has been found in the present study.

A more likely explanation requires appeal both to general flexibility of motor programming, and to language-specific realisation strategies. On the one hand, the differences seem to reflect flexible articulatory coordination directed towards achieving the particular auditory goals associated with stops and fricatives, and directed, in particular, towards resolving the noise/voicing conflict in fricatives. On the other hand, the fact that a particular implementation strategy is chosen from the set of possible implementation strategies[30] by speakers of this accent of English reflects a systematic learned aspect of the phonetic realisation of that accent of English, a feature which can only have its origin in the phonetic representation which drives the speech production mechanism (see discussion below on the effect of environment condition on medial voicing).

It should be underlined once again that the above discussion only concerns cases in which medial voicing was observed to occur, and that in both VOICED stops and VOICED fricatives there are many instances, in all of the environments studied, in which no medial voicing took place. Hence, one further point can be added to this summary, namely that an important characteristic of the timing of voicing with respect to the medial phase of stops and fricatives in SBE is that there is a good deal of variation regarding whether medial voicing occurs or not. The fact that this is one aspect of phonetic realisation which is not subject to very precise control (compared, for example, to the transition from /s/ to nasals discussed above), but which nonetheless is possibly governed by language-specific 'rules' of some sort, is discussed further below.

Place of articulation

Suomi (1980) and Westbury (1979) have argued against place of articulation having any major role in determining the duration of voicing during the early part of VOICED and VOICELESS stops in a post-vocalic environment. On the other hand, Keating (1984b) reports that longer intervals of medial voicing are observed the more advanced the place of articulation of the stop. She attributes this to differences in cavity wall surface area behind the point of occlusion and the effect which this has on the vocal folds' ability to vibrate (the greater the area, the longer voicing can be maintained). The results of this experiment (shown in Tables 3.9/3.11) confirm the findings of Suomi and Westbury. In SBE, place of articulation has no significant effect on the duration of medial voicing in VOICED and VOICELESS stops (in percentage terms) occurring initially or finally, although there is a non-significant tendency in all the subjects for labials to have less medial voicing than stops produced at different places of articulation within the same voicing category, an ordering which is opposite to that observed by Keating (the exception to this tendency is final VOICED stops occurring in environment conditions 1 and 2, in which labial stops have slightly more medial voicing (in absolute terms) than alveolar or velar stops).

Place of articulation of initial fricatives has no significant effect on the percentage of the fricative accompanied by voicing. In final fricatives, post-hoc analysis has shown that /ð/ has significantly greater voicing during its medial phase than all the VOICELESS fricatives, and that /z/ has significantly greater voicing than /s/, /ʃ/, and /f/, but not /θ/ ($p < 0.005$ in both cases). The only other acoustic study of the effect of place of articulation on the duration of voicing during a VOICED fricative is Haggard (1978). On the whole he found that /v/ had longer intervals of medial voicing than /z/. This finding is confirmed here, but in addition /ð/ has relatively more medial voicing than either of the other two VOICED fricatives (although this is quite likely to be at least partly a consequence of the relatively short mean duration of /ð/).

The finding that place of articulation of an obstruent largely does not significantly affect the duration of intervals of medial voicing argues against a hypothesis (Keating 1984b) that the duration of medial voicing is determined by the size of the post-occlusion cavity. If voicing was dying out passively in this way, a place effect such as that found by Keating would have been found. However, the lack of a place effect on duration of medial voicing does suggest that the cessation of voicing in VOICED and VOICELESS stops and fricatives is an aspect of the temporal control of obstruent production, possibly, as outlined in the previous section, part of the gestural organisation directed towards achieving the particular auditory goals for stops and fricatives.

Effect of environment condition on medial voicing

In initial stops, with the exception of prevoiced stops, medial voicing only occurs when the preceding environment is voiced. This means that the effect of environment class can only be fully evaluated with final stops, where it turns out to be a significant factor. Final VOICED stops occurring in intervocalic position have a greater percentage of their closure accompanied by voicing than stops occurring pre-pausally, or before a VOICELESS environment (an increase of greater than 50% over environment conditions 1 and 3; $p < 0.005$). This can be seen in Table 3.11, which shows the interaction between stop identity and environment class in final stops. There is no clear trend emerging in VOICELESS stops.

The voicing timing patterns observed for fricatives are slightly different in character. In VOICELESS fricatives occurring initially medial voicing only occurs with any frequency in intervocalic position, so no environment comparisons can be made. In word-initial VOICED fricatives, medial voicing occurs under all three environment conditions, having similar duration in post-pausal and intervocalic environments, but with a significantly shorter duration ($P < 0.001$) in a preceding VOICELESS environment.

The greatest mean duration of voicing in word-final VOICED fricatives occurs in intervocalic position. This is significant in the data from all the subjects with the exception of FD, who has the same pattern of results but they are not significant. Post-hoc comparison of the pooled data showed that the degree of voicing in intervocalic position is significantly higher than that which occurs in the other two environments ($p < 0.005$). As in the initial fricatives, there is a fairly strong interaction between the phonological voicing category of the fricative and the environment class (see Table 3.15). This is present in the data from all the subjects at the $p < 0.005$ level. In VOICELESS final fricatives, there is very little incursion of voicing regardless of the following environment (only /θ/ shows any increase in the intervocalic environment).

To summarise these findings, in final VOICED stops and fricatives longer intervals of medial voicing are observed in intervocalic position than when the following context is voiceless or a pause. No significant trends emerge from the final VOICELESS obstruents. No environment condition comparisons can be made with initial stops, but initial VOICED fricatives with a preceding voiceless context have a smaller percentage of their medial phase accompanied by voicing than in other conditions, although only in the case of /v/ does this show up as a reduction in the absolute duration of the voiced interval.

These findings suggest that, whenever a juxtaposition of a VOICED obstruent and voiceless context (including a pause) occurs, the VOICED obstruent frequently becomes partially or completely unvoiced in SBE. This corresponds to the findings reported by Westbury (1979) and Thorsen (1971) concerning the timing of voicing in English consonant sequences. It could be hypothesised that the fact that VOICED obstruents commonly 'lose' their voicing, but that VOICELESS obstruents do not become voiced (except for the very short incursion of voicing from a preceding vowel described earlier in this chapter) in the equivalent circumstances, could reflect the aerodynamic constraints (i.e. progressively higher intra-oral air pressure) which militate against the occurrence of vocal fold vibration during obstruents. If this were the case, as with all aerodynamically-based explanations we would expect to see similar patterns in other languages. However, what little data is available does not support this. For example, in Dutch (van den Berg 1988), voicing 'assimilation' is both regressive and progressive depending on the manner of articulation of the obstruent. 'If the second consonant in the sequence is a voiced fricative, this second consonant becomes voiceless ... if the second consonant in the sequence is a voiced plosive, the first consonant becomes voiced' (van den Berg, 1988:3).

It is likely, then, that the findings regarding the effect of environment condition on medial voicing in SBE obstruents reflect a (at least partially) rule-governed aspect of phonetic realisation, rather than a by-product of 'low-cost' motor programming or of utterance execution. Given the appropriate circumstances the domain of voicelessness encroaches on the domain of voicing -- a form of 'feature-spreading'. It is noteworthy that the extent of 'spreading' is variable, and often well within the domain of a 'segment'. This mean that if this is in fact rule-governed, the specification of the rules requires a time-base which is finer than that offered by segment-ordering alone.

Effect of position in word

In VOICELESS stops there is no significant difference in duration of medial voicing as a function of whether the stop is in initial or final position (see Table 3.31). In VOICED stops, the effect of position in the word depends on the index of medial voicing which is used, and the environment of the stop. Using the percentage index of medial voicing, and pooling across all subjects, stop identities and environment conditions, there is no significant difference in the amount of voicing during the medial phase of initial and final VOICED stops. However, when the data compared is limited to stops occurring intervocalically,[31] there is found to be a significantly greater proportion of stop medial phase accompanied by voicing in final VOICED stops than in initial VOICED stops. However, the opposite is found to be the case when intervals of medial voicing are represented in absolute terms. The duration of absolute intervals of medial voicing in initial VOICED stops is greater than that observed in final VOICED stops.

A comparison of the mean percentage of the medial phase of initial and final fricatives accompanied by voicing, pooling across subject, fricative identity and environment class revealed that there is a significantly greater degree of voicing during the medial phase of initial fricatives than during the medial phase of final fricatives. When the data for comparison is restricted to fricatives occurring intervocalically, the same tendency is observed (but is not significant), with slightly greater amounts of voicing during the medial phase of initial fricatives compared to final fricatives. These results are found regardless of which of the two indices of medial voicing are used. The figures in Table 3.31 suggest that this difference resides primarily in VOICED fricatives. There are only very small differences observed in VOICELESS fricatives.

Hence, the main effect of position in the word is that in initial VOICED obstruents there are longer intervals of medial voicing than in final VOICED obstruents. It is possible that this finding is due to the different stress characteristics of the following vowels (in the intervocalic environment condition, initial stops are followed by a stressed vowel in the carrier sentences, whereas final stops are followed by an unstressed vowel). Keating (1984b) argues that segments before stressed vowels will be characterised by relatively higher sub-glottal pressure than stops occurring before unstressed vowels. The reason put forward for this is that the increased respiratory force and consequent rise in sub-glottal pressure for stressed vowels will begin during a preceding consonant. This causes an increase in both sub- and supra-glottal pressure, but a relatively larger increase in sub-glottal pressure, thus leading to longer intervals of voicing during the preceding consonant (since it

CHAPTER 3   167

takes longer for the trans-glottal pressure to be equalised).[32] Keating found that by simulating this sequence of events with a simple vocal tract model, stops were produced with different degrees of closure voicing depending on whether the following vowel was stressed or unstressed.

Hence, it is possible that we can invoke an aerodynamic explanation for the observations described in this section, although it is evident that a good deal of further investigation is required to confirm that Keating's description of events is correct. In particular, one might look for evidence of the same patterns of voicing timing in other languages, as would be predicted by this aerodynamic account. No such data is available in the literature.

3.3.5 Effect of speaker identity

On the whole, the five speakers who provided the data for this experiment are fairly consistent in their production of the voicing timing parameters which have been the object of the present study (as evidenced by the small number of significant between-speaker differences observed). However, subject TC differs from the others in his voice onset time patterns. Of the two different modes of voice onset used in VOICED stops (prevoicing vs short lag), prevoicing only occurs in the stops from two subjects (TC and BD), but of these two, only TC produces a large number of prevoiced VOICED stops (75% of his utterance-initial VOICED stops). Subject BD only produces three cases of prevoicing in utterance-initial VOICED stops out of a sample of 26. The remaining three speakers do not produce a single case of prevoicing between them. This certainly supports the idea that speakers of the same accent of English show different preferences about which pattern of voicing to use in post-pausal VOICED stops, but it is not in accord with the claim made by Smith (1978) that no speaker will use one type of voicing timing to the exclusion of the other.

There are some differences between speakers with regard to the frequency with which different patterns of medial voicing occur, and the duration of medial voicing. An example of this is shown in Table 3.32.

There are a number of areas in which noticeable between-speaker differences can be observed. Subject PB stands out as being the only subject not to produce a single case of 100% medial voicing in initial or final stops, the contrast with other speakers being particularly noticeable in final stops. In final fricatives, there are differences between speakers with respect to the frequency with which any medial voicing occurs. For example, subject BD produces double the number of cases of medial voicing than subject FD. TC also produces a relatively high frequency of medially voiced final fricatives.

Furthermore, it is interesting to note that the speakers who produce cases of prevoicing in their utterance-initial VOICED stops (TC and BD) also have the greatest number of cases of medial voicing in final fricatives (in initial fricatives too, but the difference is less apparent). There is insufficient data in this corpus for any significant correlation to be established, but there are grounds for further investigation here, to see if other speakers of the same accent who prevoice their VOICED stops also have a tendency to have medial voicing occurring relatively frequently in fricatives. One other study (Scully & Allwood 1985) has reported significant between-speaker differences in the timing of voicing in VOICED fricatives (Scully & Allwood's study was based on five subjects). As can be seen in Table 3.33, by taking two parameters, 'prevoiced stops', and what is labelled 'fricative voicing' (this could refer to a probability of presence of medial voicing in final fricatives above a certain threshold), four classes of speakers can be identified. Given the possibility outlined above of a correlation between prevoicing of VOICED stops, and medial voicing in final fricatives, it is an empirical question whether in SBE there are any speakers of type (d).

Table 3.32: Number of cases of 100% medial voicing and >0<100% medial voicing in VOICED obstruents as a function of speaker identity and position in word.

No. of cases of 100% voicing			Subject		
	RT	PB	TC	BD	FD
initial stops	-	-	1	6	-
final stops	19	-	11	24	14
initial frics.	2	15	27	27	17
final frics.	5	11	14	16	10
No. of cases of >0<100% voicing			Subject		
	RT	PB	TC	BD	FD
initial stops	40	49	46	43	43
final stops	97	105	107	98	95
initial frics.	18	28	31	31	29
final frics.	71	74	98	112	56

Table 3.33: Illustration of a means of categorising speakers of British English as a function of the patterns of voicing timing used in VOICED fricatives and post-pausal VOICED stops. '+/-' should be interpreted as meaning 'above/below certain thresholds'.

	(a)	(b)	(c)	(d)
prevoiced stops	-	+	+	-
fricative voicing	-	-	+	+

The fact that speakers of the same accent of English use different patterns of voicing timing in their realisation of the same underlying category is of some importance for the area of speech production modelling under consideration in this study. The following remarks refer specifically to the difference in voice onset time observed in VOICED stops. Since the same speaker can produce both modes of voicing timing, between-speaker differences are not explicable on the grounds of general properties of motor control or of utterance execution, or on the grounds of between-speaker anatomical differences.

An alternative explanation might be that speakers who prevoice their VOICED stops have a different underlying contrast from the others (for example, in Keating's (1984a) terms they may use a different phonetic category ({voiced}) to that used by the other subjects ({voiceless unaspirated}). Evidence against this is the fact that the speakers who prevoice VOICED stops are not consistent in their use of that pattern of voicing timing, and there are a significant number of cases in which TC and BD produce VOICED stops with short lag voice onset times. Another possible explanation is that TC and BD have acquired an extra realisation rule for initial VOICED stops, which they are able to use in free variation with the rule which provides unaspirated VOICED stops (although TC uses it more frequently than BD). The problem with that position is that it could be the case that all speakers have acquired the potential to prevoice VOICED stops, but that only some speakers actually use that potential.[33] Despite this uncertainty, it does seem to be the case that the between-speaker difference in voice onset time is a reflection of different implementation strategies, as opposed to being a by-product of some other feature of the speakers concerned.

3.4 SUMMARY OF FINDINGS

One of the principal aims of this experiment was to make a contribution to broadening the state of knowledge concerning the timing of voicing in obstruents in SBE. The results above go some way to achieving this. In addition, they allow an evaluation of the area of theoretical difficulty outlined in Chapter 2; the question of to what extent micro-variability in voicing timing reflects properties inherent in the speech production mechanism, and to what extent it is an aspect of the linguistic control of the production of an utterance.

The results show that whether an obstruent is VOICED or VOICELESS has a powerful influence on the pattern of voicing timing which occurs in relation to its medial phase (i.e. voice onset time, and frequency of occurrence and duration of medial voicing). However, the relationship between the observations of voice onset time/medial voicing and phonological voicing category is not transparent, and systematic, within-category variability occurs as a function of many of the additional independent variables studied.

The following additional factors have a significant effect on voice onset time in SBE stops; stop place of articulation (labials have shorter voice onset times than non-labials, but there is no significant difference between alveolars and velars); vowel quality (slightly higher voice onset times before high than before low vowels); the nature of the post-stop environment (longer voice onset times are produced if the following segment is a sonorant than if the following segment is a vowel); the nature of the preceding environment (VOICELESS stops following /s/ in the same syllable have voice onset times which are not significantly different from those found for VOICED stops in other environments), speaker identity (prevoicing was only found to occur in the data from two out the five subjects). In addition there are non-significant tendencies for voice onset time to be shorter in sentence-conditions than in isolated words, and in stops preceded by /s/ across a syllable boundary.

The duration of intervals of medial voicing in stops and fricatives is affected by manner of articulation (VOICELESS fricatives seem to be more resistant to medial voicing than VOICELESS stops -- the situation is less clear in the case of VOICED obstruents), place of articulation (but only in certain final VOICED fricatives), environment condition (voiceless and pause contexts lead to shorter and less frequent intervals of medial voicing in VOICED obstruents), position in the word (in environment condition 2 there are longer intervals of voicing in initial than in final VOICED stops), and speaker identity.

In attempting to account for this wide range of micro-variability, it was pointed out that some aspects of it are likely to be the automatic consequence of properties of the speech production mechanism, such as the aerodynamic or mechanical properties of the vocal apparatus, (e.g. variation in voice onset time before different vowel qualities, effect of a transyllabic /s/ on voice onset time). However, in other cases (e.g. place of articulation effect on voice onset time, delay in voicing onset in /s/-nasal sequences, differences as a function of manner of articulation, etc.) there appears to be at least the possibility that patterns of interarticulator coordination are not explicable entirely in terms of automatic, universal phonetic processes. This opens up the possibility that some aspects of the micro-timing of voicing are part of the 'phonetic plan' which drives the speech production mechanism.

It is evident that these findings and their interpretation are in need of support from future investigation of the timing of voicing in many more speakers of a wide range of languages. However, if the present findings and interpretations are confirmed, it would suggest that the specification of the timing of voicing which is input to the (universal) speech production mechanism is rather more detailed than is the case within conventional models of voicing control. This, in turn, imposes a requirement on speech production modellers to consider what exactly the nature of the phonetic representation which drives this aspect of speech production might be.

In Chapter 5, working on the assumption that the present findings and interpretations are correct, I return to the issues raised in Chapter 2. I consider in more detail the nature of a model of the timing of voicing which would be capable of incorporating findings, such as these, that there is significant variability in the detail of voicing timing (both within and between languages) which reflects some form of phonetic control other than that embodied in the fairly abstract specifications proposed in a number of existing models.

NOTES

1. Nine of the total set of words did not conform to this template having instead either a (C)CV or VC(C) structure, or a CVC structure in which one of the Cs was not an obstruent.

2. In order to accustom subjects to the experimental procedure, they were first given a trial set of (12*3) 36 utterances to read. These tokens were not included in the analysis.

3. Of course, there is no reason why a smaller window, of less than 10 ms for example, could not be used in some of the time-domain algorithms. However, this may well give rise to a greater likelihood of an erroneous decision due to the considerable fluctuation from one analysis interval to the next which often occurs in windows which are shorter than the period of the waveform

4. The accelerometer is a mechanical device, very similar to a throat microphone, which is capable of registering glottal vibration. The difference is that whilst the throat microphone measures mechanical displacement, an accelerometer measures acceleration (Hess 1982:114).

5. Stathopoulos and Weismer (1983:396) identified the medial phase of post-vocalic VOICELESS stops as the interval between the last glottal pulse for the preceding vowel, and the burst of the stop. However, the results to be reported in the following chapter suggest that the last glottal pulse may not give an accurate representation of the point at which oral closure begins.

6. In Chapter 1 the difficulties involved in defining the medial phase of a fricative were discussed. In this experiment, I opt to use the most commonly used definition (presence of noise in the signal as a result of close approximation of articulators). This definition is the simplest from the point of view of performing measurements on acoustic data, and is the most appropriate from the point of view of encoding phonetic knowledge for speech synthesis applications.

7. The tables of results presented in this chapter show the results for the data pooled across the five subjects. Where between-subjects differences are found to be significant, this is referred to in the text.

8. Hutters (1985:4), citing Ferguson (1976), points out that 'the Scheffé procedure does not require an equal number of observations in the groups to be compared. The drawback is the procedure is more rigourous than other procedures, which consequently leads to fewer significant differences. Therefore ... a less rigourous significance level than normally required for an F test may be employed.' This is the motivation for the present use of $p < 0.005$ as the Scheffé significance level, compared to $p < 0.001$ for the analysis of variance.

9. Note that throughout this account of experiment I, most of the statistical comparisons of the duration of intervals of medial voicing are based on the percentage figures rather than on the absolute figures (where this is not the case, it is made clear). The motivation for this was discussed above.

10. This statement may be open to criticism on the grounds of circularity; i.e. it is possible that three timing patterns are observed solely because I happen to have classified the findings in terms of three different types of voicing timing (A,B, and C, in, for example, Table 3.8). From a descriptive point of view, the choice of three categories seems reasonable, firstly because it is not evident on what grounds, other than arbitrary ones, the current class C would be sub-divided, and secondly, because it captures the extremes of 'no medial voicing' and 'complete medial voicing', as well as the intermediate case of 'incomplete medial voicing'. Furthermore, it is not inevitable that all three patterns are found, as is the case with the VOICELESS fricatives in Table 3.12 which show no cases of type B.

11. If the present results were found to be applicable to continuous speech, they would have an interesting implication from the point of view of the acoustic front-end of an automatic speech recognition system. Given an unidentified pre-stressed syllable stop with a voice onset time of 45 ms, it would be difficult to use that voice onset time measure ALONE as a cue to the identity of the stop (to judge from the histograms in Figure 3.6, it could be one of /p,t,k,d,g/). However, in a multi-variate analysis with voice onset time and a robust place of articulation algorithm forming

part of the descriptive vector, the voice onset time measure could then be used relatively efficiently to indicate its underlying voicing category, due to the overall homorganic stop separation. In this respect, it is also interesting to note that the present results for VOICED stops run counter to the findings of Kewley-Port (1982) who suggested that voice onset time was a very effective means of identifying the place of articulation of an unknown VOICED stop. The results of experiment 1 suggest quite the opposite for both VOICED and VOICELESS stops. Of course, this could be due to the different techniques used for measuring the onset of voicing (waveform analysis in this case, energy threshold function in Kewley-Port's case) but the mean voice onset time figures reported are comparable across the two experiments.

12. It is interesting to note that even in reports which show the 'conventional' progression in voice onset time from /p/ to /t/ to /k/ in English, the difference between /t/ and /k/ is often far smaller than that between /p/ and /t/ or /k/ -- see Table 1.2 in Chapter 1. Given that few of the authors carry out tests to ascertain whether all three distributions are statistically different, it is possible that in some cases the /t/-/k/ distributions are not in fact different, as is found in the present data

13. In particular, Klatt's claim that there is a phonetic rule which governs the onset of glottal closure is not compatible with studies of laryngeal abduction in stops which suggest that it consists of a single integrated gesture (Löfqvist 1980).

14. The idea of a uniform glottal abduction gesture being used in all stops and fricatives (i.e. regardless of place and manner) was proposed independently, and around the same time, by Weismer (1980)

15. An alternative position, which is less open to criticism, could be to say that whilst the **absolute** duration of the voiceless interval may not necessarily correspond to the absolute duration of the laryngeal gesture, any differences in the duration of the voiceless interval presumably DO reflect differences in the duration of laryngeal activity. Since differences in duration, rather than absolute durations are the main focus of my interest, this seems to be safer ground.

16. We can, however, assume that it **does** correspond to a glottal gesture of some sort -- data reported later in 3.3.4 suggests that voicing is not interrupted passively.

17. The present results for VOICELESS stops are in agreement with Baran et al. (1977), but in that study it was found that VOICED stops had longer voice onset times in sentence conditions, the opposite to that found here.

18. In order to be absolutely certain that this tendency for longer voice onset times is a function of the fact that the test word is produced in isolation as opposed to being a function of the fact that the adjacent context is a pause, it would be necessary to carry out a further study of voice onset time in sentence-initial post-pausal stops. If the same pattern of results emerged, the interpretation offered in this section would have to be reviewed (c.f. Lisker & Abramson (1964, 1967), who found a

difference between voice onset time in isolated words and the same words in sentences, but no difference between words occurring sentence-initially or -medially).

19. Some evidence of plasticity interacting with macro-temporal factors is provided by Gay (1981). In a study of articulatory organisation at different rates of speech, he points out that speakers were capable of varying the degree of vowel 'undershoot', and that undershoot could be overridden if 'speakers were instructed to maintain syllable stress and phonetic identity of the vowel' (1981:152).

20. Klatt (1975:691) -- citing a personal communication from Lisker -- points out that there is a possibility that Lisker & Abramson's data were not appropriate for testing the effect of vowel height on voice onset time.

21. This account contrasts with that given by Summerfield (1975) of his findings that voice onset time in [pi] was shorter (but not significantly) than that in [pa]. He claimed that the upward pull on the laryngeal structures, caused by tongue fronting and raising, leads to a relatively earlier onset of voicing. The basis of this claim is an assumption that smaller amounts of glottal abduction result from greater tension in the vocal folds. Summerfield fails to consider the likelihood that greater tension in the vocal folds means that there is greater glottal resistance to be overcome before voicing can commence, and hence a possibility that this would delay voice onset; i.e. a factor which predicts the opposite to the tendency emerging from his data. In fact, on the whole, increased tension of the vocal folds tends to be more normally associated with voicelessness rather than being thought of as a process which would enhance voicing (Kohler 1984:160), although this is clearly still an empirical question..

22. The greater differences between /stop-V/ and /stop-r-V/ sequences when the stop is alveolar compared to when the stop is non-alveolar, could be interpreted as evidence that /tr, dr/ operate as a composite phonological unit (similar to /tʃ, dʒ/), and are therefore timed differently from the other stop-sonorant sequences. The possible affricate status of [tr, dr] is discussed by Gimson (1980:172ff).

23. Ohala (1983:207) lists three reasons why these changes occur over a finite length of time, and out of synchrony; (a) inertia of the vocal organs has to be overcome, (b) 'some muscular slack needs to be taken up before the articulators can move', (c) limited temporal resolution of neuro-muscular control. In the light of the discussion in Chapter 2, it may be wise not to overstate the role of (a) and (b), but there is no doubt about the importance of the third factor. Temporal resolution of control is discussed further in Chapter 5.

24. It may be that Spanish is not strictly comparable to English, since /s/-nasal sequences never occur syllable-initially. However, the results of experiment 2 show that the constrained pattern of voicing timing in these sequences in English also occurs across syllable and word boundaries.

25. Interestingly, whilst there is insufficient data to make a robust statistical comparison, intervals of voicelessness in [θr] are considerably longer than in [θV], whereas (at least in environment conditions 1 and 3) voiceless intervals in [θw] are similar in duration to [θV]. This is compatible with the interpretation offered above that lengthening of voicelessness may be a consequence of a complex transition between two segments which cannot be co-produced.

26. An attractive non-segmental explanation of this has been proposed by Browman & Goldstein (1986). This has the advantage of showing that this aspect of voicing timing is absolutely regular for speakers of English, and that it does not have to be singled out for special treatment. They suggest that a general rule of English phonology is that words begin with at most a single glottal (abduction) gesture. Additional rules specify that if a fricative is present the peak glottal opening is timed to coincide with the middle of the fricative. If the word begins with a single stop, the peak glottal opening is timed to coincide with the release of the stop gesture.

27. This requires an assumption to be made that sub-glottal pressure remains constant. Very few studies of the effect of different segmental types on sub-glottal pressure have been carried out. Netsell (1969) in a study of [t] and [d] concluded that there was no difference in sub-glottal pressure which could be attributed to the voicing category of the stops. Similar results were obtained for labial stops by McGlone & Shipp (1972). I know of know no study investigating the effect of manner of articulation (specifically stop vs fricative) on sub-glottal pressure.

28. Incidentally, the present results back up a further comment made by Ohala (1983:202) in which he suggests, on the basis of auditory impression, that /v, z/ are more likely to be 'devoiced' in word-final position than /b, d/ (in American English).

29. Bickley & Stevens (1987) point out that 'while [ð] and [v] are normally classified as obstruents there is often little evidence of frication and it is difficult to specify an acoustic correlate that provides a clear and qualitative distinction between these consonants on the one hand and liquids and glides on the other.'(:251)

30. Different strategies are used, for example, in French (e.g. Armstrong 1932:122) in which VOICED obstruents are 'devoiced' far less frequently than in English. Cross-language investigation would provide some idea of the range of possible strategies used in different languages and accents, and would allow the results presented here to be placed in some perspective.

31. The discrepancy between percentage and absolute measures for medial voicing in final VOICED stops is probably a result of the duration of those stops, which is relatively short (hence giving rise to relatively high percentage figures).

32. Note that this account is based on an assumption that voicing ceases passively, as a result of trans-glottal pressure equalisation. Results reported above suggest that this may not be the case in the present data, and therefore undermine to some extent the possibility that Keating's explanation is applicable in this case.

33. This latter possibility is backed up by other studies of between-speaker differences in VOICED stop voice onset times, which have shown that no speaker uses one realisation strategy to the exclusion of the other.

CHAPTER 4
Experiment 2

4.1 INTRODUCTION

The experiment reported in the previous chapter was designed to study the effect of the phonological category of a segment and of the nature of the phonetic environment in which it is embedded on voice onset time and the duration of any voicing occurring during the obstruent medial phase in SBE obstruents. The aim of this second experiment was to explore the effect of a different type of contextual factor on the micro-timing of voicing; the nature of the boundary between the two components of a consonant sequence. More specifically, the aim of this experiment was to evaluate claims in the literature (described in Chapter 1) that delayed onset of voicing in sonorants in stop-sonorant sequences does not occur across word-boundaries (Jones 1960, Brown 1977, Gimson 1980), or syllable boundaries (Kahn 1976). These proposed boundary constraints are not consistent with the small amount of experimental work which has been carried out in this area, which suggests that, at least the word-domain hypothesis[1] may not be an accurate characterisation of the domain in which voice onset delay is found.

However, it is not possible to fully evaluate these claims since there have been no studies of the effect of different boundary conditions on the timing of voicing in a range of different stop-sonorant sequences in British English. The relevant data which is available is of very limited scope and, on the whole, is embedded in studies which do not primarily set out investigate this aspect of phonetic realisation. It is this gap which the present experiment was designed to fill.[2]

Not only does this experiment allow some evaluation of the claims regarding the timing of voicing in stop-sonorant sequences, it also has a degree of relevance (in a way to be described below) from the point of view of the problematic areas of speech production theory described in Chapter 2. The experimental paradigm chosen for this experiment is one that has been used in the past for investigating coarticulatory phenomena in speech. It involves observing the variation which is brought about in interarticulator coordination as a function of the status of the boundary which is placed between the source of the coarticulatory accommodation and the location to which it spreads. Generally, one of two possible findings may be expected. In the first case, there may be no difference whatsoever in the frequency of occurrence or in the span of a particular type of accommodation under a range of different boundary conditions (i.e. in a sequence of segments [ab], feature 'X_b' would always be anticipated during the production of [a] regardless of the type of boundary present between [a] and [b]). This could be interpreted as evidence in favour of treating this particular form of anticipatory coarticulation as the product of a low-level component of the speech production mechanism, quite possibly being caused by the aerodynamic/bio-mechanical properties of the vocal apparatus. The second major type of observation which might be made is that there is no coarticulation, or significantly less frequent and/or shorter span coarticulation taking place between two segments, the deeper the boundary between the two segments. One interpretation of this type of finding (providing that one has excluded other possible explanations such as segmental lengthening at 'deeper' boundaries which could potentially result in less segmental interaction), involves assuming that..

> ... at some processing level, a speaker applies phonetic rules over some specified phonetic domain, such that phonetic information lying outside this domain cannot be taken into consideration in the application of the rules. Thus for a given syntactic domain 'x' including phonetic segments [S1,S2,S3,...]x, phonetic rules applied to any segment 'Si' can utilize information contained only in segments (typically adjacent to 'Si') contained within 'x'. (Cooper 1980:313)

If it is discovered that a particular type of coarticulatory interaction is blocked or inhibited across some types of boundary (i.e. the syntactically deeper ones) but not across others, and that this is not the consequence of some other aspect of the 'deeper' boundary (such as a segment duration difference), then there are at least three main ways in which such data would be interesting from the theoretical framework described in Chapter 2. The first is that the data would provide information regarding the size of the domains under which particular phonetic rules are operational -- 'blocking' would tend to take place at domain boundaries. The second is that we are given some insight into the nature of the phonetic rule itself; e.g. variability which is sensitive to linguistic juncture is unlikely to be the result of an automatic process originating in the execution of an utterance. The third is to do with the ordering of the processes which give rise to allophonic variation. If it is found that very fine coarticulatory and coordinatory activity is sensitive to 'higher' level structures and domains, it suggests that the processes which give rise to those fine-grained phenomena are activated at a stage at which the contextual information is accessible.

Previous work on boundary effects on coarticulation has produced varying results. Some types of coarticulation do appear to be sensitive to different types of boundary, others do not. For example, McLean (1973) found that word boundaries did not curtail nasal coarticulation, but that phrase, clause and sentence boundaries did. Conversely, Lewis et al. (1975) found that /n/ would be dentalised before a dental fricative across all types of boundaries, including a sentence boundary. The following experiment set out to use this experimental paradigm to investigate whether the micro-timing of voicing is sensitive to higher level factors, namely the status of the boundary which lies between two segments.

4.2 EXPERIMENTAL METHOD

4.2.1 Linguistic material

In this experiment, the timing of voicing in stop-sonorant sequences was examined with six different types of boundary intervening between the stop and sonorant.

#CCV word initial position (ie syllable-internally). As well as providing the boundary with minimum depth (and sequences which are transparently syllable-internal), this condition permits confirmation of the results obtained in experiment 1, and in other studies reported in the literature.

C+C across a morpheme boundary

C+C across a morpheme and compound boundary (this does not always involve a word-boundary due to the fact that compound nouns are not consistent in their orthographic structure).

C#C across a word boundary phrase-internally (between an adjective and noun)

C#C across a word boundary phrase-internally (between the subject of a verb and the verb)

C#C Across a word boundary which is also a clause boundary.

Hence, if the word-domain hypothesis is correct, delayed voice onset would not be expected to be found in the final three of these conditions. As was pointed out in Chapter 1, the syllable-domain hypothesis depends on how syllable margins are defined, and since this is an area of considerable uncertainty, it is difficult to ascertain exactly what its predictions would be with respect to this data (i.e. resyllabification could occur across the deeper boundaries thereby 'forcing' delayed voice onset to take place). The results of this experiment shed some light on this issue. However, the syllable-domain position does predict that there should always be a delay in voice onset in the first condition, where the sequence is transparently in syllable-internal position. The sequences investigated were as follows:

VOICELESS Sequences
/pr/ /pl/
/tr/ /tw/
/kr/ /kl/ /kw/

VOICED Sequences
/br/ /bl/
/dr/ /dw/
/gr/ /gl/

In addition, tokens of [sm] and [sn] sequences occurring under all the six conditions were also obtained from all the subjects. The purpose of including these sequences was to investigate whether the delay in onset of voicing which occurs between the fricative and the nasal in these sequences was affected by the different boundary conditions, in the same way as the delay in voicing onset in the stop-sonorant sequences.

These particular sequences were chosen because they involve little segmentation and measurement difficulty, and they allow comparison with other work which has been carried out, and evaluation of the specific claims made in the literature concerning the timing of voicing in initial sequences in English.

As was pointed out in Chapter 1, the question of stress is also an important consideration in considering the timing of voicing in these sequences. It has been shown by Dent (1984) that whether a cluster occurs in a stressed or unstressed syllable is a relevant factor for the pattern of voicing timing. Dent reports that in British English stop-lateral sequences, there is a shorter voice onset time in a lateral when the following vowel is stressed that when the following vowel is unstressed. For this reason, stress was one of the controls incorporated into the materials for this experiment. In conditions 1, 3, 4, 5, and 6, all the initial clusters occurred before a stressed syllable. In condition 2, it was not possible to maintain this control throughout the data due to the large number of unstressed affixes which were used in order to produce the correct sequences. This fact must be borne in mind during the analysis of the results. Ensuring that the sequences are followed by a stressed vowel should, if Dent's findings are replicated, lead to a more conservative measure of the voice onset time than would be the case if the following vowel were unstressed.

The following are examples of the materials used in the experiment (a full list of the test words and phrases is given in Appendix B).

Condition 1 (word-initial position) he said he wanted to pray, didn't he

Condition 2 (morpheme boundary) we all know it's upright, don't we.

Condition 3 (compound boundary)   We all know it's the tap-room, don't we

Condition 4 ([adj./noun] word boundary)   we all know it's a steep road, don't we.

Condition 5 ([subj/verb] word boundary)   we all know Philip ran, don't we.

Condition 6 (word and clause boundary)   we all saw the cap Ron bought, didn't we.

4.2.2 Database description

The sentences were randomised and collated into a single list containing two repetitions of each sentence in each of the boundary conditions. This list was read by seven subjects in 8 blocks of 28 sentences. Each block contained a number of 'filler' sentences at the beginning and end, which were not analysed (unlike experiment 1, no control for rate of articulation was used in this experiment; the subjects were asked to read the sentences at a comfortable rate). This gave a total of (15 sequences * 6 conditions * 2 repetitions * 7 subjects) 1260 utterances for analysis. The actual database used in the analysis was slightly smaller, containing 1127 utterances. There are three reasons for this difference. Firstly, 1 subject only produced a single repetition of the sentences (-90). Secondly, in three cases (/br/ and /gr/ in boundary condition 2, and /bl/ in boundary condition 4), no suitable sentences were devised, with the result that these particular combinations of sequence/condition were not produced by the subjects (-39). Thirdly, four of the sentences produced by the subjects were unusable due to background noise on the recording.

4.2.3 Subjects

The subjects were all male speakers of Southern British English, aged between 18 and 30. None reported any speech or hearing disorder, and there was no evidence of any systemic differences between their accents.

4.2.4 Recording and measurement procedures

The recording and storage of the utterances produced by the informants was identical to that carried out in experiment 1. The criteria used for extracting the measurements from each token were as follows. The duration of the delay in voice onset was measured from the point at which the stop closure was released (visible as a sudden burst of noise on the oscillogram) to the first peak of the periodic signal in the throat microphone waveform corresponding to an interval of voicing. It was assumed that at the moment at which the stop is released, the vocal tract would have adopted the configuration required for the following sonorant, therefore the delay in voice onset corresponds to an interval of unvoiced sonorant. In the cases in which delayed voice onset was not observed to occur, speakers used a range of different strategies. These were identified as follows. The replacement of the stop by a glottal stop, and glottalisation of the stop were detected auditorily. As was pointed out in the previous chapter, auditory judgement was used because of the difficulty involved in consistently distinguishing oral and glottal(ised) stops on an oscillographic representation, and the same reservations apply concerning the accuracy of auditory judgement. A pause was taken to have occurred if there was an interval of silence in the time waveform between the release of the stop closure and the onset of voicing for the sonorant. An incomplete stop closure was identified by a continuous noisy signal throughout the period in which the stop was being produced (i.e. there was no silence and no stop release indicative of a complete closure).

4.2.5 Data analysis

Data analysis consisted of two main tests. A non-parametric chi-square test was used to examine whether delayed voice onset occurred with significantly greater frequency in any of the boundary conditions. Analysis of variance was used to see if the duration of voice onset time was significantly affected by the boundary condition.

4.3 RESULTS

4.3.1 Frequency of occurrence of delayed voice onset

The results of this experiment show that a delay in voice onset in sonorants in a stop-sonorant sequence occurs with varying frequency according to the status of the boundary which is present between the two components of the sequence.

Table 4.1 shows the number of cases of VOICED and VOICELESS sequences in which delayed voice onset occurs in the six conditions investigated (pooled across all the subjects). The deeper the boundary between the consonants, the fewer the cases of delayed voice onset, and consequently the higher the number of cases in which an alternative strategy is used (see below). The results are now considered in more detail by focusing separately on VOICELESS clusters and VOICED clusters.

Table 4.1 also shows the frequency with which delayed voice onset occurs in VOICELESS clusters as a function of the boundary condition between the components of the CC sequence. Associated chi-square measures are shown in Table 4.2.

Table 4.1: Number of cases of delayed voice onset for the sonorant in VOICELESS and VOICED stop-sonorant sequences in the pooled data as a function of boundary condition. The numbers in parentheses indicate the number of cases as a percentage of the total for each cell, and the number of cases in which an alternative realisation strategy was used (see Tables 4.2/4.3).

Boundary Condition	Voiceless Sequences		Voiced Sequences		Total	
1	89	(99% 1)	69	(88% 8)	158	(94% 9)
2	79	(87% 12)	28	(54% 24)	107	(75% 36)
3	73	(80% 18)	32	(42% 45)	105	(63% 62)
4	58	(64% 33)	22	(34% 43)	80	(51% 76)
5	64	(70% 25)	22	(28% 56)	86	(51% 1)
6	40	(45% 48)	18	(23% 58)	58	(36% 106)

Table 4.2: Results of chi-square analysis of VOICELESS clusters.

Comparison	Chi-Square	d.f.	significance
all voiceless clusters independently	21.577	5	0.001
boundary condition 1 vs 2-6	8.848	1	0.003
boundary condition 6 vs 1-5	12.291	1	0.001
boundary conditions 1-3 vs 4-6	15.197	1	0.001

In VOICELESS clusters occurring syllable-initially,[3] there is always a delay in voice onset for the following VOICED sound. In clusters with a deeper medial boundary (conditions 2 through 6), this occurs progressively less frequently. The chi-square analysis shows that the boundary condition is a significant factor in determining the frequency with which delayed voice onset occurs (in the pooled data, and in the individual subject data). It is found consistently more frequently when clusters occur in boundary condition 1 compared to when they occur in boundary conditions 2-6. This is due to the fact that under the former boundary condition, a voice onset delay always occurs, whereas in the other conditions, a range of different realisation strategies are observed, only one of which is a delay in voice onset for the following sonorant. The clause boundary condition always produces by far the fewest cases of delayed voice onset.

The fourth chi-square effect shown above appears to suggest that there is a significant effect depending on whether the sequence occurs word-internally or not (conditions 1-3 are all word-internal). However, it seems likely that this effect is produced purely as a result of the extremes shown by boundary conditions 1 and 6.

In the cases in which delayed voice onset did not occur, the most frequent strategies were insertion of a pause between the release of the stop and the onset of voicing for the following sonorant (especially in the clause boundary condition), replacement of the stop by a glottal stop or glottalisation of the stop, and an incomplete stop closure. The frequency of occurrence of the various alternative strategies observed is shown in Table 4.3.

Table 4.3: Frequencies of occurrence of alternative realisation strategies in VOICELESS sequences in the pooled data as a function of boundary condition. A = pause, B = glottalisation, C = incomplete stop closure, D = voicing throughout stop closure and release, E = other strategies.

Alternative Strategy	Boundary condition						
	1	2	3	4	5	6	total
A	-	4	4	6	9	27	50
B	-	4	10	19	11	13	57
C	1	4	4	7	7	6	29
D	-	-	-	-	-	-	0
E	-	-	-	1	-	2	3
	1	12	18	33	25	48	139

Table 4.1 shows for the pooled data the frequency with which delayed voice onset of the sonorant occurs in VOICED stop-sonorant sequences as a function of varying the status of the boundary between the two consonants. Related chi-square measures are shown in Table 4.4.

In syllable-initial VOICED clusters, a voice onset delay in the sonorant occurs almost as reliably as it does in VOICELESS clusters under the same boundary condition (this is a reflection of the fact that phonemically VOICED stops in British English are frequently not accompanied by vocal fold vibration throughout their duration, as was shown earlier in Chapter 3). However, it is not the case that it **always** occurs in VOICED clusters in syllable-initial position. When deeper boundaries intervene between the components of the cluster there are still cases of delayed voice onset, but these are far less frequent than in VOICELESS clusters under the same conditions.

Table 4.4: Results of chi-square analysis of VOICED clusters.

Comparison	Chi-Square	d.f.	significance
all voiced clusters independently	49.261	5	0.001
boundary condition 1 vs 2-6	41.07	1	0.001
boundary condition 6 vs 1-5	9.925	1	0.002
boundary conditions 1-3 vs 4-6	28.12	1	0.001

The main effect to emerge from the chi-square analysis is that the frequency of occurrence of delayed voice onset is significantly greater in VOICED clusters occurring in boundary condition 1 than in VOICED clusters occurring in the other five boundary conditions. The other two analyses shown in Table 4.4 are possibly artefactual, as a result of the large difference between boundary condition 1 and conditions 2 - 6.

In the instances in which delayed voice onset did not occur, the most frequent strategy which was observed in its place was continuation of voicing unbroken right through the closure and release phases of the stop (see Table 4.5). This occurred in almost one third of the VOICED clusters in boundary conditions 2-6. It was also subject to considerable between-speaker differences, with three out of the seven subjects accounting for 72% of the instances of complete voicing (this backs up the comments made earlier in this chapter about patterns of medial voicing being a possible source of between-speaker variability).

4.3.2 Duration of voice onset time

Table 4.6 shows the mean delay in voice onset following the release of the stop in VOICELESS clusters as a function of the boundary condition. Boundary condition is not a significant factor with respect to voice onset time. Voice onset time is affected by the place of articulation of the stop and the identity of the sonorant, thus confirming the results of experiment 1. In every case, with the exception of /pl/, there is a greater delay in voice onset when the sequence occurs in syllable-initial position compared to when the same sequence occurs across deeper boundaries. There is no consistent trend across the remaining boundary conditions, and no replication of Dent's (1984) finding that longer voice onset times are found before unstressed vowels (i.e. boundary condition 2) than before stressed vowels. In some cases, the delay in voice onset becomes gradually less as the boundary is deepened, whilst in others the values vary seemingly at random. However, in every case, the shortest delays occur under the deepest boundary. Further investigation is required in order to establish whether this is a result of a phonetic 'rule' specifying shorter voice onset times in deeper boundaries, or whether the shorter voice onset times are produced as a result of lengthening of the stop closures under the deeper syntactic boundaries.

Table 4.5: Frequencies of occurrence of alternative realisation strategies in VOICED sequences in the pooled data as a function of boundary condition. A = pause, B = glottalisation, C = incomplete stop closure, D = voicing throughout stop closure and release, E = other strategies.

Alternative Strategy	Boundary condition						
	1	2	3	4	5	6	total
A	-	-	1	1	2	7	11
B	-	-	4	1	5	1	11
C	-	2	-	3	2	2	9
D	7	22	39	38	47	48	201
E	1	-	1	-	-	-	2
	8	24	45	43	56	58	234

In VOICED clusters (see Table 4.7), the duration of the voice onset delay is affected by the place of articulation of the stop and the identity of the sonorant, as established in experiment 1 (particularly noteworthy is the fact that the voice onset times for /dr/ sequences are almost double those for other VOICED stop clusters, thus confirming the findings of Experiment 1). With regard to the effect of the boundary condition, no clear tendencies emerge from the data. Unlike the findings for VOICELESS clusters, the highest delays in voice onset are not observed when the sequence occurs in syllable-initial position.

Table 4.6: Mean duration (ms) of the delay in voice onset in VOICELESS stop-sonorant sequences in the pooled data as function of boundary condition.

	Boundary condition					
	1	2	3	4	5	6
/pr/	60.92	46.00	58.60	42.43	35.00	32.67
/pl/	47.58	50.56	37.75	44.14	40.00	35.57
/tr/	105.38	91.62	85.67	76.75	79.80	70.00
/tw/	91.62	76.70	82.11	63.50	67.63	57.00
/kr/	87.92	84.92	70.23	78.00	69.00	60.50
/kl/	68.33	58.83	51.85	51.27	55.75	45.71
/kw/	82.92	74.00	77.91	80.00	74.36	56.00

Table 4.7: Mean duration (ms) of the delay in voice onset in VOICED stop-sonorant sequences in the pooled data as function of boundary condition.

	Boundary condition					
	1	2	3	4	5	6
/br/	19.08	-	18.67	21.33	17.00	18.83
/bl/	16.33	16.80	17.67	-	-	10.00
/dr/	51.83	47.78	51.75	72.33	35.50	40.00
/dw/	17.33	28.00	24.75	20.00	16.50	15.00
/gr/	30.58	-	36.44	31.00	35.80	31.33
/gl/	21.75	23.25	16.44	35.33	22.00	23.17

4.4 DISCUSSION

In summary, the results of experiment 2 show that the timing of voicing in VOICED and VOICELESS clusters in SBE is affected by medial boundary status. Specifically, the nature of the boundary between a stop and a following sonorant has an effect on the probability of there being a delayed voice onset for the sonorant. The crucial factor determining this aspect of the timing of voicing in stop-obstruent sequences is that it should occur syllable-initially; in the other boundary conditions voice onset delay occurs less frequently, and a variety of alternative realisation strategies are employed.

In VOICELESS clusters, voice onset time is largest when the sequence occurs in syllable-initial position, with shorter delays occurring under the other boundary conditions. In VOICED clusters, voice onset time does not vary in a predictable manner as a function of boundary condition.

It is instructive to compare these results with the data shown in Table 4.8 concerning the frequency of occurrence of a 'voiceless transition' in /s/-nasal sequences under the same set of boundary conditions. In these sequences, the frequency of occurrence of delayed voice onset is approximately the same under all of the different boundary conditions. This suggests that the delay observed in these clusters is a different sort of context-sensitivity to that observed in the stop-sonorant sequences, and indeed, supports the interpretation given to the findings in experiment I, that the timing of voicing in /s/-nasal sequences is governed by a tight temporal constraint which allows for very little variability, even, it would appear, across different boundary conditions.

Table 4.8: Number of cases of delayed voice onset for the sonorant in /s/-nasal sequences in the pooled data as a function of boundary condition. The figures in parentheses indicate the number of cases as a percentage of the total for each cell.

Boundary condition	Number of Cases
1	26 (100%)
2	26 (100%)
3	26 (100%)
4	25 (97%)
5	26 (100%)
6	24 (92%)

These results allow some light to be shed upon the claims in the literature concerning the domain in which delayed voice onset in these sequences takes place in English. No support is provided for the claim that it can only occur word-internally, since it is found to occur under all of the boundary conditions investigated. It is not the case that delayed voice onset occurs only within words or between words that form a 'close-knit entity' (Gimson 1980:287). This backs up the findings of Dent (1984) and Bladon & Al-Bamerni (1976) who provided a small amount of data showing delayed voice onset in /l/ following stops across word boundaries in English. These results also suggest that the presence or absence of delayed voice onset in a sonorant in stop-sonorant sequences is not, in itself, a very reliable cue to word juncture, in the sense described by Nakatani & Dukes (1977). However, as pointed out by Randolph & Zue (1987), it may be that the intensity of the stop burst or the voice onset time (although the present results show no significant differences in voice onset time) may be stronger correlates of the presence or absence of a word-boundary.

Evaluation of the syllable-domain hypothesis is less straightforward. The results could be interpreted in two ways. The syllable-domain hypothesis could be preserved by arguing that resyllabification is taking place on a fairly major scale in the present data. However, apart from the fact that there are no means (other than circular ones) of verifying when resyllabification has taken place (i.e. whatever measure was used would have to be evaluated with respect to the definition of a syllable, which in turn would require another means of identifying the syllable-boundary, etc.), this requires a further account of why resyllabification occurs progressively less frequently under boundary conditions 2-6, and why it is that mean voice onset times tend to be shorter in boundary conditions 2-6 than in the transparently syllable-initial boundary condition 1.[4]

A second interpretation is that syllable boundaries are not being redrawn, and that therefore it is not the presence or absence of delayed voice onset which marks a sequence as being syllable-internal or not (as is claimed), but the fact that in syllable-internal position a delay ALWAYS occurs, whereas in other positions it is optional. This interpretation is compatible with the data, and has the advantage of not requiring any further complex argumentation (as would be the case with the former interpretation). It suggests, however, that the syllable-domain hypothesis is need of some revision.

Furthermore, this latter interpretation is compatible with the idea (Fujimura 1987, Randolph & Zue 1987, Nolan 1987) that some aspects of allophonic variation (including syllable-based voicing variation -- Randolph & Zue 1987) are more of a gradient process as opposed to being an all-or-nothing alternation as suggested by rules such as the word- and syllable-domain hypotheses being tested here.

These findings suggest that if it is the case that this aspect of the timing of voicing in English is rule-governed, the nature of the rule is rather different from that which is suggested by either the 'word-domain' or 'syllable-internal' hypotheses. Both these claims suggest that delayed voice onset does not occur across particular types of boundary. However, delayed voice onset has been shown to occur across all of the boundaries investigated, and is therefore not restricted in the way suggested by either (unless we could prove that resyllabification was frequently taking place across boundary conditions 2-6).

These claims imply that delayed voice onset is a process which is present in some circumstances and never in others, whereas the experimental results suggests that it is more accurate to think of it as a gradient process, capable of occurring in all of the conditions observed, but occurring progressively less frequently across deeper boundaries.

In summary, these results suggest that the timing of voicing in stop-sonorant sequences is not constrained in the manner suggested by the claims in the literature. However, whilst the present results allow some evaluation of these specific claims, they only paint part of the picture, since they reveal the effect of medial boundary status on only one of the parameters involved in producing stop-sonorant sequences. A stronger account of the timing of voicing in these sequences might be achieved by analysis of a wider range of acoustic and articulatory parameters. In particular, it would be interesting to investigate not only the presence and duration of delays in voice onset with respect to the stop release, but also the effect of medial boundary status on the duration of the supralaryngeal gestures for the stop and sonorant, and (by making use of electropalatography) on the extent of coarticulatory overlap between the stop and sonorant. This would allow the construction of a more complete picture of inter-articulator coordination in these sequences, and may reveal regularities which could not be observed in the present experiment.

NOTES

1. As was pointed out in Chapter 1, the syllable-domain hypothesis is harder to evaluate due to the difficulty in identifying syllable margins.

2. The only other similar study which has been carried out (to the best of my knowledge) is that by van Hoof and van den Broecke (1983) on the effects of different types of juncture on voicing 'assimilation' in Dutch.

3. In the description of these results, 'syllable-initial' refers to boundary condition 1, in which the sequences are transparently in syllable-initial position. The question of possible resyllabification is considered in the discussion of the results.

4. An argument based on increased duration of the stop closure would not necessarily provide an answer to this latter point, since a further account would then be needed of why, if the stop is now in syllable-initial position, it should be temporally different from stops in boundary condition 1.

CHAPTER 5

Discussion

The aim of this chapter is to elaborate on the theoretical issues raised earlier in this book in the light of the experimental results described in Chapters 3 and 4. In the first section, I concentrate on the general phonetic description of the timing of voicing, outlining a set of proposals for a parametrically-based descriptive framework for the timing of voicing which overcomes a number of the features of the conventional descriptive apparatus which, in Chapter 1, were identified as being problematic. The proposals which I make are themselves not problem-free, and directions for future work in this aspect of general phonetic theory are identified.

In section 5.2, I discuss the timing of voicing in the context of a model of speech production, and present a number of minimum requirements which it is important to attain in devising an explicit account of how the timing of voicing is specified in the phonetic representation. I outline one possible means in which many of these requirements could be achieved, and some further investigation which would allow the proposals to be tested.

5.1 A DESCRIPTIVE TOOL FOR THE TIMING OF VOICING

In Chapter 1, I pointed out that the major problems with the conventional segmental descriptive framework from the point of view of the timing of voicing is descriptive labelling which does not match the complexity of the phenomena which are the object of the description, particularly in the area of temporal resolution. The results of the experiments reported in Chapters 3 and 4 underline these difficulties. It would be impossible to provide a full and accurate description of these results using the conventional descriptive apparatus, since the systematic variability which has been observed is too fine to be captured by a segmental time-base, and an essentially binary labelling procedure. The proposals outlined in this section attempt to remedy this, by showing one possible way in which a more detailed account of the timing of voicing could be achieved, by the incorporation of an element of parametric organisation within the descriptive framework.

Before outlining the proposals, a number of general points should be made concerning their scope. These proposals are not intended to be a wholesale replacement for the conventional descriptive framework. The aim of the proposals below is to provide a supplementary tool for the descriptive phonetician, allowing an account of the timing of voicing which is more detailed than that possible with a conventional transcription.[1] The aim is to provide the level of detail required in describing subtle between- and within-language variability in the timing of voicing, such as that described in Chapter 3.

It is also important to underline that the motivation for these proposals is purely descriptive. They do not represent a model of the phonology of the voicing contrast in languages, nor are they intended to represent the phonetic representation which drives the speech production mechanism. However, one prerequisite to advancing the state of our knowledge in both of these areas is a detailed descriptive account of phonetic realisation, such as that provided by the proposed framework.

Two further limitations of the proposals should be pointed out. Firstly, only obstruents are dealt with. This is because the framework is based on the data on the timing of voicing in SBE stops and fricatives described in the previous chapter. Secondly, for the same reason, the framework only gives an account of the **timing** of intervals of voicing in relation to supralaryngeal events, and no account is given of the different types of glottal gesture associated with different sounds.

5.1.1 A framework for the detailed description of the timing of voicing

The basis of the approach to be described is the incorporation of greater temporal resolution into descriptions of the timing of voicing by performing a finer-grained division of the time base, and specifying the timing of voicing in terms of whether there is any voicing during the medial phase of an obstruent (a), and the timing pattern occurring at phase 1[2] (b), and at phase 3 (c) of an obstruent. The method adopted involves establishing a set of possible **templates** of voicing timing at stages (a), (b), and (c), and observing which combinations of medial and transitional **templates** are observed under a range of contexts in a given accent or language (the exemplification given below relates to English, and specifically to the results described in Chapter 3).[3] It can be seen that by sub-dividing a segment in this way I am not completely dispensing with vertical divisions in the time domain. Hence, the framework is only partially parametric (however, in a sense, every parametric description of speech must include at least some form of vertical division as a reference point, even if it is only the time scale).

Phase 3 templates

Two basic templates are sufficient to capture the findings regarding the timing of voicing in the transition phase between stops and fricatives and following VOICED sounds. These are shown in Figure 5.1. In type (i), voicing commences after the end of the obstruent medial phase. The results of the experiment described in Chapter 3 show that long delays in voice onset are characteristic of VOICELESS stops. Short delays (of less than 40-50 ms) are characteristic of VOICED stops, VOICELESS stops when preceded by /s/ in the same syllable, and of fricatives when they are followed by a nasal consonant or other sonorant. In type (ii) voicing is present from the end of the obstruent medial phase. This is found in both VOICELESS and VOICED fricatives in SBE (with the exception of VOICELESS fricative-sonorant sequences). It is found frequently in the VOICED stops produced by one of the subjects (TC), in conjunction with medial templates (ii) and (iv), described below.

Figure 5.1: An illustration of the two templates used to represent the timing of voicing in phase 3 of obstruents in obstruent-vowel sequences.

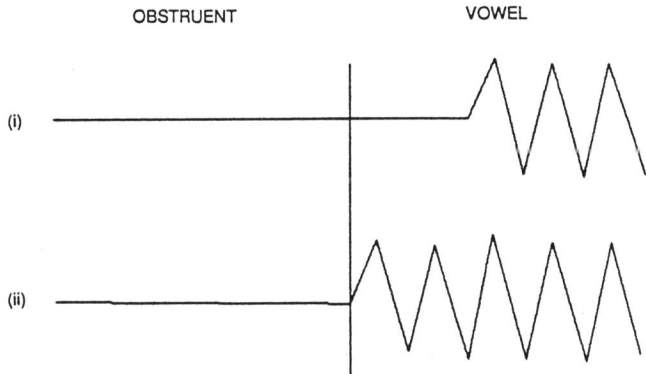

It could be argued that the first category (delayed onset of voicing) should be split into two sub-categories, in order to capture the difference between aspirated and unaspirated stops. Initially, this would certainly appear to be a problem with the position just described. However, later in this outline I show how this apparent difficulty can be avoided.[4]

Phase 1 templates

These are a mirror image of the phase 3 patterns (see Figure 5.2); the first possibility is that voicing ceases prior to the end of phase 1, as in pre-aspirated stops. The second possibility is that voicing continues all the way through phase 1. The latter is most commonly the case in SBE obstruents.

Figure 5.2: An illustration of the two templates used to represent the timing of voicing in phase 1 of obstruents in vowel-obstruent sequences.

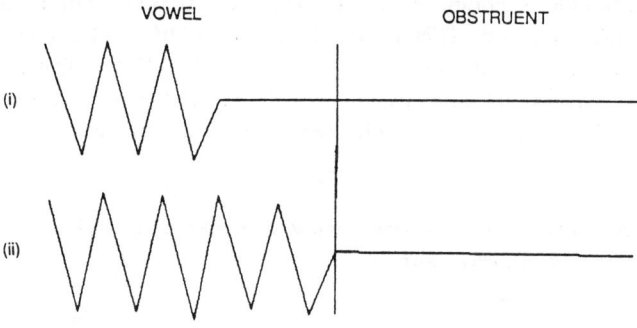

Medial templates

A set of four stylised patterns is sufficient to summarise the main types of voicing timing observed during the medial phase of obstruents occurring in the environments studied. These are shown in Figure 5.3. In type (i), voicing continues into the medial phase of an obstruent from a preceding VOICED sound. In the present study, this is found to occur in all the obstruents investigated (in post-vocalic/sonorant position), with the duration of medial voicing being influenced by the phonological voicing category of the obstruent, and its manner of articulation (on the whole it occurs more frequently and to a greater degree in stops than in fricatives). In type (ii), voicing commences prior to the end of the obstruent medial phase in anticipation of a following VOICED segment. This is compatible with type (ii) of the phase 3 templates shown above. In type (iii), there is no voicing at all during the medial phase of the obstruent. This is commonly found with word-initial stops and fricatives preceded by a voiceless environment, regardless of whether they themselves are VOICED or VOICELESS. In type (iv), voicing occurs throughout the duration of the obstruent medial phase. This only ever occurs with intervocalic VOICED stops and fricatives, although it is far from inevitable that in such sequences this pattern will occur. Depending on the environment, and on whether the obstruent is in word initial or final position, patterns (i) and (ii) are also commonly found.

Figure 5.3: An illustration of the four templates used to represent the timing of voicing in the medial phase of obstruents.

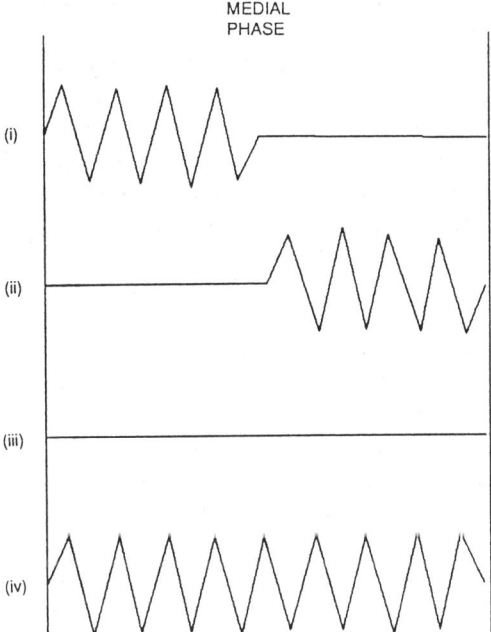

One logical possibility which has not been included in this preliminary formulation is the occurrence of an interval of voicing which starts and stops within the medial phase of an obstruent. The experimental results suggest that a template of this sort is not required for the description of the timing of voicing in the accent of English investigated, but of course, it could well be necessary for the description of other accents and languages, and would therefore have to be incorporated into the set of medial templates.

Having identified a preliminary set of potential combinations of medial and transitional voicing types, it is then possible to indicate in a table the combinations of medial and transitional voicing timing observed for the segments which are under investigation (in this case, obstruents in SBE in range of environments).

Binary Assignment

As a first step, a binary assignment could be carried out. A '+' indicates which of the medial and transitional categories gives the most appropriate description of the pattern of voicing timing observed for a given segment in a given environment. Figure 5.4 shows the tables for stops and fricatives in British English as observed in experiment 1. For segments occurring in pre-pausal position, only the medial and phase 1 templates are indicated, since none of the phase 3 categories are appropriate. Conversely, for segments occurring in post-pausal position, only the medial and phase 3 templates are indicated, since none of the phase 1 categories are appropriate. By simply using a binary assignment, this framework is reasonably successful at indicating the major similarities and differences in the timing of voicing as a function of manner of articulation and environment. It also has the potential, given appropriate templates, to give a descriptive account of differences in the timing of voicing between languages and accents, and even between speakers, e.g. /s/ before vowels and nasals in SBE, and speaker preference for pre-voicing in initial VOICED stops.

However, one obvious criticism of the framework as it stands at this point, is that the description which is produced is too abstract, mainly as a consequence of the use of a '+/-' to indicate the occurrence of a particular type of medial and transitional voicing timing pattern. The fact that the distinction between aspirated and unaspirated obstruents is lost by being absorbed into the single transitional category of delayed voice onset has already been mentioned. It is also clear that, without further elaboration, the framework provides no indication of the absolute or even of the relative amounts of delay in voice onset, or duration of prevoicing, or amount of voicing incursion observed in the production of obstruents.

Figure 5.4: Illustration of the use of a binary template assignment to describe the timing of voicing in English obstruents (A) in post pausal position with a following voiced sound (B) in the environment of a preceding and following voiced sound (C) in the environment of a preceding voiced sound.

Template

	Phase 1		Medial				Phase 3	
[p,t,k]	−	+	+	−	−	−		
[b,d,g]	−	+	+	−	−	−		
[f, θ, s, ʃ]	−	+	−	−	+	−		
[v, ð, z, ʒ]	−	+	−	−	+	−		

Template

	Phase 1		Medial				Phase 3	
[p,t,k]			−	−	+	−	−	+
[b,d,g]			−	−	+	−	−	+
[f, θ, s, ʃ]			−	−	+	−	+	−
[v, ð, z, ʒ]			−	−	+	−	+	−
[v, ð, z, ʒ] if voiced			−	+	−	−	+	−
[b,d,g] prevoiced			−	+	−	−	+	−
[s] before nasal			−	−	+	−	−	+

Template

	Phase 1		Medial				Phase 3	
[p,t,k]	−	+	+	−	−	−	−	+
[b,d,g]	−	+	+	−	−	−	−	+
[f, θ, s, ʃ]	−	+	−	−	+	−	+	−
[v, ð, z, ʒ]	−	+	+	−	−	−	+	−

Scalar Assignment

One possible remedy for this would be to replace the binary assignment with scalar values. This requires a cutting up of the three continua which are being used in the description in order to represent the appropriate amount of detail which is required for a particular task. It is conceivable that different tasks would require different divisions of the continua. A small number of divisions could be used if the aim was restricted to giving a description of the types of contrastive voicing timing patterns used by different languages (something similar to the multi-valued features proposed by Ladefoged 1971[5]). At the other extreme, an investigator interested in the very fine detail of the timing of voicing could divide up the continua into far smaller portions (such as 10 ms units) and thereby provide a detailed account of fine within- and between-language variability. An intermediate possibility might be to use a normalised scale, such as 1-10, which could indicate in the medial categories the relative percentages of the obstruent medial phase accompanied by voicing, and in the transitional categories, the relative amounts of delay in voice onset. These figures would have to be obtained by careful analysis of a representative corpus of data from speakers of the accent being described. When combined with a slight rationalisation of the proposed categories, the tables shown earlier could then be revised as shown in Figure 5.5.

5.1.2 Evaluation

Undoubtedly, the proposed framework is more complex than the conventional terminology used to describe the timing of voicing (this, of course, is largely due to the complex variability of the phenomena which it sets out to describe). A further drawback is that whilst it is capable of giving a descriptive account of the timing of voicing, it provides no insight into the co-variation of laryngeal and supralaryngeal gestures which, to judge from the experimental data described in Chapters 3 and 4, would seem to be an important factor in accounting for the observed variability. It is possible that this problem could be solved (at the cost of even greater complexity) by quantifying in some way the duration of the medial phase templates. However, whilst the descriptive tool which has been proposed is not without its problems, it is also important to underline the advantages it has over the terminology and concepts already in existence.

Firstly, it means that the description of different types of temporal coordination which is permitted is much closer to the empirical observations upon which the description is based, but at the same time using a relatively small number of parametrically-based categories.

Figure 5.5: An example of the use of scalar values to describe the timing of voicing in English obstruents.

Template	Range	Examples/Comments
Phase 1	$0 - n$	Always 0 in SBE. >0 in accents and languages with preaspiration.
Medial — VTT	$0 - n$	0 in VOICELESS fricatives. n in VOICED stops and fricatives which are fully voiced. $0<n$ in partially 'devoiced' VOICED stops and fricatives, and in VOICELESS stops following a VOICED environment.
Medial — PV	$0 - n$	0 in VOICELESS stops and fricatives. >0 in VOICED stops produced by certain speakers, and sometimes in VOICED fricatives.
Phase 3	$0 - n$	0 in VOICED and VOICELESS fricatives. >0 in stops (the value of n depends to a large extent on the factors studied in Chapter 3).

VTT = voice termination time (i.e. the amount of incursion of voicing into an obstruent medial phase). PV = prevoicing (i.e. the duration of intervals of voicing which start up during the medial phase of an obstruent).

Secondly, the fact that the transitional category 'delayed onset of voicing' is not sub-categorised ceases to be a problem, since the difference between aspirated and unaspirated obstruents is now captured by a difference in the scalar value associated with the transitional template. This allows aspiration to be treated not as an all-or-nothing process (as is conventionally the case), but more accurately, in production terms, as a gradient phenomenon, and it also allows for a specification of the different degrees of aspiration observed in the literature, and in the data gathered in this investigation. The fact that, in this framework, modal voice onset time phenomena are embedded within a more general description of laryngeal timing, reflects the position that voice onset time is only a 'special case' (Abramson 1977:297) of laryngeal timing in general.

Thirdly, the framework allows for a more detailed account of the fine-grained differences in the timing of voicing between languages, accents and speakers; i.e. between languages which use the same category, but in slightly different ways. Furthermore, by comparing the scalar values for the same segments in different contexts, at slow and fast rates and in connected speech, and under different stress conditions, it would be possible to discover which aspects of the timing of voicing are subject to greater or lesser variation as a function of these different conditions, and thereby build up a clearer picture of the nature of the variability of this aspect of phonetic realisation.

As stated above, this represents, in the first instance, an attempt to describe the timing of voicing only in the data which has arisen from this study (i.e. stops and fricatives in SBE). However, the framework which has been tentatively proposed may provide the basis for a more general descriptive account of voicing timing, allowing comparisons of the timing of voicing in different languages. This is an area for future research. In specific terms, this would involve working towards a definition of the optimum set of templates, and deciding on the best way to cut up the continua for particular tasks.

A further comment can be made concerning the relationship between descriptive phonetics and phonological theory. One of the criticisms of a linear segmental phonetic taxonomy is that it is guided too much by phonological considerations; i.e. it consists of discrete, steady-state, phoneme-sized time slices, and the symbols used to describe sounds are often determined more by phonological structure than by phonetic rigour (e.g. the use of [h] vs [ḁ], [ç] vs [i̥] -- a usage which seem to have at least as much to do with phonology as phonetics). It could be argued that a parametric taxonomy goes too far to the other extreme, and does not do much more than summarise a series of experimental observations, and that it largely obscures the relationship between surface realisations and underlying phonological units. This objection would be based on a view of phonology by which a phonemic unit is represented as a simultaneous bundle of features. At least in the case of voicing, this would seem to be an unrealistic stand to take. The phonological categories VOICED and VOICELESS are associated with a constellation of asynchronous articulatory and acoustic events (not just vibration of the vocal folds), and a fully parametric representation of speech allows observation of all of these events, and of the ways in which they interact. Furthermore, it is not necessarily the case that a parametric taxonomy serves no purpose for phonological analysis. A non-segmental representation of this sort is potentially quite compatible with non-linear tiered phonological representations such as that proposed by Browman & Goldstein (1986).

A final point here concerns the control of the voicing parameter in speech synthesis systems. In developing a system which is to approximate as closely as possible the acoustic characteristics of human speech, the timing of voicing represents a major area of allophonic variation which has to be accurately modelled. A preliminary to achieving this is formulation of our knowledge concerning variability of glottal activity in speech both in terms of the nature of the glottal gesture (pulse shape, amplitude, etc.), and of the alignment of different types of glottal gesture with acoustic events produced by other parameters, such as stop bursts, noise generation for fricatives, etc. This descriptive framework represents one possibility within which, at least this latter type of information, could be formulated, and applied in a synthesis-by-rule system (see Appendix A for an example of such an application).

5.1.3 Summary

A tool for describing the timing of intervals of voicing in relation to the supralaryngeal events associated with obstruents has been proposed. It is intentionally very limited in scope, concentrating only on the findings of the experiments reported in Chapters 3 and 4, and not referring at all to the different types of glottal gesture associated with obstruents. However, it does overcome some of the disadvantages of the traditional means of describing the timing of voicing, and it permits a somewhat clearer picture to be built up of how voicing is timed in a language, and of the differences in timing between languages, accents and speakers. Whilst it is certainly the case that the parametrically-based framework proposed above is designed purely for descriptive purposes, it is interesting to note that a parametric view of articulation has recently received considerable attention in speech production modelling (Browman and Goldstein 1986), phonology (e.g. Goldsmith 1990, Broe in press), and speech synthesis (Local in press). The means by which, in speech production, the phonetic 'plan' might govern the relative timing of events in different articulatory 'tiers' (i.e. different parameters) is discussed in the second half of this chapter.

5.2 THE TIMING OF VOICING IN A MODEL OF SPEECH PRODUCTION

In Chapter 2 I pointed out that work on speech production modelling has largely failed to provide a comprehensive account of micro-variability in phonetic realisation. This situation was underlined in the discussion of three recent models of the timing of voicing. Despite differences in detail, all three models concentrate on describing essentially a level of contrast (in their own different ways), with little if any attention being given to accounting for variability both within- and between-languages in the details of the implementation of that contrast. It was concluded that, unless they are further elaborated, such models predict that observed patterns of voicing timing should be explicable either as a function of the underlying phonological contrast, or as a function of universal phonetic processes.

One aim of the experimentation described in the Chapter 3 was to investigate the extent to which patterns of voicing timing in SBE correspond to that prediction, and to identify any phenomena which fall outside the scope of models such as those described in the earlier chapter. In summary, it was found that whilst underlying phonological category and universal phonetic processes (at the execution and motor programming stages of speech production) could account for some of the observed variability, there were other observations which fell into the gap between these two explanations -- i.e. systematic micro-variability not capable of explanation on bio-mechanical or inertial grounds.

Hence, the experimental results provide some support for the claim that there is a gap in the models of voicing timing discussed in Chapter 2. In the rest of this chapter, in the light of these findings, I consider what is required in order for this gap to be filled. The main implication of these results (and of the results of other studies of micro-variability, some of which were referred to in Chapter 2) is that the phonetic representation, which sets the goals for the speech production mechanism, is significantly more complex than suggested by models such as those reviewed above, and in particular may govern many aspects of allophonic variation, both spatial and temporal, at a fine-grained level.

Many of the comments made below are of a rather tentative nature, raising as many new questions as they attempt to answer, but as a result, I outline a number of areas in need of future investigation, which could lead to a fuller account of the timing of voicing than is currently possible.

5.2.1 Minimum requirements for an account of the timing of voicing

I begin this discussion by defining a number of minimum requirements for an explicit account of the way in which the timing of voicing is specified in the phonetic representation. These can be considered to be a set of 'benchmarks' which could be used to evaluate any attempt to model the specification of voicing in the phonetic representation.

Compatibility with properties of the vocal apparatus

In attempting to model the control of the timing of voicing, it is necessary to establish, and make some allowance for, the extent to which speakers are capable of controlling the relevant parameters. This is necessary for defining the granularity of control which has to be incorporated into the model; i.e. in order to avoid proposing a model which is too powerful, predicting speaker control of aspects of articulatory coordination which are actually beyond their capability, or a model which is not powerful enough (as is the case in the three models of voicing timing reviewed in Chapter 2).

This involves characterising what Nolan (1983:60) labels the 'dynamic and configurational constraints' of the system being modelled. The dynamic constraints consist of the 'upper limits on rate and acceleration of articulators, and on the rate of change of vocal tract configuration, including upper limits on the transmission of neural impulses.' Configurational constraints are determined by the 'physical limits on the size and shape of the vocal tract configuration.'

This task can be broken down into three sub-tasks; it is necessary firstly to establish what the relevant control parameters are (in this case, those which are manipulated in the control of the timing of voicing), secondly, to demarcate the extremes within which those parameters can be manipulated, and finally to quantify the accuracy with which control can be exerted over those parameters. Taken together these factors lead to a definition of the 'space' within which the timing of voicing can potentially be controlled and the resolution of the control exerted on interarticulator coordination within that space. Each of these sub-tasks is now considered in turn.

At the articulatory level, it could be argued that in modelling the space within which the timing of voicing is controlled, every relevant independently controllable parameter should be taken into consideration, including, for example, not only relative timing of diverse articulatory gestures, but also degree of glottal aperture, velocity of glottal abduction/adduction, duration and velocity of supralaryngeal gestures, etc. The implication of this approach would be that the control system underlying the timing of voicing is extremely complex with multiple degrees of freedom. In addition, if this assumption is made about this aspect of speech production it would presumably be applicable to other parallel features of speech production thus multiplying the complexity of the control problem.

Accounting for a human's ability to manipulate multiple degrees of freedom in motor activity has long been an area of central concern for physiologists and psychologists interested in motor control in general, but it is a topic which has only relatively recently had a significant impact on the thinking of investigators concerned with modelling speech motor control (originating in particular from Fowler's (1977) thesis). However, there is now a degree of consensus among those working in this area (including investigators who fundamentally disagree with Fowler's overall theoretical orientation) that it is unlikely that all of the potential degrees of freedom of the vocal apparatus are independently controlled (e.g. Fowler et al. 1980, Nolan 1982b, Abbs 1986, Kelso et al. 1983).

> ... there are too many points in time in an act for a like manner of control to be workable. Clearly there must be some way in which many degrees of freedom can be automatically regulated through the control of very few. (Fowler et al. 1980:385)

If this is the case, it is likely that the dimensions involved in controlling the timing of voicing are only a subset of those which are potentially independently variable.[6]

At the other extreme, it has been argued by Weismer (1980) that the only relevant glottal parameter for the control of voicing timing is whether there is a laryngeal abduction gesture or not This would allow for a direct mapping between a binary phonological feature specifying laryngeal activity, such as [+/- VOICED] and the level of articulation. As was pointed out in Chapters 1 and 3, there is considerable evidence suggesting that this is a rather simplistic account of the laryngeal contribution to control of voicing timing in speech production, and that many of the assumptions on which it is based are not in fact found to be the case in speech production.

Therefore in identifying the articulatory dimensions which are manipulated in the timing of voicing, it seems that what is required is a framework which falls between these two extremes. However, for the moment, it is difficult to conclude much more than this. Much further work is required in order to establish which laryngeal and supralaryngeal parameters are actually controlled in speech production. The ongoing debate, described in Chapter 1, concerning the nature of controllable laryngeal parameters, represents a move in that direction, but any firm conclusions in this area are still some way off.

It is also important to consider the possibility that the control space has an auditory as well as an articulatory component. It is possible, therefore, that temporal control at the level of the phonetic representation consists of specifying auditory goals rather than precise articulatory configurations and temporal relations. As a first approximation, it could be claimed that the dimensions of the auditory space relevant to the timing of voicing might consist of those parameters which can participate in the voicing contrast in languages, such as voice onset time, duration of medial voicing, closure duration, preceding vowel duration, etc. (c.f. Watson 1983). It is conceivable that these auditory parameters are correlated with a set of articulatory parameters which are manipulated at the motor programming stage in order to produce an acceptable auditory output. For example, it may not be accurate to claim that the acoustic interval corresponding to voice onset time is actively controlled -- since the results suggest that observed voice onset times are a function of co-variation of the duration of laryngeal and supralaryngeal gestures -- but that the articulatory dimensions underlying voice onset time (which may itself be best classified as an auditory dimension) are manipulated in order to produce an appropriate voice onset time.

The picture which emerges from this discussion is rather imprecise, mainly due to the uncertainties concerning the extent to which the degrees of freedom involved in the timing of voicing are independently controlled in speech production. However, it is probably appropriate to (provisionally) consider the dimensions of the space as being auditory-motor in nature; i.e. a relatively small number of auditory parameters (such as those mentioned above) together with the articulatory parameters which can be manipulated in order to achieve the auditory goals.

The second sub-task involves defining the extremes of the space, i.e. the range within which the set of controllable parameters can be manipulated. These are determined by the physical properties of the articulators; for example, the fastest/slowest rates of laryngeal abduction and adduction, or of oral constriction. One means of approximating this information would be to consider the extreme values observed in experiments as being indicative of the performance limits of particular parameters. However, this may not give a complete picture, since even the extreme observations are likely to be within the range of what is possible, given the tendency to avoid extremes in articulation; i.e. they will reflect the extremes of control in speech, rather than absolute extremes in a physical sense. For example, observations of voice onset time in VOICED stops in English might suggest that there is a gap in performance capability in the ⁻30-0 ms zone of the voice onset time continuum (see Flege (1982), and discussion in Chapter 3). However, the fact that speakers of other languages (as is reflected in some of the cross-language data presented by Lisker & Abramson 1964), and trained performers such as phoneticians, can produce voice onset times of that order suggest that the findings for English reflect a pattern of control rather than a limitation on performance potential.

Another task to be performed in quantifying the bounds of the space is to consider limits placed on the interaction between different parameters. For example, given oral occlusion at a particular point in the oral cavity, for how long is it possible to maintain phonation (i.e. the trans-glottal pressure difference required for phonation)? This of course is one area which has received a certain amount of investigation (Rothenburg 1968, Bell-Berti 1975, Westbury 1979), one of the major findings being that speakers use a range of strategies for delaying the instant at which trans-glottal pressure falls below the minimum required for phonation (these were outlined briefly in Chapter 1). Another example might be, given a stop closure of n ms, what are the range of possible voice onset times which can be produced such that the stop is voiceless throughout?

The third sub-task involves quantifying the resolution of the control which speakers can exert within the extremes identified; i.e. with what degree of accuracy are speakers capable of controlling laryngeal-supralaryngeal timing? As was briefly pointed out in Chapter 2, it is very likely that neuro-muscular 'noise' gives rise to a core of random micro-variability of temporal coordination. One way of investigating this would be to look at the amount of token-to-token variability in a large number of multiple repetitions of a syllable or word. The extent of random variability in the relevant temporal intervals (e.g. voice onset time, closure duration, overall syllable duration, etc.) could give some indication of the resolution of control exerted by speakers on those parameters. The fact that phonetic realisation is subject to random neuro-muscular perturbation suggests that speakers do not have absolutely accurate control over the temporal intervals concerned (e.g. to the nearest ms).

Another important neurophysiological consideration in determining this aspect of the 'space' is the likelihood that different intervals of time are required for innervation to reach the larynx and the oral structures. As pointed out by Roach (1980), there are conflicting accounts of the neural transmission times involved (the most extreme being the observation made by Lenneberg (1967:96) that a difference of 30 ms may be the case), but the consensus seems to be that the difference involved is somewhat smaller, of the order of less than

10 ms. However, this does suggest that the temporal structure deducible from articulatory or acoustic observations of the timing of voicing may not correspond exactly to that specified in the phonetic representation, and conversely, it is therefore not the case that temporal intervals specified at the control level will necessarily emerge unaltered at the level of realisation.

We are clearly a long way from a full account of the characteristics of the dynamic and configurational constraints pertaining to voicing, which define the limits of the control task performed by the phonetic representation, i.e. of the 'space' within which the timing of voicing can be manipulated. This situation could be improved by carrying out two types of investigation in tandem; acoustic and physiological studies of voicing in different languages and different accents (so that aspects which are common to all languages and which are hence possibly a reflection of universal constraints on the 'space', can more easily be identified), together with more sophisticated articulatory synthesis to try to reproduce the findings and thereby refine our account of them.

In determining the contribution of the speech production mechanism to microvariability of the timing of voicing, it is important to take into consideration not just the dynamic and configurational properties of the relevant control parameters, but also the contribution made by motor programming, specifically by the fact that motor programming appears to operate on a general principle of 'cost-effectiveness', avoiding extremes where possible, and using the most economical set of gestures in a given set of circumstances; i.e. producing efficient motor organisation. From the point of view of spatial configuration, an economical gesture may be defined (Lindblom 1983) as being one which produces a relatively small degree of displacement of the criterial articulator from a 'neutral' position. However, from the point of view of temporal coordination, it is not clear what the criterion for efficiency would be; i.e. what would be the 'neutral' timing pattern? Does maximal synchrony, or asynchrony of coordinated gestures make for a more economical articulation?[7] Is it more complex than this, with different considerations applying to different articulators? We can be sure that efficiency considerations do have a role in determining interarticulator coordination, but unless we discover what the criteria for efficient motor programming in the temporal domain actually are, it will be difficult to precisely ascertain the nature of that role.

To summarise this section, it is proposed that one requirement of a model of the specification of the timing of voicing in the phonetic representation is that it should be compatible with the characteristics of the speech production mechanism. However, in practical terms, our relatively poor understanding of those characteristics makes it very difficult for this requirement to be met in the short term with any degree of certainty. The remaining minimum requirements of an explicit model of the timing of voicing all concern the characteristics of the phonetic representation itself, and it is elaborating this aspect of a model of speech production which is the focus of the rest of this chapter.

Within- and between-language variability

An account of the specification of the timing of voicing within the phonetic representation must be able to account for variability of two types. Firstly, the account must provide some means of explaining within-language context-determined variability (not capable of explanation on other grounds), some examples of which were observed in the experiment reported in Chapter 3. Secondly, the fact that languages differ in a number of significant (but often very subtle) ways in their patterns of voicing timing is also a feature which has to be taken into consideration in specifying the nature of temporal control of voicing. Furthermore, a model of the control of the timing of voicing should also account for the fact that, both across-and within-languages and accents, certain aspects of voicing timing seem to be subject to tighter temporal constraints than others; e.g. compare the highly constrained patterns of timing observed in English /s/-nasal or /s/-stop sequences (as evidenced by small standard deviations) with the wide variation observed in the frequency of occurrence and duration of medial voicing in VOICED stops and fricatives.

Segment-based limitations

It is likely that a model which has a rigid segmental time base will not provide adequate temporal resolution for specifying the timing of voicing. This is not to say that the notion of a segment should not have a role in the phonetic representation, but that certain limitations emerging from a segmental approach need to be sidestepped. In this respect, there are three requirements to be made of a model. Firstly, the resolution of the time-base must be finer than that offered by the serial-ordering of segments. Secondly, unlike the situation existing in most segment-based models, it should be possible to co-vary the domains of the component gestures of a 'segment'. The experimental results point to significant asynchronies and co-variation of laryngeal and supralaryngeal articulatory gestures which can only be captured in a phonetic representation if this possibility is allowed. Thirdly, the phonetic representation should allow for the possibility of allophonic variability being a gradient process, involving some form of fine parameter tuning rather than being exclusively the result of categorial segment transposition, substitution, or deletion rules.

Broad scope

In Chapter 1, I pointed out that voice onset time has been the object of the great majority of studies of the timing of voicing. However, as was shown in the experiments in Chapters 3 and 4, this is only one aspect of the coordination of laryngeal and supralaryngeal activity, and it is important that this is taken account of in modelling the control of voicing timing. In formulating such an account, the aim should be to address wider issues of voicing timing, not just timing of voice onset in relation to stop release (and of course as mentioned above, it is in any case, conceivable that voice onset time is not actively controlled by speakers as an independent articulatory parameter).

Normalisation

Following Nolan (1982a), it seems reasonable to assume that the phonetic representation of an utterance is remote in some ways from its physical realisation. One basis of this assumption is an acknowledgement that phonetic realisation is a function not only of the goals set in the phonetic representation, but also of properties of the motor programming and execution stages of speech production. In attempting to describe the nature of the phonetic representation, it seems reasonable not to endow it with responsibility for aspects of phonetic realisation which are in fact generated by the speech production mechanism (Nolan 1983:54). This reasoning interacts strongly with the points made above concerning the need for compatibility with the dynamic and configurational constraints of the vocal apparatus.

There are three principal ways in which the phonetic representation may be remote from phonetic realisation. Firstly, systematic (and, of course, random) variability generated by the dynamic and configurational constraints of the vocal apparatus do not need to be specified in the phonetic representation. It was pointed in Chapter 2 that there is considerable uncertainty regarding the extent of the role these factors have in determining phonetic realisation. However, if we assume that there is a core of such effects, then there seems to be no reason to attribute them to the phonetic representation.

Secondly, aspects of phonetic realisation generated by organic differences between speakers (the 'invariant, absolutely uncontrollable physical foundations of a speaker's vocal apparatus' Laver 1976:57) are likewise not required to be accounted for in the phonetic representation.

Thirdly, we might argue that systematic features of phonetic realisation which are the result of speech motor programming strategies need not be specified in the phonetic representation. This area is less transparent than the two just described. On the one hand it seems reasonable to exclude from the phonetic representation consequences of motor programming that are characteristic of all speakers of all languages whenever they produce speech; for example, the use of different (combinations of) gestures to achieve the 'same' goal in different contexts; efficient organisation of motor activity in the form of coarticulation, economy, and plasticity; motor reorganisation as a result of macro-temporal or prosodic constraints, for example in order to produce the same utterance at different rates, or the same syllable in phrase-final position, or the same syllable in mono- and poly-syllabic words. However, given the existence of language-specific patterns of coarticulation (see references in Chapter 3) and rate variation (Fletcher 1988), it seems more appropriate to argue that the fact that these features of speech production inevitably occur does not have to be represented in the phonetic representation. However, aspects of the instantiation of these processes which are characteristic of a given language must, in some way, originate in the phonetic representation.

In Chapter 2, I pointed out that the phonetic representation which is commonly used in models of the timing of voicing (and in general) is too abstract to account for systematic, fine-grained patterns of phonetic variability. The points just made suggest that it is equally inappropriate to go to the other extreme, and propose a model which generates absolutely every systematic characteristic of realisation which can be instrumentally observed. What is required is a representation which embodies an appropriate level of specification, that level being one which allows a characterisation of all of the phonetic systematicities of a particular language which cannot be accounted for by appeal to properties of the speech production mechanism.

5.2.2 Incorporating the timing of voicing into the phonetic representation

Limitations of previous attempts

As was pointed out in Chapter 2, the inability of segment-based models of speech production to account for micro-variability, especially of temporal aspects of phonetic realisation, has been realised for some time. But very few attempts have been made to provide a solution. The limitations of these attempts become apparent in the light of the minimal requirements outlined above.

Klatt (1976a, 1979), Port & Rotunno (1979), and Port et al. (1980) proposed that temporal variability in speech production was the result of temporal 'implementation rules'. Klatt's rules involved specifying for each segment an 'inherent duration' and a set of rules for modifying (either by expansion or compression) that duration as a function of a wide range of contextual factors. The timing rules are described by Klatt (1979) as follows:

> the phonological component specifies inherent durations for each phonetic segment type of English and executes a set of rules that modify the inherent durations according to phonetic context and the other factors mentioned above (rate [arising from psychological & semantic variables], syntactic structure, lexical stress). The discrete phonetic string is then transformed into a temporal sequence of motor commands to the muscles controlling the articulators, resulting in a temporal sequence of articulatory motions. (1979:287)

The approach described by Port & Rotunno (1979) is similar in effect, although the two authors claim that their rules are somewhat of an elaboration of Klatt's basic position.

> Assuming that the phonology of a language yields a matrix of segmental features as output, the phonetic temporal implementation rules would convert these into descriptions of the durations of various prominent temporal intervals (such as consonant constriction durations, vowel durations, and VOT) as observed in speech production. (1979:655)

The phonetic implementation rules described by Klatt and Port & Rotunno fail to fulfil the minimum requirements outlined above on a number of counts. The authors make no reference to the fact that the power of a model of temporal implementation has to be compatible with the dynamic and configurational constraints of the parameters involved. In fact, it could be argued that both approaches are too powerful since there are no limits placed on the capabilities of the rules (except through the notion of segmental incompressibility).[8]

Secondly both proposals make use of an essentially segmental time-base, i.e. they do not allow for the fact that there may be different temporal domains associated with the different component gestures of a segment (a feature which it would be necessary to incorporate in order to model variability in the timing of voicing in obstruents, for example). Within the proposed frameworks, this would require separate inherent durations for each component feature, plus rules for differentially modifying them.

The notion of 'inherent duration' is also rather a suspect component of a model of speech production. Whilst a language may have a tendency to produce certain durational patterns, it is not clear in what sense they are 'inherent' (since it is perfectly possible for different durational patterns to be produced). The 'inherent' duration is merely a theoretical construct which provides a basis for the subsequent modification/compression rules.

A further problem is that these proposals do not address any aspect of interarticulator timing, providing instead rules manipulating independently a diversity of mainly acoustic intervals, without any recognition of the fact that they may, in fact, be best considered to be part of the same coordinatory process (e.g. voice onset time and stop closure durations would be treated as independent, separate intervals without any acknowledgement that there is a certain amount of interaction between the two, as was seen in Chapter 3). Hence, these approaches adopt an essentially mono-stratal view of the timing of voicing based on measurement of temporal intervals in the speech signal, and fail to capture the fact that, from the point of view of a speech production model, the timing of voicing may be best thought of as a multi-stratal activity, consisting of complex patterns of laryngeal and supralaryngeal coordination. Perhaps the major problem with these approaches is that having compiled rules which capture *some* of the temporal systematicities present in the speech signal, the authors then assume (as evidenced in the above quotations) that these are the **same** rules used by speakers in speech production, thereby implying that the acoustic features manipulated by the rules are the same parameters manipulated in speech production.

In summary, the implementation rules proposed by Klatt and Port & Rotunno are more suited to a synthesis-by-rule duration assignment module (which requires adequate acoustic segment durations) than an account of the phonetic representation in a speech production model (which requires specifications for the parameters governing interarticulator coordination). In the previous section I claimed that it was probably the case that the phonetic representation is remote from phonetic realisation in a number of respects, and for this reason it is unlikely that temporal intervals are specified in absolute terms. It seems then that what is required is an essentially relational (as opposed to absolute) specification[9] of temporal aspects of articulatory coordination, but one which is far less abstract than that which is proposed in the models reviewed in Chapter 2 (i.e. it has to go beyond the stage of just specifying contrast, in order to approximate the systematic non-universal characteristics of the implementation of that contrast).

Some accounts of timing rules which involve relative timing of different articulatory gestures, and which are therefore more appropriate than the proposals just reviewed, have been tentatively put forward in recent years. Port (1986) and Fourakis & Port (1986) recognised the difficulties of applying 'temporal implementation' rules such as those just described to modelling speech production, and the need to formulate rules relating to interarticulator coordination rather than arbitrary acoustic intervals. The basis of their proposal is very similar to that put forward independently by Browman & Goldstein (1986), described in Chapter 3. They consider the basis of fine temporal control as being a 'syllable cycle' with temporal relations between different articulatory gestures being expressed as phase angles within that cycle, normalised for tempo and stress. The implementation rules which they devise manipulate the phase angles, and hence interarticulator timing. Their 'phase rules' are envisaged to be language specific and learned, and controlled by phonological and contextual factors.[10]

These proposals may eventually represent a more plausible account of the phonetic representation than the 'temporal implementation rules' described in the previous section, but, as they stand, they only take us a certain distance towards an understanding of temporal aspects of a phonetic representation. The difficulties with the account formulated by Browman & Goldstein were discussed in Chapter 2. Fourakis and Port, by not specifying which gestures form part of the gestural score and by leaving open the timing intervals which are available (i.e. the possible phase angles) offer a model which is potentially more powerful, but in need further elaboration. However, as they stand, neither model is sufficiently specified in order to be fully evaluated along the lines described above.

5.2.3 Towards a 'window model' of the timing of voicing

In the remainder of this chapter I discuss one possible means in which the timing of voicing could be specified in the phonetic representation. The formulation which is presented is schematic and speculative in nature, but it does have a number of features which suggest that it might be worth following up in greater detail, with the benefit of a far broader database. It gives rise to a number of predictions which could be tested, possibly leading to a better understanding of temporal control in speech production. Of course, it also leaves many questions unanswered.

The proposal involves applying some of the ideas put forward by Keating (1990) to modelling the temporal control of interarticulator coordination. Keating proposes that spatial targets (for vowels, for example) consist of 'windows' of acceptable configurations located within articulatory 'space'. The position of the window in space, and its width are determined on a language-specific basis. The production of a sequence of spatial targets therefore involves navigating through the windows in the most 'cost-effective' way. Different trajectories are observed as a function of the juxtaposition of windows at different positions in articulatory space, and different amounts of configurational variability are observed as a function of the different widths of windows (narrow windows permit little variability, wide window permit extensive variability). Figure 5.6 (adapted from Keating 1990) shows examples of possible trajectories for a single articulator through windows with different specifications. The implications of a model of this sort are described by Keating (1990):

> In traditional models each segment is viewed as having an idealised target or variant that is uncontaminated by contextual influences ... the window model stands this view on its head. Context, not idealised isolation, is the natural state of the segments, and any single given context REDUCES NOT INTRODUCES variability in a segment. (1990:461)

How could an approach of this sort be applied to the present modelling task? In her paper, Keating is concerned almost entirely with configurational aspects of speech production. It is evident that a full account of configurational variability cannot be given without reference to the temporal constraints under which speech production must operate. The proposals made here suggest one way of characterising those temporal constraints in such a way that they are similar in form to the articulatory constraints which Keating proposes.

If we accept that it is possible to identify a 'space' within which the timing of voicing can potentially be controlled by speakers (as described in the previous section, the nature of the 'voicing timing space' is in need of empirical verification, but as a first approximation we might consider the dimensions of the space to consist of auditory parameters -- such as those which participate in the voicing contrast -- and their articulatory correlates), then it is possible that the timing specification within the phonetic representation can be thought of as defining 'windows' within that 'space' which delimit 'acceptable' equivalence classes of timing patterns for a particular language; for example, acceptable voice onset times, intervals of medial voicing, pre-aspiration, etc.

Speech production, then, consists not only of navigating through spatial and configurational windows, as suggested by Keating, but of doing so within the temporal windows also defined in the phonetic representation.

Figure 5.6: Possible trajectories for a single articulator through a sequence of three configurational windows of different widths (adapted from Keating 1990).

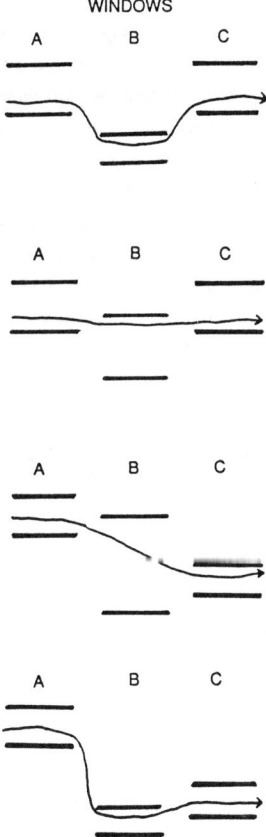

In the examples given by Keating, the temporal domain of the windows are constant. Figure 5.7 shows the effect of interaction of spatial and temporal windows. By independently adjusting window width in the two dimensions, it is possible to define precise configurational targets associated with broad temporal constraints (or vice versa), targets which are highly constrained in spatial and temporal terms, and targets which are relatively underspecified in both of the dimensions.

Figure 5.7: Illustration of the means by which temporal windows can interact with configurational windows in order to define sets of acceptable trajectories (in each case, the configurational target x must be achieved at some point within the time interval delimited by t). (i) shows a relatively narrow spatial window in conjunction with a relatively narrow temporal window (i.e. a highly constrained spatial and temporal target). (ii) shows the same narrow spatial window with a wider temporal window (i.e. a highly constrained spatial target but with the possibility of greater temporal variability). (iii) shows a wide spatial window associated with a narrow temporal interval (i.e. a spatial target which is free to vary within a wide range but which must be achieved in a fairly precise temporal slot). (iv) shows a conjunction of wide spatial and temporal windows (i.e. a target subject to considerable spatial and temporal variability).

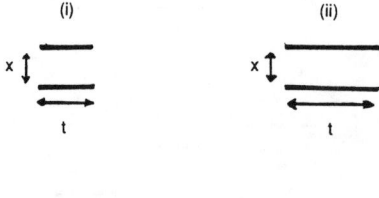

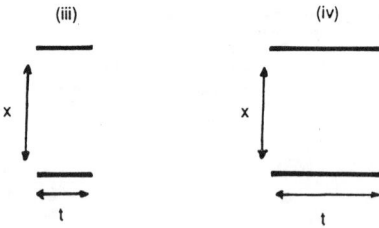

These examples illustrate the general notion of temporal windows, but it is clear that the notion of temporal targets is somewhat different from the configurational targets described by Keating. From the point of view of describing the timing of voicing, it seems useful to hypothesise that temporal windows define sets of acceptable inter-articulator temporal relationships (i.e. they specify the relative timing of laryngeal and supralaryngeal gestures).

Let us consider the characteristics of the hypothesised temporal 'windows' in a little more detail. Their positioning within the 'voicing timing space', would be determined by language-specific rules governed by phonological and contextual factors, as suggested by Fourakis & Port (1986) (thus capturing the fact that languages differ in the patterns of voicing timing which they use). For example, the windows governing voice onset time (assuming, on a strictly provisional basis, that voice onset time is in fact a relevant parameter) in utterance-initial VOICED and VOICELESS stops in Spanish and English, would be positioned differently reflecting the major differences in the timing of voicing in those two languages (in Spanish, post-pausal VOICED stops are prevoiced, and VOICELESS stops are unaspirated). However, not only would window position capture differences of this sort (on its own, this would hardly be a spectacular improvement, since the difference involved is fairly coarse-grained, and could quite likely be captured by any of the three voicing models described in Chapter 2), it would also capture fine-grained differences, such as that between voice onset time in Danish and English, requiring a slightly different window positioning to account for the slightly longer voice onset times observed in aspirated stops in Danish than in English (Hutters 1985).[11]

The 'width' of a window (i.e. the amount of variability permitted for a particular temporal interval) would likewise partly be a result of language-specific rules, reflecting not only the fact that certain parameters are more free to vary in some languages than in others, but also the fact that within a language different temporal parameters vary to different degrees.[12] It is possible that window width could partially be governed by the importance of that temporal parameter for conveying the voicing contrast within a particular language. One might expect to see larger windows (greater variability) associated with parameters which carry little perceptual weight. If this is the case, we might also predict that the area of a window would vary within a language in different contexts reflecting the shifting of importance from one set of cues to another in different contexts (e.g. initial and final stops in English).[13] In this way, the trade-off between the different cues for the voicing contrast could be thought of as consisting of co-variation of the width of windows in the 'voicing contrast space' (of which the 'voicing timing space' may be best considered to be a subset), and that the differences in the way in which languages realise the voicing contrast merely involve the use of different window parameter values within the same 'space', rather than categorially different realisation strategies.

These comments concerning window width can be exemplified from the results reported in Chapter 3. A wide range of variability is observed in VOICED obstruent medial voicing (both in terms of whether medial voicing occurs or not, and when it does occur in terms of the duration of intervals of medial voicing). According to the window model outlined here, this is a reflection of a wide window specification for the temporal parameter(s) which determine(s) the timing of voicing vis-a-vis the medial phase of VOICED obstruents (see Figure 5.8).[14] This in turn could be due to the fact that in the accent of English studied, medial voicing does not have a crucial role in conveying the voicing contrast. This is not to say that medial voicing cannot be used to distinguish VOICED and VOICELESS obstruents, just that it is not one of the principal cues normally used in English. Indeed, one test of the claims made here would be to investigate obstruent medial voicing in languages, such as French, where it plays a more significant perceptual role. The present proposals predict that the more perceptually relevant medial voicing is, the less variability it should display (as the result of being governed by a narrow window). A further test would be to examine the degree of variability shown by speakers of English in the parameters which are relevant perceptually (e.g. preceding vowel duration), the prediction being, once again, that it should be considerably less, and hence indicative of smaller temporal windows. One case where a perceptually relevant temporal interval shows (as predicted) relatively little variability in the data described in Chapter 3, is VOICED stop voice onset times (excluding prevoicing, a matter which is addressed below).

In Keating's definition of configurational windows 'the window is not a mean value with a range round that mean, or any other representation of a basic value plus variation around that value' (1990:455). No further comments are made concerning the nature of the distribution of observed cases corresponding to a particular window. The temporal windows proposed here define patterns of temporal coordination which are undifferentiated with respect to their auditory acceptability (i.e. they are auditorily equivalent for that particular language). However, given the tendency (described in Chapter 3) to avoid the extremes of the permitted range, one might expect to see certain characteristic patterns of distribution in the window to emerge, reflecting the most economical path through the range. Hence, the distribution of observed cases corresponding to a particular window might be expected to reflect the 'cost-effective' constraints applying at the motor programming stages, producing fewer cases (dips in the distribution) of the more 'extreme' components of the windows.

Figure 5.8: An illustration of a possible window specification governing the timing of medial voicing in post-vocalic VOICED obstruents in English.

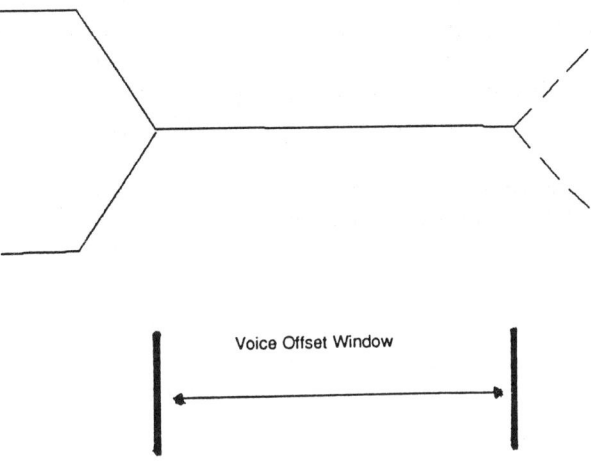

It is likely that the nature of the 'cost-effective' constraint would depend on the types of gestures being coordinated. Figure 5.9 compares the distribution of cases within the windows which could hypothetically govern medial voicing in VOICED stops and fricatives. In fricatives virtually any interval of medial voicing entails a significant 'cost', given the incompatibility of fricative noise and vocal fold vibration (described in Chapter 3). Therefore one might expect to see a large area of relatively 'costly' possibilities. In stops, medial voicing does not meet any obstacles until the trans-glottal pressure difference has fallen below a certain threshold, requiring the activation of compensatory strategies. Therefore, it is possible that the distribution curve would not begin to fall off until relatively later than in VOICED fricatives.

The shape of the rest of the window distribution is a matter for further empirical study. One possibility is that if windows are defined to govern all of the conditioned variability in temporal parameters, cases within a window should be normally distributed, with the distribution reflecting random (execution-induced) variability. If this were the case, this would provide a means of identifying the lower limit of the control which needs to be specified in the phonetic representation; (i.e. once a normal distribution is achieved, there would be nothing left to be accounted for). However, this is complicated by the fact that, as pointed out in Chapter 3, conditioned (i.e. non-random) variability is also generated at the execution and motor-programming stages of speech production, and therefore outside the realms of the phonetic representation. For example, the most 'cost-effective' temporal pattern will not always be identical in different contexts and as a result we might expect the peak(s) of the window distribution to encompass the range of 'cost-effective' temporal patterns for the different circumstances which apply.

Figure 5.9: A comparison of the possible window distributions for the timing of medial voicing in post-vocalic VOICED stops and fricatives in English.

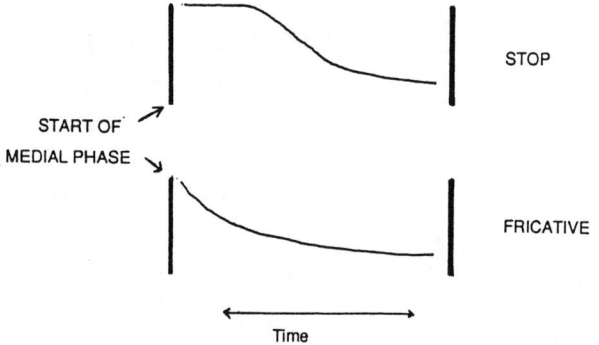

In addition, one might hypothesise that it is the position and width of a window in phonetic 'space' that are characteristic of a particular language or accent (i.e. normalised across speakers), but that the shape of the observed distribution within the window (position of peaks and skewness) is subject to between-speaker variation (Laver, personal communication); i.e. the distribution within each window would always have peaks and valleys but the precise location of these within any given window may vary across speakers. This hypothesis may give a means of rationalising the findings described in the previous chapter concerning the bi-modal distribution of voice onset time in VOICED stops in English. If we assume that this temporal parameter is governed by a wide window, as shown in Figure 5.10, speakers who never or only rarely produce negative voice onset times could be characterised as having a single (finely tuned) distribution peak, whereas speakers who produced both types of voice onset time could be characterised as having two peaks with an intermediate dip reflecting the area of the voice onset time continuum which is rarely used in English. This allows us to claim that the two groups of speakers have in common the 'rules' which determine the position and width of the temporal window, and that the difference between the groups lies in the pattern of distribution within that window.

Figure 5.10: Illustration of the temporal windows governing voice onset time in initial VOICED stops, showing that speakers may differ with regard to window distribution. Speakers who prevoice stops in this environment are characterised by a bi-modal distribution as in (a). Speakers who rarely or never prevoice VOICED stops are characterised by a uni-modal distribution, as in (b).

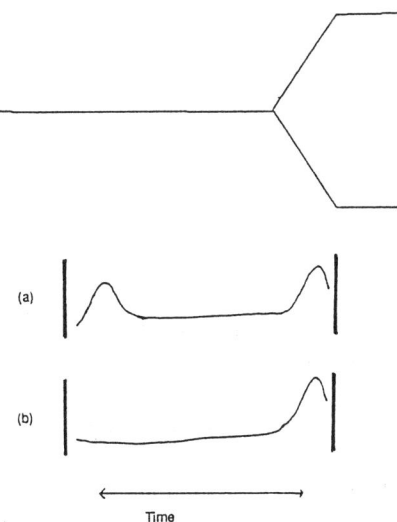

In formulating this preliminary account it is possible to envisage two ways in which fine-grained variability such as that observed in this investigation could be generated. One possibility is that there could be window specifications for each significantly different timing pattern (e.g. separate ones for /p/, /t/ and /k/ -- with a good deal of overlap between the three windows, and especially the latter two), as shown in Figure 5.11.

Figure 5.11: A representation of window targets for voice onset time in English stops.

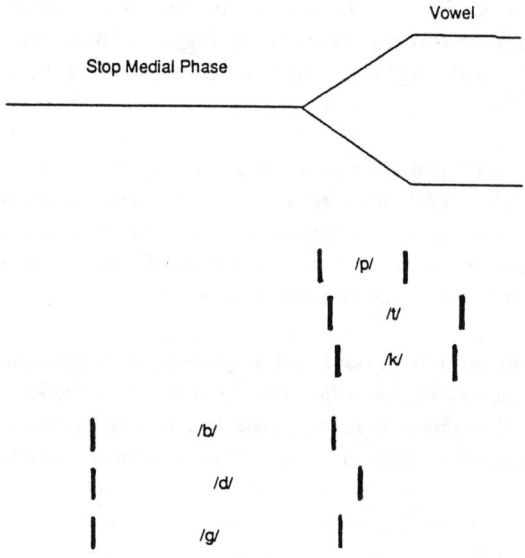

Alternatively, it could be the case that window-definition has a hierarchical structure; firstly a level of 'category-rules' which define the general pattern for VOICED and VOICELESS obstruents (without differentiating between the members of those sets), followed by 'within-category rules' which result in language-specific within-category systematic variability, such as that observed in the experiments reported in Chapters 3 and 4. Regardless of which of these two approaches is adopted, it is inevitable that quite a large number of detailed language-specific rules are required in order to define the width and location of windows.

These two alternatives point to two ways in which a window model of timing could be interfaced with a model of the voicing contrast, and thereby to a phonological representation. If it was interfaced with a model such as that proposed by Keating (1984a), described in Chapter 3, it is possible to conceive of coarse-grained window specifications corresponding to the 'phonetic categories' described by Keating, with fine-grained window specifications governing sub-category variation being introduced at a 'lower' level. This would be compatible with Keating's model of the timing of voicing (at least with relation to voice onset time which is the only aspect of the timing of voicing she deals with). On the other hand, the model of timing outlined here could also interface with a tiered, non-linear phonological representation such as that proposed by Browman & Goldstein (1986). The relatively abstract phase angles which specify inter-gestural sequencing in their phonological representation could be translated (by language specific rules) into equivalence classes of phase angles, or 'windows' within the syllable cycle.

A further feature of the windows is that they are remote from phonetic realisation in the ways suggested in 5.2.1 above. In particular the windows are assumed to be normalised for prosodic and macro-temporal factors, such as rate, final lengthening, polysyllabic shortening, and stress (i.e. factors which are characteristic of the 'prosodic modulation' of an utterance; Fujimura 1987). The difficulties associated with this assumption were outlined above, and are discussed further in Section 5.2.4.

5.2.4 Evaluation

How does this preliminary set of proposals perform against the minimum requirement conditions established earlier in this chapter?

One important feature of the proposal is that it is not limited to providing an account of voice onset time (in this respect it is different from Keating 1984a). It addresses the timing of voicing in general, and emphasises that voice onset time is just one aspect of laryngeal - supralaryngeal coordination.

Another positive aspect of the proposal is that it allows for the specification of temporal intervals in the phonetic representation without having to make reference to real-time. As has already been pointed out, this is one drawback of the temporal implementation rules proposed by Klatt (1976a) and Port & Rotunno (1979), and in addition, it would not be possible to normalise across speakers, different rates, stress conditions, if real-time temporal targets were manipulated at the level of a phonetic representation. This also allows for the fact that the real-time intervals observed instrumentally reflect the intervention of the properties of the motor programming and execution phases of speech production.

However, on the other hand, the proposals are not tantamount to an 'intrinsic' model of timing, as proposed by Action Theory and Task Dynamics (Fowler 1980, Kelso & Tuller 1987, Hawkins in press). In that approach, the phonological input to motor programming is claimed to contain no temporal specification, and temporal aspects of interarticulator coordination arise entirely from properties of motor programming;

> .. the temporal orchestration of articulatory events in the speech motor system unfolds as a consequence of its dynamic parameters ... as in a candle and a watch, time is not a possessed, programmed, or represented property of the speech production system. (Kelso & Tuller 1987:218)

Whilst the present proposals involve relational temporal control, along the lines suggested by the action theorists, the crucial difference is that this is considered to be part of the phonetic representation, and rule-governed. As was explained in Chapter 2, the reason for this is that it is only by incorporating a temporal component into the phonetic representation that an account can be given of systematic temporal micro-variability which is not universal, and not explicable in terms of properties of motor programming or execution. The present proposals are not necessarily incompatible with the notion of motor programming being based on tuning parameters in coordinative structures, but they do differ quite substantially from the strict Action Theory and Task Dynamics position concerning the nature of the phonetic representation.

A further feature of this approach is that variability is seen as something which is built-in to the phonetic representation rather than being something which originates at a more peripheral level as the result of properties of the speech production mechanism (as is the assumption in a good deal of the work on speech production modelling). This is the point made by Keating in the first quote from her paper given above. This suggests that the role of the phonetic representation is not to define precise articulatory, acoustic or auditory targets, but rather to delimit acceptable ranges within multi-dimensional phonetic 'space'. The path through the space which is taken in a given instance is a function of properties of execution and motor programming, and possibly also subject to speaker-specific variability. Furthermore, by associating acceptable limits of variability with window width, a model of this sort captures the fact that some temporal parameters vary a good deal more than others, and gives a possible means of explaining why the amount of variability observed in a parameter is not uniform across different contexts in the same language, or different languages.

In her account of configurational windows, Keating draws a parallel between her proposal that window width defines acceptable limits of variability, and a proposal by Bladon & Al-Bamerni (1976) (later amplified by Bladon 1979, and Nolan 1983), that part of the characterisation of a segment in the phonetic representation is an index of 'coarticulation resistance' which accounts for the fact, that within a language, different segments show greater propensity to accommodate to context, and that languages are found to differ in the extent of inter-segmental interactions which take place. The present proposals suggest that a parallel notion of 'temporal resistance', incorporated into the phonetic representation, may be one way of accounting for the fact that both within- and across-languages, certain temporal intervals are more variable than others (as has been observed in this study), with greater amounts of 'resistance' to variability corresponding to narrow temporal windows, and less 'resistance' to wider windows.

The framework described overcomes a number of the difficulties associated with a segmental time base. It offers greater temporal resolution, since the window specifications can govern intra-segmental temporal intervals. It allows for co-variation of the features (or articulatory gestures) which make up a segment, something which was not possible in a conventional segmental model (this is because in this model, temporal constraints are local to the parameters involved, and do not effect all aspects of the production of a segment; i.e. everything does not have to change at once, as is the case in a conventional feature matrix). Also, a model such as this gives a means of achieving allophonic variation other than by considering it to be a process of categorial segmental deletion, substitution, etc. It allows for independent modification in a continuous fashion of one or more of the temporal parameters defining the windows. For example, a partially 'devoiced' /z/ would be produced not by replacing [z] with [z̥] in the phonetic 'plan' (there would need to be an allophone for different degrees of 'devoicing' in that case), but merely by altering the window parameter affecting the timing of voicing, whilst leaving everything else the same. This, then, is rather similar to the approach advocated by Fujimura (1987:20 -- quoted in Chapter 2). However, whilst the proposals do manage to overcome some of the difficulties inherent in the use of a segmental time base, they do not necessarily mean jettisoning the segment as a useful component of a model of speech production. All they do is to allow for the specification of constraints on the temporal coordination of the different tiers or features, which make up a segment, and allow for their independent variation.

These proposals are on the whole compatible with the observations made in Chapter 2, specifically with the suggestion that the phonetic representation contains a rather more detailed specification of the timing of voicing than has hitherto been the case, and with Keating's (1990) model of configurational targets. However, a good deal of further empirical work is required in order to evaluate and considerably refine what has been proposed. The model is based on a number of assumptions which, if they proved not to be the case, could undermine it. In addition, it makes a number of predictions which could be tested experimentally. The following areas in particular would be interesting to follow up in the light of the present discussion.

In formulating the proposals, I have assumed that the phonetic representation is normalised for the effects of a range of prosodic and macro-temporal factors such as rate, stress, polysyllabic shortening etc. This greatly simplifies the phonetic representation, by suggesting that the explanation for these effects is to be found at the levels of motor programming and utterance execution. Evidence showing that 'prosodic modulation' of fine-grained temporal coordination occurs in different ways in different languages, would suggest that this aspect of the proposals would have to be reconsidered. The experiments which could be performed in order to assess this possibility would include studies of relevant acoustic or articulatory temporal parameters at different rates or under different stress conditions, in order to observe whether the variation of voicing timing parameters as the result of a particular type of 'prosodic modulation' (e.g. rate, or final lengthening) is the same across a range of accents and languages (a descriptive phonetic framework such as that described earlier in this chapter may give one means of structuring such data). Hence, as a first approximation, these proposals provisionally assume that the effects of prosodic modulation can be accounted for outside the phonetic representation. However, future work along these lines must evaluate the extent to which this assumption is tenable.

A further assumption which has been made is that there is a negative correlation between window width and the importance of a particular parameter in conveying the voicing contrast, with narrow windows being applied to temporal parameters which are perceptually more important. The main way in which this could be tested has already been mentioned above -- namely investigating the distributions of the parameters which have been shown to be of greater or lesser significance in perceptual terms in a particular language, and ascertaining if the extent of variability which they show is as predicted.

The claims made regarding the correlation of window-width and perceptual salience could also be tested by a study of the performance of non-native speakers of a language. Port & Mitleb (1980) have shown that native temporal implementation strategies persist even in advanced learners of a second language. The window model of timing outlined here predicts not just that inappropriate temporal intervals will be used by non-native speakers (as was found by Port & Mitleb 1980), but also that there will be greater or less variability in temporal control reflecting those features which are perceptually significant in the native language. To give a specific example, one might compare the frequency of occurrence of medial voicing in the English spoken by native speakers of a language in which medial voicing plays a perceptually more important role (e.g. French). The prediction is that the non-native English speakers would show far less variability (i.e narrower distributions) than native speakers. If found to be the case, this would argue against any model which postulated precise temporal targets together with variability being induced at the periphery, outside the domain of the phonetic representation. However, this would support a model such as that proposed here which specifies in the phonetic representation (on a language-specific basis) 'acceptable' ranges of variability.

One further aspect of the proposal which is subject to empirical verification concerns the nature of the distribution of the observations within the temporal windows. Two separate aspects of this are in need of clarification. Firstly I have claimed there should be dips in the distribution corresponding to the least 'cost-effective' members of the set of acceptable temporal patterns within a given window. It is necessary to establish whether such dips exist, and if they in fact do, whether they can be attributed to general properties of motor programming and execution. Secondly, the shape and location of the peak(s) of the distribution curve is a further feature which can only be established as a result of the analysis of a large corpus of data. In particular, it would be of interest to investigate the possibility that detailed characteristics of the distribution within a window could reflect differences between speakers, as suggested above.

5.2.5 Summary

In the second half of this chapter I have focused on two aspects of the timing of voicing in a model of speech production. Firstly I have outlined a set of benchmarks for the evaluation of any attempt to model the specification of the timing of voicing in the phonetic representation. Models which fail to meet the requirements described are likely to give an inadequate account of the timing of voicing. Secondly, I have provided a tentative and rather speculative formulation of one way in which many of these requirements might be met, and I have pointed to a number of ways in which this could be investigated further.

This limited set of proposals is in response to data on the timing of voicing which suggest that the phonetic representation which drives the speech production mechanism governs more detailed aspects of the relevant parameters than is acknowledged in previous attempts to account for this aspect of phonetic realisation. In a number of senses, this study has only breached the surface of an issue which has potentially far-reaching implications for speech production modelling, and phonetic theory in general. Firstly, I have only dealt with limited aspects of the timing of voicing. Future work has to continue to approximate an account of what the relevant control parameters are with respect to the timing of voicing, and to provide detailed descriptive accounts of the systematic characteristics of the timing of voicing observed in different accents and languages. Secondly, as was pointed out in Chapter 2, there is an increasing body of data suggesting that many other fine-grained aspects of speech production may be best accounted for by being incorporated in some way into the phonetic representation; i.e. the timing of voicing is just one aspect of interarticulator coordination, and detailed quantitative investigation is required to show the extent to which other aspects are part of the learned phonetic characteristics of a language or accent. Thirdly, one important area of further research which has not been touched on at all in this book is the need to determine the role of systematic micro-variability of the sort investigated in this project. If it is not crucial for lexical identity (something which remains to be shown), does it have some other function, possibly acting as an accent or social marker? This opens up a wide area of research, quantifying the systematic phonetic differences between accents (on a geographical and social basis for example), and investigating listeners' responses to accents with subtly different phonetic characteristics (e.g. their ability to detect a non-native accent, or social class on the basis of fine-grained phonetic differences).[15]

Investigations such as these may mean that our conceptualisation of the nature of the phonetic representation is likely to have to be modified in a number of ways. Amassing the relevant data, and evaluating their implications set a challenging agenda for future research.

NOTES

1. Given the breadth of interests encompassed by the discipline of phonetics, it is unlikely that a single descriptive framework and transcription system will cover every requirement.

2. In order to avoid confusion in the use of the terms 'onset' and 'offset' (arising from the fact that these terms can be used to refer both to voicing, and the supralaryngeal gestures in obstruents), henceforth I restrict the use of those terms to voicing alone, and I adopt the convention (suggested by Abercrombie 1967:140) of referring to the onset phase of an obstruent as phase 1, and the offset phase as phase 3. The term 'medial phase' can still be used, since there is no possible confusion. It is equivalent to Abercrombie's phase 2.

3. Westbury (1979) used a similar means of subdividing sequences of stops in order to describe his data, but he did not explore the possibilities this offers from the point of view of the description of the timing of voicing in general.

4. One problem with attempting to sub-divide phase 3/template (i) would be where to draw the line between aspirated and unaspirated obstruents. A figure could be used to reflect the findings of psychophysical experiments (e.g. Stevens & Klatt 1974, Pisoni 1977) that listeners show a discrimination peak in VOT-like continua at around +20 ms. But there would be at least two problems with this -- (a) it has been shown that the location of peak discrimination depends on the language being investigated (Flege & Eefting 1986); (b) within a single language, speakers do show overlap in the voice onset times which they produce corresponding to the two modal patterns of voice onset time (i.e. aspirated/unaspirated). In the present study, many of the VOICED stops, normally labelled as unaspirated in the literature, had voice onset times of well above 20 ms. Since the aim of the typology presented here is to give an account of phonetic realisation and not of perceptual categories as evidenced by listener response to synthetic stimuli, it is proposed initially to continue on the basis of a single delayed voice onset category. In a later section, an alternative method of indicating the difference between relatively long and short delays is described.

5. There is a difference between the scalar values incorporated into the descriptive framework proposed here and those used by Ladefoged in his work on multi-valued features in the late 60's and early 70's (Ladefoged 1971). Firstly, Ladefoged's aims were quite different to mine. He was interested in giving an account of the 'contrasts available at the systematic phonetic level'(1971:1). My aim is not to provide a tool which merely characterises potential CONTRASTS, but one capable of providing an accurate and comprehensive account of one aspect of phonetic REALISATION. Ladefoged's approach leads him to place insufficient emphasis on the temporal aspects of voicing control, with the labels 'voiced', 'voiceless' and 'aspirated' being classed as linguistically significant STATES (1971:9). Voice onset time is dealt with separately, but once again with possible contrasts uppermost in mind -- i.e. it would be possible for two languages/accents to be assigned the same scalar voice onset time feature within Ladefoged's framework, and yet for these two languages to use significantly different portions of the voice onset time continuum.

6. There is currently a lively debate in progress concerning the nature of the motor control strategy whereby a small number of parameters are actively controlled, leaving the others to be autonomously regulated (Kelso et al. 1986, Lindblom & MacNeilage 1986, Hawkins in press).

Progress in this area is dependent on the provision of a good deal of additional data in order for the various theoretical positions (e.g. coordinative structures; see Chapter 3) to be tested and refined. Little reference will be made to this debate in the remainder of this chapter, since the emphasis of this discussion is on the nature of the phonetic representation which drives the speech motor control mechanism (as opposed to strategies of motor control).

7. Kent & Minifie (1977:132) claim that motor organisation attempts to 'maximise the number of simultaneous movements within an articulatory sequence.'

8. Klatt proposed that each segment was defined with a 'minimum duration' beyond which it could not be shortened. This is described (Klatt 1976a:1215) as 'the absolute minimum duration ... that is required to execute a satisfactory articulatory gesture'.

9. This is similar to some of the suggestions made by investigators working within the Action Theory framework (Kelso & Tuller 1987), but, as is explained in 5.2.4 below, there are fundamental differences between the approach adopted here, and that taken by Action Theory.

10. Nolan (1983:56, 119), in a similar vein, proposes that the phonetic representation can be thought of as consisting of tiered auditory phonetic dimensions. Phonetic goals are defined in terms of three components; 'v' the 'value' in a given dimension, 'r' resistance of the value to coarticulatory perturbation, 't' the temporal domain associated with 'v'. However, Nolan is not specific about the means by which the tiers of the representation are assigned their 't' specifications. Earlier in his account (1983:51), he adopts a position similar to Klatt (1976a) and Port & Rotunno (1979): 'a phoneme may be thought of as having firstly an intrinsic duration associated with it which is then adjusted by the realisation rules according to segmental environment.' However, it should be underlined that Nolan's outline is (deliberately) schematic, and the temporal domain is not the chief focus of his discussion.

11. It is not inconceivable, too, that some form of maximal auditory dispersion tendency (such as 'polarisation' described by Keating (1984a) and reviewed in Chapter 2) could also have a role in determining window position, although theories of auditory dispersion have only met with limited experimental verification (Disner 1983).

12. One aspect of the data in Chapter 3 which might reflect a difference of this sort is the small level of variability observed in voice onset delay in /s/-nasal sequences, compared to voice onset time in stop-vowel sequences.

13. This idea is similar to Kohler's (1984) proposal that the components of the [+/-fortis] coordinative structure which he proposes would receive different weightings depending on their position and context.

14. This is another way of saying that these stops have a potential for being voiced (c.f. Catford 1977:112), but that the potential need not be realised.

15. For an example of a project which takes an approach of this sort in a study of phonetic variability, see Kerswill (1985).

Conclusion

In the introduction to this study, I pointed out that it sought to contribute in three ways to the objectives of phonetic theory. In these concluding remarks, I summarise what has been achieved in each of those areas.

The results of the experiments described in Chapters 3 and 4 represent one of the few instrumental studies of the timing of voicing in obstruents in an accent of British English. It is the only study, with the exception of Hanninen (1979), in which stops and fricatives have been investigated together, and it is one of the few studies in which a range of contextual and structural variables have been examined for their effect on the timing of voicing, and which attempts to provide a detailed explanation of the patterns of systematic variability which are observed to occur. This database goes some way towards filling the gaps in our knowledge concerning the systematic characteristics of the phonetic realisation of Southern British English.

However, this work has also had the result of revealing significant gaps in our knowledge of the factors governing the timing of voicing in obstruents. A number of areas are in particular need of future investigation. It is necessary to establish the extent to which the effects found in the highly controlled utterances studied here are also found in natural conversational speech. This would allow for the necessary corroboration (or otherwise) not only of the findings of this study, but also of the basis on which inferences were made (in Chapter 5) concerning control of the timing of voicing in speech production. It would also lead to an account of how the timing parameters investigated in this study interact with coarse-grained macro-temporal constraints, which are more apparent in natural speech than in the controlled 'laboratory' utterances analysed here. In addition, considerable physiological investigation is required to further investigate some of the assumptions made in Chapter 3, on the basis of acoustic data, about physiological aspects of voicing. In summary, the experimental sections of this work have served to partially fill the gap in our knowledge, but equally to highlight areas in need of further investigation.

The experimental results have also served to illustrate the relatively weak descriptive power of the framework which is conventionally used to describe voicing related phenomena in obstruents. There seem to be three basic problems. The temporal resolution of the conventional framework is inadequate for capturing fine-grained systematic characteristics of the timing of voicing. The phonetic categories used in relation to the timing of voicing are capable of giving no more than a very approximate idea of patterns of voicing timing. The segmental underpinning of the conventional framework is incompatible with any attempt to specify differential temporal domains for laryngeal and supralaryngeal activity.

I have proposed one means by which some of these problems may be overcome, and by which a more detailed description of the timing of voicing can be obtained. Whilst the proposed framework is more complex than that which is conventionally used, this is a reflection of the complexity of the phenomena being described (much of which is lost in the conventional framework). The practical utility of the proposed framework remains to be tested with data from different accents of English and different languages, as does the adequacy of the descriptive categories which it offers. However, there is no doubt that it does allow for a more detailed description of the timing of voicing than is possible with conventional labelling. The fact that it can be of some use other than as a purely theoretical exercise is shown by the way in which it could interface directly with the rule base for producing naturalistic patterns of voicing timing in a speech synthesis-by-rule system described in Appendix A.

A study of the implications of the data for speech production modelling has been a major strand of this volume. The experimental findings support the assertion that there is a gap in speech production theory which results in certain types of systematic fine-grained variability not receiving an adequate explanation. Much of the systematic variability observed in the experimental data does not appear to be the product either of properties of the execution or motor programming stages of speech production, or of the phonological voicing category of the obstruent concerned. The results suggest that certain aspects of the micro-timing of voicing must originate in the phonetic representation.

On the basis of these findings, I have made a preliminary attempt to define a set of minimum requirements which must be fulfilled by any account of how fine-grained variability of the timing of voicing could be incorporated into the phonetic representation. I have put forward a tentative set of proposals which fulfil many of these requirements, but which, of course, require further evaluation and refinement. One important point emerging from this strand of the study is that a major obstacle to progress in this area is the relatively scarce empirical data which is available. In particular, we are still a long way from being able to characterise the parameters of the 'control space' for the timing of voicing, and for the voicing contrast in general. A fully specified model is still a rather distant goal.

CONCLUSION

The unifying theme of this study was to show the inadequacies of the way in which the timing of voicing is handled in phonetic theory, and to work towards possible solutions. Each area investigated was found to offer an inadequate treatment of the fine-grained systematic properties of the timing of voicing which are characteristic of a language. There appear to be two fundamental problems. The widespread adherence to a segmental approach automatically makes it difficult to handle sub-segmental variability. Inadequate categorisation of voicing related phenomena, such as the use of binary categories for phenomena which appear to be more continuous in nature, masks their complexity, and, at best, permits no more than a simplistic reflection of the systematic variability observed in speech.

In each of the areas discussed, the solution which I have proposed suggests that a better account of the timing of voicing can be achieved by representing the fact that the temporal domains of intervals of voicing and voicelessness are not necessarily the same as those corresponding to the supralaryngeal correlates of obstruents. This leads to accounts which are more in keeping with experimental observations, but which break from the segmental mould which has dominated past work in all of the areas studied. A good deal more experimental work is required to investigate in greater detail the temporal domains of a range of phonetic parameters in order to more fully evaluate the power of such an approach, and to develop a sufficient empirical foundation for devising and refining theoretical frameworks (in phonetic theory, speech production modelling, and phonology) which reflect this characteristic of phonetic realisation.

APPENDIX A
Modelling the Timing of Voicing in Synthesis-by-rule

A.1 INTRODUCTION

In this appendix I describe an exploratory attempt to design a set of rules for reproducing naturalistic patterns of timing of voicing in a speech synthesis-by-rule system. Given the existence of systematic fine-grained variability in the timing of voicing (as demonstrated in this study), speech synthesis allows at least two further related questions to be addressed; (a) does the inclusion of fine-grained allophonic variability into a synthesis-by-rule system lead to more intelligible and natural synthetic speech? (b) to what extent are listeners capable of hearing fine-grained differences of the timing of voicing in synthetic (and, of course, in natural) speech -- i.e. is it the case that speakers produce systematic fine-grained variability of timing in their vocal performance which are below the threshold of sensitivity of a listener? A preliminary to both these lines of investigation is the design of a set of rules which can generate fine-grained variability of the sort described earlier in this book. In this appendix, I outline one possible means of achieving this. A preliminary evaluation of the synthesis rule-base illustrates some of the difficulties involved in addressing the two research questions outlined above.

There are two aspects to be considered in attempting to control the voicing parameter in synthesis-by-rule; (i) the shape and amplitude of the glottal waveform; (ii) the timing of the onset and offset of intervals of voicing. Dynamic control of glottal pulse shape is not discussed further here, given that the emphasis in this study is on the control of the timing of the onset and offset of intervals of voicing in relation to the synthesis parameters corresponding to the medial phase of obstruents (c.f. Rosenburg 1971, Holmes 1973, Allen et al. 1987 for further discussion of glottal shaping in speech synthesis).

The section of the phonetic rule base within a synthesis-by-rule system dealing with voicing is not an area that is given much coverage in the literature, with the result that it is difficult to evaluate what methods are used, if any, to model variability of the timing of voicing. It is certainly the case that early synthesis-by-rule systems (Holmes et al. 1964, Rabiner 1968) merely specified sounds as being voiced or voiceless, and an appropriate source was used by the synthesiser throughout the duration of each segment (this of course is why Holmes et al. had to resort to using extra 'sub-elements' for modelling phenomena such as aspiration in stops). There is some evidence that rules were used to substitute voiced with voiceless segments and vice versa in appropriate contexts (e.g. Rabiner 1969, Klatt 1976b), but on the whole, very little discussion is given in the literature regarding this type of allophonic variation.

The fullest account of the allophonic rules embedded within a synthesis-by-rule system is provided by Allen et al. (1987), in an account of the MITalk text-to-speech system. A small number of these rules do provide some allophonic variation of the timing of voicing. One set of rules varies the duration of intervals of aspiration as a function of a limited number of contexts, including whether a following vowel is stressed or not, and whether a sonorant intervenes between a stop and a following vowel (1987:190). A second section of the rule base 'devoices'[1] voiced stops and fricatives, for example, when they are not followed by a vowel (1987:195). These rules go some way towards providing naturalistic patterns of voicing timing. However, when they are considered in the light of the data described in this study and in the literature in general, it is evident that they only cover a small subset of the contextual effects on the timing of voicing.

In summary, control of the timing of voicing in obstruents is not an area which is considered in any detail in the majority of the accounts of speech synthesis-by-rule systems. What little information is available suggests that even the most comprehensive systems currently in existence still fall some way short of modelling anything like the full range of contextual variability observed in this study, and in the literature.

A.2 MODELLING THE TIMING OF VOICING IN SYNTHESIS-BY-RULE: A TEMPLATE APPROACH

The basis of the rule base to be described is the acoustic analysis of the timing of voicing in English described in Chapter 3. There are three aspects of the results which are particularly relevant from the point of view speech synthesis: intervals of voicing and voicelessness are not synchronously aligned with the supralaryngeal correlates of obstruents, VOICED obstruents are commonly realised as partially or completely 'devoiced'; the timing of voicing is subject to fine-grained systematic variability as the result of a number of contextual and structural factors. In modelling these features, the aim must be to assign appropriate temporal domains to the synthesiser parameters corresponding to the laryngeal and supralaryngeal levels. This line is pursued in the set of rules for the timing of voicing in speech synthesis-by-rule described below. This approach permits the modelling of a wide range of allophonic variants using a relatively small set of rules, with the added attraction of breaking to a certain extent with the segmental constraints normally encountered in synthesis-by-rule systems. There are strong parallels between the approach outlined here for producing natural voicing timing in synthesis-by-rule and the descriptive framework for voicing timing outlined in Chapter 5. Indeed the following rule base represents one possible application for a descriptive tool such as that proposed.

The rule set is presented in detail below, and is summarised in Figure A.1. The effectiveness of the procedures described below remains to be tested by being fully implemented within a synthesis-by-rule system. This is an area of future work. Hence, the following description has the status of a 'blueprint' for a computer program which could be embedded within a synthesis-by-rule system. There are three main stages to the voicing timing assignment; parameter generation; template assignment; template tuning.

Parameter generation

The input to a synthesis-by-rule system is a string of allophones with their associated acoustic targets. The actual acoustic parameters which are specified depends on the synthesiser which is being used, but at the very least there will be some formant parameters and some excitation parameters. The parameter which is the object of the following rule base is, for the present purposes, labelled 'V'<oicing>. In the LSI parallel formant synthesiser (Quarmby & Holmes 1984), for which these rules were initially conceived, the 'V' specification can be in the range '1' (fully voiceless) to '63' (fully voiced). Normally, VOICED and VOICELESS obstruents have different 'V' targets, resulting in either fully voiceless or voiced realisations. However, in the rule base proposed here, the 'V' target for all obstruents, regardless of their phonological category, is set to '1'.

Parameter generation involves the conversion of a string of discrete allophone acoustic targets into a stream of synthesiser parameter values specified at 10 ms intervals (or thereabouts -- depending on the frame rate of the synthesiser being used). This is achieved by the use of a transition algorithm such as that described by Holmes et al. (1964) or Allen et al. (1987). The stream of synthesis parameter values is used as the input to the voicing timing rule base.

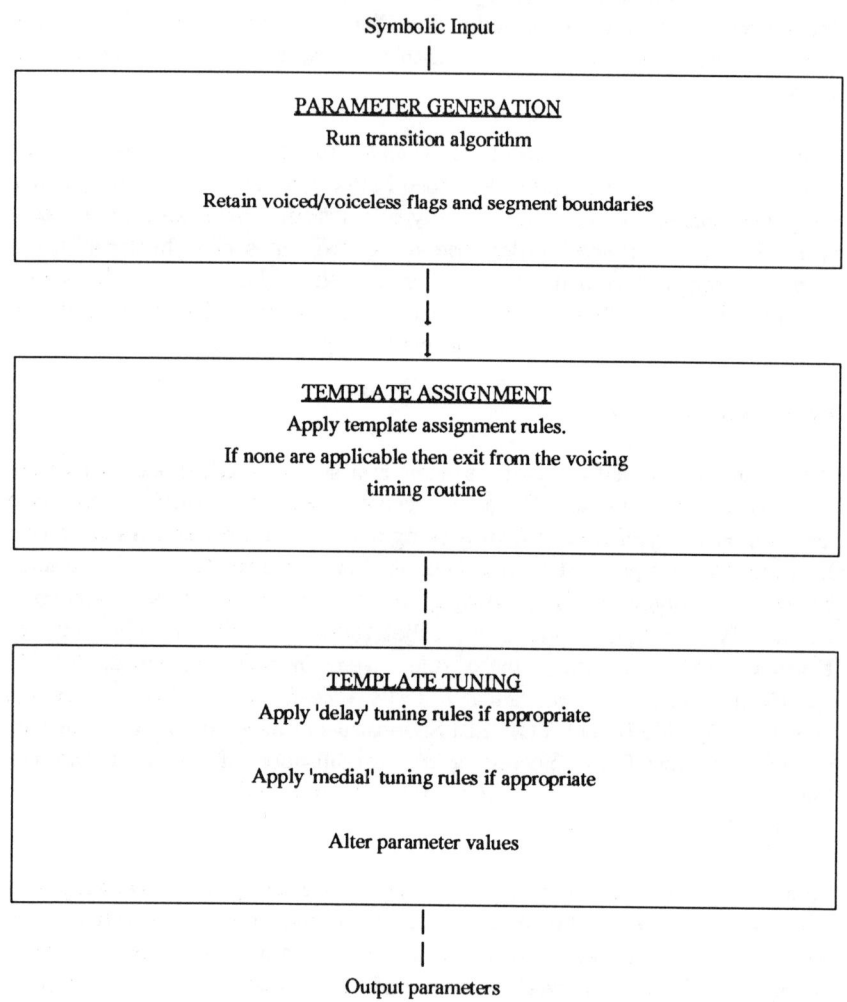

Figure A.1: A flow chart showing the principal stages of the proposed routine for for generating naturalistic patterns of voicing timing in a synthesis-by-rule system.

Since the 'V' target for obstruents is uniformly '1', after parameter generation has taken place the value of the 'V' parameter for all obstruents remains unchanged at '1'. Figure A.2 shows an example of a VCV string as it is input to the next stage of the voicing timing rule base. Note that obstruents are still flagged as belonging to different underlying voicing categories, and that the margins of segments are still marked (or at least are accessible) at this stage. This information is required at the next stages of the rule base.

Figure A.2: A schematic representation of the stream of values for the 'V' synthesiser parameter which is input to the template assignment and tuning stages of the voicing timing rule base.

```
Parameter         Vowel         VOICED C         Vowel
                              |              |
    F1                        |              |
                              |              |
    F2                        |              |
                              |              |
    F3                        |              |
                              |              |
    'V'    63 63 63 63 63  |  1  1  1  1  1  |  63 63 63 63 63
                              |              |
    etc.                      |              |
                              |              |
    etc.                      |              |
```

Template assignment

The context of the obstruent is then examined. If neither the preceding nor the following segment is voiced, the voicing timing rules rules described below are not applicable, and the default procedure is used -- that is, the parameters are then output unchanged.

If the voicing rules are applicable for a segment (i.e. if it has an adjacent voiced context), one voicing template is then chosen from a set (for SBE, a set of no more than four templates are required). The templates specify the *gross* patterns of the timing of the voicing parameter relative to supralaryngeal features in SBE stops and fricatives. Each template consists of two parts; one describing the characteristics of the obstruent medial phase, and the other characterising the offset phase, as follows;

(1) medial voicing -- no delay
(2) medial voicing -- delay
(3) no medial voicing -- no delay
(4) no medial voicing -- delay

Table A.1 shows the default template choice for stops and fricatives occurring in a number of environments in SBE. Note that in the case of VOICED fricatives adjacent to a pause or voiceless environment (where in natural speech the occurrence of medial voicing is subject to a good deal of variation), the template choice specifies a completely 'devoiced' realisation. This allows the template choice for VOICED and VOICELESS fricatives to be collapsed, as is the case with stops (it does not, of course, mean that cognate fricatives will sound exactly the same, since their fricative noise levels will be different). These are labelled 'default' choices since there are certain instances in which they would be overriden. An example of this is the case of /s/ occurring before sonorants which requires a 'no medial voicing -- delay' template, and initial VOICED stops to be produced with prevoicing which require a 'medial-voicing -- no delay' template.

Table A.1: The default template choice for stops and fricatives in post-pausal, pre-pausal and intervocalic position.

		Stops			Fricatives		
		#__V	V__V	V__#	#__V	V__V	V__#
	(1)			*		*	
Template	(2)		*				
	(3)				*		*
	(4)	*					

Template tuning

This stage is responsible for computing the appropriate amount of voice onset delay and medial voicing. The templates are refined on the basis of information contained within a small database, which lists default voice onset times and medial voicing values for the obstruents of English, and which also contains a set of rules for modifying these default values as a function of context. Table A.2 illustrates the contents of the database, showing the default values (obtained from the experimental results reported in Chapter 3), and a subset of the rules which could apply.

The default voice onset time for the element is read in, and is then altered as a function of the voice onset time rules. When the final value has been obtained, the values of the voicing parameter at the start of the following segment are altered as appropriate -- i.e they are changed to '1' during the appropriate interval.

If the template selected contains a 'medial voicing' specification, the routine then enters the medial tuning stage. The default medial voicing value is obtained from the look-up table. It is then modified by the context-sensitive rules if these are applicable. Once the final value has been achieved, the values of the voicing parameter during the medial phase of the obstruent are changed appropriately (after conversion of the percentage value into an absolute value); e.g. a segment which is assigned a 10% medial voicing specification will be voiced during the first 10% of its duration. Table A.3 gives a number of examples of how these rules would operate on English obstruents.

Table A.2: Examples of the rules used to tune the templates for English stops and fricatives.
===

Voice onset time section (only activated if the 'delay' template is chosen)

default values (ms): /p/ 42   /t/ 63   /k/ 63

rules:
[1] if in $s_V/sonorant context, use default and rules for VOICED cognate
[2] if in s$_V/sonorant -10%
[3] if in _r/l/w/j +20%
[4] if in isolated word +10%
[5] if following vowel is unstressed -20%

default values (ms): /b/ 19   /d/ 26   /g/ 31

rules:
[1] if following syllable is unstressed -20%
[2] if sequence is /dr/ +75%
[3] if in _r/l/w/j +20%

Medial voicing section (only activated if 'medial voicing' template is chosen)

default values (expressed as a percentage of the medial phase which is to be voiced):
/p/ 14   /b/ 52   /t/ 18   /d/ 59   /k/ 18   /g/ 66   /v/ 78   /ð/ 100   /z/ 84

rules:
if in syllable-final position   -10% (VOICELESS stops) or -20% (VOICED stops) or -50% (VOICED fricatives).
===

The result of the procedures just described is that the temporal domains of voicing and voicelessness are altered independently of the other synthesis parameters, thus capturing some of the asynchronies between voicing and supralaryngeal parameters. However, this is achieved without having to abandon essentially segment-based approach to synthesis-by-rule, which is still dominant in that brand of speech synthesis. This means that this set of rules could be implemented within any of the major segment-based systems that have been developed, and furthermore, it shows that non-linear segmental variability can be produced within an essentially segmental framework.

Table A.3: Examples of the application of the English voicing timing rules.

/b/ in word-initial position
    -underlyingly VOICED
    -template choice --> no medial voicing:delay. Voice onset time rules only activated and appropriate voice onset time is generated.

/z/ adjacent to a voiceless sound
    - underlyingly VOICED
    - template choice --> no medial voicing:no delay. No change to input specification required.

intervocalic /p/
    - underlyingly VOICELESS
    - template choice --> medial voicing:delay. Voice onset time activated and appropriate VOT generated. Medial voicing section activated and appropriate % medial voicing generated.

/p/ in a /$s_V/ environment
    - underlyingly VOICELESS
    - template choice --> no medial voicing:delay. Voice onset time routine activated and appropriate voice onset time generated by application of context rule [1].

/g/ in a /_#s/ environment
    - underlyingly VOICED
    - template choice --> no medial voicing:no delay. No changes to input specification required.

It should be emphasised that this set of rules is only responsible for assigning more natural **temporal coordination** of intervals of voicing with the acoustic parameters related to supralaryngeal aspects of obstruents. It is assumed that at some other level of the system, there is a set of rules for varying the shape of the glottal pulse and its intensity as a function of the type of sound being produced.[2]

A.3 EXPLORATORY EVALUATION

In this section I describe an exploratory attempt to carry out a limited form of assessment of the effects of implementing the rules described above generating fine-grained variation in voicing timing. This is based on a comparison of listeners' responses to tokens of words which have been generated by a speech synthesiser, in which some of the above rules have been applied (referred to henceforth as 'template' tokens), and other tokens (referred to as 'non-variant' tokens), which have been generated by the same system but with patterns of voicing timing which reflect the state of affairs of most current speech synthesis-by-rule systems.

The limited nature of this exercise is quite transparent. Altering the timing of voicing whilst leaving all the other parameters unchanged is a somewhat crude means of evaluation, given that, in a more complete system, there would have to be some modelling of the co-variation of voicing intensity and other parameters such as burst intensity, and level of frication. The experiments described in this section were performed not to prove that the voicing timing rules lead to more natural speech output, but in order to gauge whether listeners are sensitive to the effects of generating speech with and without fine variation of voicing timing such as that generated by the above rules.

The listening tests were designed to look at two very specific questions. In the first test I set out to see if listeners could suspend their categorial mode of perception and consistently detect the fine-grained differences between synthetic tokens of the same word which had been produced with and without the voicing timing rules described above (to the trained ears of a phonetician, the differences are audible, the aim of this test was to see if this was the case with untrained listeners). In the second task, I attempted to look at the link between intelligibility and naturalness, and specifically at whether subjects' performance on a standard intelligibility test was affected by the different patterns of voicing timing present in the two sets of tokens which were compared. If micro-variability such as that generated by the above rules does not affect the intelligibility of speech (as indexed by subjects' ability to discriminate between VOICED and VOICELESS cognates), due to the fact that it is non-distinctive from the point of view of the phonological system of a language or accent, intelligibility scores for synthetic tokens should not be significantly different (better or worse) if such rules are implemented within a system.

A.3.1 Stimulus preparation

All of the synthetic tokens used in the listening tests were generated using an LSI parallel formant synthesiser (Quarmby & Holmes 1984) in conjunction with the SYNCON synthesis-by-rule software written by John Holmes (version 4.2).

In this system, control of the timing and amplitude of voicing is achieved by manipulation of a single synthesiser parameter identified as 'V'. For any frame of the synthesis, this parameter may be assigned a value between 1 and 63. An assignment of '1' switches off the glottal excitation. Assignments of 2-63 produce glottal excitation of increasing intensity

There are two ways in which the voicing assignment may be changed for a given segment; target alteration and parameter tuning. In the first case, the 'V' target corresponding to a particular element can be altered, thereby changing the overall voicing characteristics throughout the production of that segment. In the second, alterations to the 'V' parameter can be made on a frame-by-frame basis permitting very fine tuning of the timing and intensity of voicing. Both of these methods were used in preparing the stimuli for these tests.

Since SYNCON requires stops to be constructed from 'sub-elements' corresponding to closure, release, and (optionally) aspiration (as described in Holmes et al. 1964), it is possible to set/alter the 'V' target and the duration of each of these stop components independently.

The 'template' rules consisted of a slightly modified version of the voicing timing rules described above. These were modified in order to conform to the 10 ms frame rate which is a characteristic of the LSI parallel formant speech synthesiser. These modifications consisted of rounding the values which are used to tune the templates to the nearest 10 ms. The original values used in these rules were shown in Table A.2.

The 'non-variant' rules were designed to generate the voicing patterns which would be produced by a speech synthesis-by-rule system which did not make any attempt to vary voicing timing as a function of context (as is the case in the majority of synthesis-by-rule systems). Obstruents generated in this way had the following characteristics.

-all VOICED elements had periodic excitation throughout their medial phase

- the amplitude of voicing during the medial phase of obstruents was set to V = 20, in order to model the attenuation of voicing level which takes place during intervals of constriction of the oral cavity.

- all VOICELESS elements were synthesised with no voicing during any of the medial phase.

- voicing was present through the release burst of initial VOICED stops.

- no voicing was present through the release burst of final VOICED stops.

- delay in voice onset following the release of VOICELESS stops was held at a constant value of 50 ms.

In order to produce tokens which differed only in their patterns of voicing timing, the following procedure was adopted. Firstly the 'non-variant' token of the word was generated. This was a relatively simple task since the VOICED obstruent parameter targets provided by the SYNCON system are fully voiced (the only difference was to incorporate a uniform 'V' target of '20'), and the VOICELESS obstruents have a target of '1' for the 'V'oicing parameter. Likewise the default voicing targets for the bursts of VOICED stops provide bursts which are fully voiced. The only tuning that it was necessary to do in producing these tokens was of the duration of the aspiration following the release of VOICELESS stops in order to achieve a uniform voice onset time (50 ms) across the three places of articulation, and of the 'V' parameter in the burst element of final VOICED stops in order to produce final unvoiced releases.

The 'non-variant' tokens were then used as the basis for generating the 'template' tokens, as follows.

Initial VOICED stops were produced by changing the 'V' target for the closure element and the burst element to '1'. The burst element was given a duration of 10 ms for initial /b/ /d/ and /g/.

Initial VOICELESS stops were assigned variable voice onset times corresponding to those which would be generated by the rules in Table A.2

Initial VOICED fricatives were produced by altering the 'V' target for each of the fricatives to '1'.

Initial VOICELESS fricatives required no change.

Final VOICED stops (partially voiced) were produced by altering the generated parameter files on a frame-by-frame basis. The 'V' parameter was assigned the value '1' during the interval in which the stop was 'devoiced'.

Final VOICELESS stops, with slight voicing incursion, were also produced by altering the generated parameter files on a frame-by-frame basis. The 'V' parameter was assigned the value '20' during the short interval in which the stop was voiced.

Final VOICED fricatives were produced by altering the 'V' target for each of the fricatives to '1'.

Final VOICELESS fricatives required no change.

A.3.2 Discrimination experiment

The aim of this test was to discover whether listeners are capable of consistently perceiving any difference between stimuli generated using the voicing timing rules described above, and other stimuli which are identical in every way except that the voicing timing in an initial or final obstruent has been generated using a set of 'default' voicing timing patterns, which do not reflect natural context-sensitivity of voicing timing.

This listening test used an AX discrimination test format (Repp 1984), involving presentation of pairs of stimuli which were sometimes identical and sometimes different, with subjects being asked to say whether the stimuli were identical or not.[3] The data analysis consisted of recording the percentage correct/wrong judgements as a function of the type of rule (voice onset time assignment, or medial voicing), the type of segment involved (stop vs fricative), and whether the segment was in initial or final position.

Two synthetic tokens of each of the following words were generated, one using the 'template' rules and one using the 'non-variant' rules.

	(1) be	(2) zinc	(3) cup
	do	vault	seat
	gap		lack
	bride	(4) robe	
	drunk	seed	(5) lose
	grate	league	live
	blank		teethe
	glue		

These words were chosen in order to allow evaluation of the voicing rules affecting segments in word-initial/post-pausal position and in word-final/pre-pausal position.

The words in group 1 contain initial VOICED stops occurring pre-vocalically or before sonorants. The 'non-variant' rules produce tokens with prevoiced stops, the 'template' rules produce tokens with short lag voice onset times which vary according to the voice onset time tuning rules described in section A.2 above. The words in group 2 contain initial VOICED fricatives. These are voiced throughout when produced with the 'non-variant' rules, and completely 'devoiced' when produced with the 'template' rules.

The words in group 3 contain final VOICELESS stops. The difference between tokens produced with the two sets of rules consists of a short period of incursion of low energy voicing into the closure phase of the stop.[4] The words in group 4 contain final VOICED stops. When produced with the 'non-variant' rules these stops have voicing throughout their closure period. The 'template' tokens have partially 'devoiced' final stops, with the amount of 'devoicing' being determined by the medial voicing tuning rules described in section A.2 above. The words in group 5 contain final VOICED fricatives. With the 'non-variant' rules these are generated with voicing throughout, with the 'template' rules they are completely 'devoiced'.

All of the synthetic stimuli were recorded on magnetic tape, and then low-pass filtered at 5KHz, digitised at a sampling frequency of 16KHz, and stored on a MASSCOMP computer.

The two versions of each word were combined into pairs in four different ways, as shown below.

x = stimulus with 'non-variant' voicing timing
y = stimulus with 'template' voicing timing

combination 1 --> x - x
combination 2 --> y - y
combination 3 --> x - y
combination 4 --> y - x

This made for a total of (19 words * 2 versions) 38 stimuli, and (19 words * 4 combinations) 76 comparisons per subject. Of these 76 comparisons, half consisted of pairs of identical stimuli of either types 'x' or 'y', and the rest were of different stimuli. The 76 pairs of stimuli were then randomised and a test tape was generated automatically such that each pair was separated by an interval of 4 seconds, and such that the inter-stimulus-interval within each pair was 800 ms.

Sixteen subjects took part in the listening test. They were all Edinburgh University undergraduates. The instructions given to subjects were as follows:

In this experiment you will be played a tape which contains a series of pairs of words produced by a speech synthesiser. Each pair consists of two repetitions of the same word. Your task is to indicate whether you think the two versions of the word are identical, or whether they are different in some way. The order in which the words are presented is listed on the answer sheet. You should write your response ('s' if you think the stimuli are the same, 'd' if you think they are different) next to the corresponding word on the answer sheet. It is important that you provide a response for every word that you hear. The words are presented in four groups of 19, with a short interval between each group. If you have any doubts or questions about this technique, ask me now.

In each case these verbal instructions were backed up verbally by the author, pointing out to the subjects that if they heard any difference at all, even a very slight one, they should indicate that with a 'd'.

A.3.3 Intelligibility test

The aim of this experiment was to assess listeners' performance on a standard[5] closed response 'intelligibility' test, as a function of the type of voicing timing present in the synthetic stimuli. Subjects were played series of single synthetic stimuli, and they were asked to indicate which of two possible words they thought they had heard, with the two candidate words differing only in the phonological voicing category of the initial or final obstruent. This experiment was split into two subsections, because in final obstruents it was necessary to co-vary the durations of the syllabic nucleii in order to attempt to control for the very powerful effect of vowel duration on listeners' perceptions of the voicing category of final obstruents in English (Raphael 1972, Denes 1955).

Word-initial stops

Three versions of each of the following words were produced. The words form rhyming word pairs, differing only in the phonological voicing category of the initial stop.

bee	pea	do	to	gap	cap
bride	pride	drunk	trunk	grate	crate
blank	plank			glue	clue

The first version of each word was a natural token produced by an adult male speaker (the author). The other two versions of each of the above words were synthesised using an LSI parallel formant synthesiser and the procedure described in A.3.1 above. The second version of each word had voicing timing generated by the 'non-variant' rules. In the third version of each word, voicing timing was generated by the 'template' rules.

The (16 * 3) 48 tokens were digitised and stored on computer, using the same procedure as in the discrimination test. They were then randomised and recorded on magnetic tape with an interval of 5 seconds between each word. An answer sheet was prepared containing a list of 48 pairs of rhyming words corresponding to the random order of the stimuli on the tape. Subjects were given the following instructions:

In this experiment you will be played tapes containing a series of single words, some of which are spoken by a speech synthesiser, and some of which are spoken by a male speaker. On the answer sheet, you will be given a choice of two words for every word that you hear. Your task is to say which of the two words you have heard. You can indicate this by placing a tick at the side of the word which you have chosen. It is important you don't miss out any of the words. If you have any doubts or questions about this procedure, ask me now.

Word-final obstruents

Five versions of the following words were produced. As in the first part of this experiment, these words form rhyming word pairs, differing only in the phonological voicing category of the final stop.

robe	rope	live	life
seed	seat	teeth	teethe
league	leek	laze	lace

- a natural token produced by an adult male speaker (the author)

- with 'non-variant' voicing during medial phase of the final obstruent and with a long vowel duration (the actual vowel durations used in this test were the same as those measured in tokens of the same words spoken by the author).

- voicing during the final obstruent medial phase assigned by 'template' rules and with a long vowel duration.

- with 'non-variant' voicing during final obstruent medial phase and with a short vowel duration.

- voicing during final obstruent medial phase assigned by 'template' rules and with a short vowel duration.

Only three versions were produced of the words ending in a VOICELESS fricative, since they do not change as a result of the application of the application of one set of voicing rules or another. These were therefore used as a control in order to observe the independent effect of the different vowel lengths. The ([9 * 5] + [3 * 3]) 54 tokens were digitised and stored on computer, using the same procedure as in the discrimination test. They were then randomised and recorded on magnetic tape with an interval of 5 seconds between each word.

An answer sheet was prepared containing a list of 54 pairs of rhyming words corresponding to the random order of the stimuli on the tape. Subjects were instructed (as above) to indicate which one of the pair of words he/she thought he/she had heard.

A.3.4 Experimental procedure

The same subjects took part in both the discrimination and the intelligibility experiments, and the tests were performed during the same session in the following order; intelligibility test I (word-initial rules), intelligibility test II (word-final rules), discrimination test. Each subjects was seated in a sound-proofed listening booth, and the stimuli were played through headphones (EAGLE SE540) at a comfortable level.

A.3.5 Results

Discrimination Task

In general, subjects found it difficult to discriminate between stimuli produced by the different sets of voicing timing rules (see Table A.4). In only two cases (initial VOICED stops, and final VOICED fricatives) were more than 50% of combinations of different stimuli correctly identified as being different. However, this relatively more successful discriminatory ability was only found when the different stimuli were presented in one order (combination 3: x-y), but not in the reverse order.

Intelligibility Task

In the section of this test dealing with initial obstruents (See Table A.5), the rate of correct lexical identification was extremely high under all conditions, and the type of stimulus, or its identity had no effect on subjects' ability to correctly identify which of the two possible words they had heard. Indeed the highest error rate occurred with the natural stimuli.

In the second part of the intelligibility test, pertaining to final obstruents (see Table A.6), the stimulus type had a highly significant effect on the number of correct responses made by subjects ($p < 0.001$). The level of correct response however, appears to be largely a function of the appropriateness or otherwise of the vowel duration rather than of which of the two sets of voicing timing rules were used to generate the final obstruent.

Table A.4: Results from the discrimination test -- number and percentage of correct answers (pooling across subjects), as a function of obstruent type and position in word.

		Stimulus Combination			
		x-x	y-y	x-y	y-x
All Data		270	264	105	69
	%	88.8	86.8	34.5	22.7
Initial Voiced		46	41	30	9
Stops	%	95.8	85.4	62.5	18.8
Initial Voiced		29	29	9	7
Fricatives	%	90.6	90.6	28.1	21.9
Initial Voiced		70	69	30	13
Clusters	%	87.5	86.3	37.5	16.3
Final Voiced		41	42	6	15
Stops	%	85.4	87.5	12.5	31.3
Final Voiced		42	38	24	16
Fricatives	%	87.5	79.2	50.0	33.3
Final Voiceless		42	45	6	9
Stops	%	87.5	93.8	12.5	18.8

Summary of results

In the discrimination test, despite the fact that (with the exception of final VOICELESS stops) the differences between the two different types of tokens are audible and that instructions and mode of presentation attempted to steer subjects away from listening purely categorially, the results do suggest that in most cases subjects responded purely on categorial grounds. Stimuli produced with the 'template' rules are on the whole difficult to tell apart from those produced with the 'non-variant' rules. The highest rate of success was found with initial VOICED stops and final VOICED fricatives. This is quite likely due to the fact that in both cases the differences between the output of the two sets of rules are relatively salient (70 ms of prevoicing vs. no prevoicing in the case of the stops; voicing throughout the fricative vs. no voicing during the fricative in latter case). However, this finding is tempered by the fact that discrimination is relatively successful only when one particular ordering of the stimuli is presented to the subjects.[6] In addition, low discrimination scores are observed with initial VOICED fricatives, where the differences between the two types of stimuli are similar to those for final VOICED fricatives.

Table A.5: Results from the 'word-initial obstruent' section of the intelligibility test -- the number and percentage of **correct** answers (pooling across subjects) as a function of whether the obstruent occurred singly or in a cluster.

		STIMULUS TYPE		
		[1]	[2]	[3]
All Data		231	244	239
	%	90.2	95.3	93.4
Initial Voiced		44	48	47
Stops	%	91.7	100	97.9
Initial Voiced		59	79	74
Clusters	%	73.8	98.9	92.5
Initial Voiceless		48	46	39
Stops	%	100	95.8	81.3
Initial Voiceless		80	71	79
Clusters	%	100	88.8	98.8

Stimulus Key: [1] natural; [2] 'non-variant'; [3] 'template'.

Table A.6: results from the 'word-final obstruent' section of the intelligibility test -- number and percentage of **correct** answers (pooling across subjects) as a function of obstruent type and of whether it is VOICED or VOICELESS.

		[1]	[2]	[3]	[4]	[5]
All Data		187	126	109	166	78
	%	97.4	65.6	75.7	86.5	54.2
Final Voiced		46	46	43	40	24
Stops	%	95.8	95.8	89.6	83.3	50.0
Final Voiced		47	45	39	33	8
Fricatives	%	97.9	93.8	81.3	68.8	16.7
Final Voiceless		46	19	27	46	46
Stops	%	95.8	39.6	56.3	95.8	95.8
Final Voiceless		48	16	-	47	-
Fricatives	%	100	33.3	-	97.9	-

Stimulus key: [1] natural; [2] 'non-variant' with relatively long vowel duration; [3] 'template' with relatively long vowel duration; [4] 'non-variant' with relatively short vowel duration; [5] 'template' with relatively short vowel duration.

The results from the 'intelligibility test' show that subjects' ability to determine which of two rhyming minimally different synthetic words they have heard is not affected by the type of voicing timing rule which is used. The effects which are found are almost entirely due to the variation of vowel duration in the synthetic stimuli.

A.3.6 Discussion

If viewed at a superficial level, these results could possibly lead to the conclusion that designers of a phonetic rule base for a speech synthesis-by-rule system do not have to concern themselves with sub-categorial variability of voicing timing, because subjects cannot reliably hear a difference between tokens which differ only in the fine detail of the timing of voicing, and these subtle differences do not make the speech output any more intelligible.

However, a more cautious approach is advisable. The results described above permit an evaluation of the tests themselves as much as of the synthetic tokens. It is possible that on its own embedded within an otherwise mediocre synthesis system, the variability of voicing timing generated by the 'template' rules does not make a difference. The subtle differences between stimuli were very likely swamped by the general poor quality of the synthesis. However, in conjunction with higher quality speech synthesis (and other forms of low-level variability especially of parameters which are known to co-vary with voicing timing such as fricative and stop burst intensities), rules such as this may well have a significant effect, and clearly it would be a mistake to discount this level of variability until such a test has been carried out.[7]

This leads to a second factor which must be considered in the light of these results. It may be that non-distinctive variability such as that examined in this study does improve the quality of speech synthesis-by-rule, but **there are no means available of demonstrating this**. A feature shared by most available evaluation metrics is that none of them are designed to test for the improvement which might be brought about by fine-grained variability of the sort described. Until such techniques are developed, it will not be possible to carry out quantitative assessment of the effect of fine-grained parameter tuning in synthesis-by-rule systems. Equally, until such techniques are developed it would be wrong to discard the potential value of incorporating such variability into synthesis-by-rule, on the basis of crude intelligibility-oriented metrics which do not address key factors associated with naturalness.

A procedure suitable for evaluating rules such those proposed above would seem to require two features: it would allow some absolute measure of the accuracy which the synthetic speech signal reflected natural speech; and it would give an indication of whether listeners considered the output to be more or less natural.

Perhaps the ultimate means of assessing the absolute naturalness of synthetic speech would be to perform distance measures (a procedure similar to that commonly performed in isolated word recognition involving spectral analysis and matching of dynamically time warped parameters; McInnes & Jack 1988) between synthetic tokens before and after the criterial modification and the same word or phrase produced by a human. This could potentially provide an objective measure of the extent to which synthetic speech was capturing the systematic properties of natural speech. One evident problem with this method which certainly makes it unsuitable for the type of evaluation currently required for the voicing timing rules (i.e. of one sub-component of a synthesis-by-rule rule base) is that the distance between the synthetic speech and the real speech is likely to be so large due to the overall mediocre quality of current synthesis-by-rule systems that it is unlikely that the introduction of fine-grained changes such as those described above would result in sufficient difference for this to be treated as a significant improvement (i.e. the improvements that are made would be lost in the general poor quality of the speech output). Hence, this technique may not be a practical proposition from the point of view of synthetic speech, for a number of years.

In the meantime, an idea of the absolute naturalness of synthetic speech can be achieved by comparing, in an informal way, synthetic tokens with corpora of natural speech. For example, in the present case, it can be said that the patterns of voicing timing generated by the 'template' rules are objectively more naturalistic than those produced by the 'non-variant' rules. This judgement is based on the available knowledge of the timing of voicing as supplied in experimental studies such as that carried out in this study. However, the shortage of quantitative instrumental accounts of many aspects of fine-grained phonetic variability means that even this relatively simple and informal means of assessing the naturalness of synthetic speech is not possible.

Different types of problems have to be confronted in developing strategies for evaluating subjects' responses to synthetic speech. The key issue is what judgement to elicit from subjects. If it is the case that phonological categories will always override subjects' attempts to report on any finer differences between tokens, then the emphasis of these tests should be placed less on contrast (although the problem of subjects listening categorially to stimuli which they are presented is always going to be difficult to solve), and more on the other functions which this level of variation might have. This however, is the crux of the problem, and it is linked to the theoretical discussion in Chapters 2 and 5 of this volume; the status and role of this level of variability in natural speech has not been established, and until it is, it will not be possible to fully evaluate any effect it might have on the quality of synthetic speech. There are, therefore, fundamental phonetic and phonological questions to be addressed before the optimum evaluation metric can be designed.

A.4 CONCLUSION

In this appendix, I have outlined a set of rules for producing naturalistic patterns of voicing timing in a synthesis-by-rule system. These are potentially capable of generating a wide range of the systematic variability of the timing of voicing with respect to obstruents in English, significantly more than that which is apparently captured in other currently available synthesis-by-rule systems. The exploratory evaluation of these rules which was carried out produced inconclusive results, illustrating the difficulty involved in assessing such fine-grained variability. I have pointed out the directions in which future developments might proceed. Two fundamental problems to be encountered are a shortage of quantitative accounts of the fine detail of phonetic realisation, and the need to establish the status of such variation in speech communication, in order to determine what sort of responses to elicit from listeners.

NOTES

1. One of the MITalk 'devoicing' rules does not actually make obstruents voiceless, but rather, attenuate the level of voicing during the obstruent medial phase.

2. An example of this is the MITalk system which uses a completely different shaped glottal pulse (quasi-sinusoidal) for voicing during the occlusion phase of obstruents; Allen et al. 1987).

3. AX tests are most often used to test within/between category discrimination of points within a continuum. This experiment is slightly different; (a) because there is no continuum (b) because it is not clear if there are any category boundaries involved. Nevertheless, the method of stimulus presentation corresponds to the AX paradigm.

4. Two trained phoneticians were unable to detect the differences between 'template' and 'non-variant' final VOICELESS stops. However, it was decided to include the words in the test for the purpose of control.

5. This test has a format very similar to that used in the diagnostic rhyme test (Voiers 1983).

6. An ordering effect of this sort is a common occurrence in AX categorial perception experiments. Batliner & Schieffer (1987) discuss the possible causes of this, concluding that, in pitch

discrimination at least, this may not just be an artefact of the AX paradigm, but a result of features of the stimuli (specifically they found that 'stimuli are better discriminated if the stimulus with the greater change in F0 comes last.' 1987:49).

7. The results of this experiment do, however, suggest quite strongly that the ordering of development work on a synthesis-by-rule system should ensure that attention is given first of all to providing overall reasonable quality output prior to fine tuning of the type described here.

Appendix B

Alphabetic listing of the words used in experiment 1 (described in Chapter 3).[1]

bags	bank	bash	bath	bathe	belt	bibs
bid	bids	bins	bland	blank	bled	bliss
brand	bread	breath	breathe	brit	bulb	cabs
cans	cash	chris	clamp	clank	class	cliff
clive's	crave	craze	crib	crick	dab	damp
dams	daz	dig	dip	div	dove	drab
drat	drills	drip	dross	dwell	dwindle	else
fad	fags	false	felt	fibs	figs	filled
flab	flag	flip	float	frank	freeze	frill
frills	frizz	gaffe	gags	gash	gills	gives
glad	glance	gland	glass	glib	grid	grids
grilled	grills	grins	guild	help	kath	kelp
key	kids	kiff	killed	love	loves	month
pam's	pant	pass	pat	pig	pills	pink
pip	plans	plead	please	pleb	plinth	police
prat	prince	print	prog	proves	quaint	queen
quid	quids	quills	quilt	sag	salp	sash
shack	shall	shams	shank	shelf	shilp	shins
shoves	shows	sick	sid	since	sins	sip
skids	skimp	skimo	skint	skive	slab	slave
sleaze	slid	smack	smash	smelt	smit	smith
smoke	snazz	sneeze	snib	sniff	snooze	space
spas	spif	spit	spiv	stab	stamp	stand
stealth	stiff	tabs	tack	tans	that	these
thick	think	this	thought	thread	three	through
thaite	tiff	tilled	tint	tip	trash	trend
trick	trims	trish	twice	twif	twig	twins
vamp	van	vat	vax	vibes	vilp	vince
viv	wealth	welsh	zag	zig	zinc	zip
zoos						

---

1. In preparing the randomised word list for the reading task, duplicates of 'drip', 'flip', and 'dig' were inadvertently included in the master list. Hence the actual word-list consists of 207 items, as described in Chapter 3. This also explains the discrepancy between the number of cases of initial /d, dr, fl/ and final /p, g/ shown in Table 3.2 and the number shown below in this appendix.

Appendix C

Sentences produced by subjects in Experiment 2 (see Chapter 4 for full details)

Condition 1 = word initial or final position
Condition 2 = across morpheme boundary
Condition 3 = across compound boundary
Condition 4 = across word boundary (adjective/noun)
Condition 5 = across word boundary (subj/verb)
Condition 6 = across word and clause boundary

Condition 1

he said he wanted ___, didn't he
to pray, to play, to breed, a blade, a tray, a twin, a drop, to dwell, a crate, to climb, a quail, to grin, to glance, to smoke, to sneak.

Condition 2

we all know ____, don't we.
it's upright, it's a stripling, it's sublet, it's nitrate, it's outward, it's a midriff, she's a midwife, it's gimmickry, he's sickly, he's backward, he's legless, it's a mismatch, it's misnamed.

Condition 3

we all know _____, don't we.
it's the tap room, it's a strip light, it's mob rule, he's a club leader, he's an out-rider, he's a light-weight, he's a lead-rider, it's a side-walk, it's a smoke ring, it's quick-lime, it's an ink-well, it's a dog-race, it's a fog lamp, she's a dress-maker, it's a bass note.

Condition 4

we all know _____, don't we.
it's a steep road, it's a steep lane, it's a drab road, it's hot rice, it's hot work, it's a bad road, it's bad work, it's thick rope, he's a thick lad, it's thick wool, it's a big road, it's a big leaf, he's a fierce man, it's a fierce knife.

Condition 5

we all know _____, don't we.
Philip ran, Philip left, Bob ran, Bob left, Pat ran, Pat went, Fred ran, Fred went, Dick ran, Dick left, Dick went, Meg ran, Meg left, Chris moved, Chris knew.

Condition 6

we all saw the _____ bought, didn't we.
cap Ron, cap Len, cab Ron, cab Len, cat Ron, cat Will, pad Ron, pad Will, shack Ron, shack Len, shack Will, bag Ron, bag Len, house Mike, house Neil.

Appendix D

This appendix contains listings of results from experiment 1 which for reasons of space it was not possible to include in the main body of the text. The tables of results are presented in two sections;

(I) tables showing the duration of intervals of medial voicing in stop-sonorant and fricative-sonorant sequences.

(II) tables showing the results corresponding to the nasal-obstruent and lateral-obstruent sequences which were investigated.

Section I

Table D.1: Frequency of occurrence (number of cases) of main patterns of medial voicing (A/B/C) in initial VOICELESS stop-sonorant sequences in the pooled data as a function of environment condition (1/2/3). Timing pattern A = no medial voicing; B = voicing throughout medial phase; C = voicing only during part of medial phase.

	Environment	/pl/	/pr/	/tr/	/tw/	/kr/	/kw/	/kl/	total
A	1	28	23	25	20	25	28	25	174
	2	2	1	1	1	1	-	3	10
	3	26	23	23	19	25	31	23	170
B	1	-	-	-	-	-	-	-	0
	2	-	1	-	-	-	-	-	1
	3	-	-	-	-	-	-	-	0
C	1	-	-	-	-	-	-	-	0
	2	25	20	23	18	24	29	22	161
	3	-	-	1	-	-	-	-	1
		81	69	73	58	75	88	73	517

Table D.2: Mean percentage of stop duration accompanied by voicing in stop-sonorant sequences for each subject.

	Pool	RT	Subject PB	TC	BD	FD
/p/-son	18.4	19.44	17.00	35.22	8.9	12.71
n	46	8	11	9	11	7
s.d.	14.6	4.36	7.34	29.25	3.11	6.85
/t/-son	22.33	22.22	10.99	40.44	20.44	15.33
n	42	9	9	9	9	6
s.d.	14.6	7.87	5.62	17.82	5.68	12.12
/k/-son	21.52	20.40	25.56	27.13	16.5	17.54
n	75	15	16	15	16	13
s.d.	9.25	6.79	9.27	11.45	5.94	7.28
/b/-son	67.15	58.86	73.11	68.578	7.00	4.13
n	38	6	9	7	9	7
s.d.	22.44	24.86	17.27	15.94	13.52	16.73
/d/-son	73.00	80.00	47.37	82.88	87.0	71.00
n	34	6	8	6	7	7
s.d.	27.09	9.38	9.24	31.26	34.39	22.16
/g/-son	57.23	65.50	51.10	49.67	81.6	32.62
n	47	10	10	9	10	8
s.d.	24.25	15.08	11.26	12.54	28.63	21.05

Table D.3: Frequency of occurrence (number of cases) of main patterns of medial voicing (A/B/C) in initial VOICED stop-sonorant sequences in the pooled data as a function of environment condition (1/2/3). Timing pattern A = no medial voicing; B = voicing throughout medial phase; C = voicing only during part of medial phase.

Environment		/br/	/bl/	/dr/	/dw/	/gr/	/gl/	total
A	1	22	18	28	8	24	24	124
	2	-	1	1	-	-	1	3
	3	24	17	27	8	24	24	124
B	1	-	-	-	-	-	-	0
	2	2	3	5	3	3	1	17
	3	-	-	-	-	-	-	0
C	1	-	-	-	-	-	-	0
	2	19	14	20	5	20	23	101
	3	-	-	1	-	-	-	1
		67	53	82	24	71	73	370

Table D.4: Mean percentage of fricative duration accompanied by voicing in /s/-nasal sequences for each subject.

Subject	Pool	RT	PB	TC	BD	FD
/sn/	9.67	14.8	6.0	7.0	5.2	13.5
n	24	5	5	3	5	6
/sm/	8.77	10.83	7.5	6.2	6.0	13.2
n	26	6	4	5	6	5

Table D.5: Frequency of occurrence (number of cases) of main patterns of medial voicing (A/B/C) in initial VOICELESS fricative-sonorant sequences in the pooled data as a function of environment condition (1/2/3). Timing pattern A = no medial voicing; B = voicing throughout medial phase; C = voicing only during part of medial phase.

	Environment	/sn/	/sm/	/fr/	/fl/	/sl/	/θr/	/θw/	total
A	1	21	28	23	21	15	12	4	124
	2	2	5	8	8	1	7	3	34
	3	23	29	17	21	12	11	4	117
B	1	-	-	-	-	-	-	-	0
	2	-	-	-	-	-	-	-	0
	3	-	-	-	-	-	-	-	0
C	1	-	-	-	-	-	-	-	0
	2	23	25	14	16	13	5	2	98
	3	1	1	-	-	1	-	-	3
		70	88	62	66	42	35	13	376

Table D.6: Frequency of occurrence (number of cases) of main patterns of medial voicing (A/B/C) in word-initial /s/-stop-V sequences in the pooled data as a function of environment condition (1/2/3). Timing pattern A = no medial voicing; B = voicing throughout medial phase; C = voicing only during part of medial phase.

	Environment	/sp/	/st/	/sk/	total
A	1	23	20	24	67
	2	2	3	7	12
	3	23	22	23	68
B	1	-	-	-	0
	2	-	-	-	0
	3	-	-	-	0
C	1	-	-	-	0
	2	21	20	18	59
	3	-	-	-	0
		69	65	72	206

Section II

Table D.7: Frequency of occurrence (number of cases) of main patterns of medial voicing (A/B/C) in final sonorant-fricative sequences in the pooled data as a function of environment condition (1/2/3). Timing pattern A = no medial voicing; B = voicing throughout medial phase; C = voicing only during part of medial phase.

		/ns/	/nθ/	/ls/	/lʃ/	/lf/	/lθ/	/mz/	/nz/	/lz/	total
	Environment										
A	1	11	6	4	2	-	6	9	2	10	70
	2	14	3	3	1	2	4	1	3	1	32
	3	8	2	2	2	3	7	5	8	5	42
B	1	-	-	-	-	-	-	-	-	-	0
	2	-	-	-	-	-	-	16	22	17	55
	3	-	-	-	-	-	-	-	-	-	0
C	1	2	-	2	2	1	2	12	17	18	56
	2	2	1	3	3	2	4	6	13	6	40
	3	8	2	4	2	1	3	19	29	19	87
		45	14	18	12	9	26	68	114	76	382

Table D.8: Mean duration (in percentage-of-medial-phase terms) of intervals of medial voicing in VOICELESS fricatives following /m/, /n/, and /l/, in the pooled data pooling across environment conditions (for all cases when the percentage of medial phase accompanied by voicing is greater than zero).

		/ns/	/nθ/	/ls/	/lʃ/	/lf/
	%	10.33	9.33	12.25	8.3	7.4
	n	12	3	9	7	4

Table D.9: Mean duration (msecs) of voiceless intervals in nasal-stop and lateral stop sequences as a function of environment condition in the pooled data.

		Environment Condition			
		1	2	3	1/2/3
/mp/	ms	73.09	24.76	32.18	43.63
	s.d.	27.1	10.7	18.8	29.2
	n	22	21	22	65
/nt/	ms	78.48	13.43	24.05	39.64
	s.d.	23.1	12.4	15.9	33.9
	n	23	21	22	66
/nd/	ms	25.40	0.00	2.16	9.8
	s.d.	32.4	-	4.52	22.5
	n	20	17	19	56
/nk/	ms	81.20	19.74	28.68	42.68
	s.d.	25.5	11.74	19.1	33.4
	n	35	38	34	107
/lp/	ms	99.16	61.63	59.32	71.26
	s.d.	22.2	18.5	17.5	25.8
	n	19	24	25	68
/lb/	ms	65.5	29.00	44.40	46.15
	s.d.	6.1	35.7	19.4	26.0
	n	4	4	5	13
/lt/	ms	81.62	22.08	39.92	48.78
	s.d.	25.3	14.5	25.0	33.5
	n	13	12	12	37
/ld/	ms	17.93	3.46	18.80	14.3
	s.d.	14.8	7.64	16.6	15.4
	n	14	13	20	47

Table D.10: Mean duration (in percentage-of-medial-phase and absolute terms) of intervals of medial voicing in VOICED fricatives following /m/, /n/, and /l/, in the pooled data as a function of environment condition (for all cases when the percentage of medial phase accompanied by voicing is greater than zero).

		Environment Condition			
		1	2	3	1/2/3
/mz/	%	10.0	78.09	20.58	42.06
	ms	12.83	50.82	13.68	28.9
	n	12	22	19	53
/nz/	%	9.8	71.43	23.59	41.38
	ms	12.47	49.91	15.52	29.7
	n	17	35	29	81
/lz/	%	10.15	80.26	14.84	38.62
	ms	15.83	55.35	10.32	29.2
	n	18	23	19	60

References

Abbs, J. (1986) Invariance and variability in speech production: a distinction between linguistic intent and its neuromotor implementation. in Perkell, J., & Klatt, D. (eds) *Invariance and Variability in Speech Processes:* 202-219 Hillsdale NJ: Lawrence Erlbaum Associates.

Abbs, J. & Eilenberg, G.R. (1976) Peripheral mechanisms of speech motor control. in Lass, N.J.(ed), *Contemporary Issues in Experimental Phonetics:* 139-168 New York: Academic Press.

Abercrombie, D. (1967) *Elements of General Phonetics.* Edinburgh: Edinburgh University Press.

Abramson, A. (1977) Laryngeal timing in consonant distinctions. *Phonetica,* 34: 295-303.

Allen, J., Hunnicutt, M.S., & Klatt, D. (1987) *From Text to Speech: the MITalk System.* Cambridge: Cambridge University Press.

Anderson, S.R. (1981) Why phonology isn't "natural". *Linguistic Inquiry,* 12:493-539.

Arkebauer, J., Hixon, T., & Hardy, J. (1967) Peak intra-oral air pressure during speech. *Journal of Speech and Hearing Research,* 10:196-208.

Armstrong, L. (1932) *The Phonetics of French.* London: G. Bell & sons.

Askenfelt, A., Gauffin, J., & Sundberg, J. (1980) A comparison of contact microphone and electroglottograph for the measurement of vocal fundamental frequency. *Journal of Speech and Hearing Research,* 23:258-273.

Baer, T. (1979) Vocal jitter: a neuromuscular explanation. in Lawrence, V., & Weinberg, B. (eds) *Transcripts of the 8th Symposium on Care of the Professional Voice, Pt1:* 19-22 New York: The Voice Foundation.

Baken, R. (1987) *Clinical Measurement of Speech and Voice.* Boston, Ma.: Little, Brown and Co.

Baran, J.A., Zlatin-Laufer, M., & Daniloff, R. (1977) Phonological constrastivity in conversation: a comparative study of voice onset time. *Journal of Phonetics,* 5:339-350.

Barry, M. (1985) A palatographic study of connected speech processes. *Cambridge Papers in Phonetics and Experimental Linguistics,* 4.

Barry, W. (1981) Internal juncture and speech communication. *Arbeitsberichte, Institut für Phonetik, University of Kiel,* 16:229-288.

Barry, W., & Kunzel, H. (1978) A note on the devoicing of nasals. *Journal of the International Phonetics Association,* 8:47-55.

Batliner, A., & Schiefer, L. (1987) Stimulus category, reaction time and order effect - an experiment on pitch discrimination. *Proceedings of the Eleventh International Congress of Phonetic Sciences, Vol 5:* 46-49.

Beckman, M., & Shoji, A. (1984) Spectral and perceptual evidence for CV coarticulation in devoiced /si/ and /syu/ in Japanese. *Phonetica,* 41:61-71.

Bellugi, U., & Studdert-Kennedy, M. (1980) *Signed and Spoken Language: Biological Constraints on Linguistic Form.* Deerfield Beach Fla.: Verlag Chemie.

Bell-Berti, F. (1975) Control of pharyngeal cavity size for English voiced and voiceless stops. *Journal of the Acoustical Society of America,* 7:456-461.

Bell-Berti, F. (1980) Velopharyngeal function: a spatio-temporal model. in Lass, N.J.(ed), *Speech and Language: Advances in Basic Research and Practice, Vol IV:* 291-316 New York: Academic Press.

Benguerel, A.-P., & Cowan, H. (1974) Coarticulation of upper lip protrusion in French. *Phonetica,* 30:41-55.

Berg, R. van den (1958) Myoelastic-aerodynamic theory of voice production. *Journal of Speech and Hearing Research,* 1:227-244.

Berg, R. van den (1968) Mechanisms of the larynx and laryngeal vibrations. in Malmberg, B. (ed) *Manual of Phonetics:* 278-308 Amsterdam: North Holland.

Berg, R. van den, Vennard, W., Berger, D., & Shervanian, C. (1960) *Voice Production. The vibrating larynx.* Film. SFW-UNFI Utrecht.

Berg, R.J. van den (1988) *The Perception of Voicing in Dutch Two-Obstruent Sequences.* Unpublished dissertation, University of Nijmegen.

Bickley, C., & Stevens, K. (1987) Effects of a vocal tract constriction on the glottal source: data from voiced consonants. in Baer, T., Sasaki, C., & Harris, K. (eds) *Laryngeal Function in Phonation and Respiration:* 239-253 Boston: College Hill.

Bladon, A. (1979) Motor control of coarticulation: linguistic considerations. in *Proceedings of the Ninth International Congress of Phonetic Sciences, Vol 2:* 325-331.

Bladon, A., & Al-Bamerni, A. (1976) Coarticulation resistance in English /l/. *Journal of Phonetics,* 4:137-150.

Broad, D. (1973) Phonation. in Minifie, F., Hixon, T., & Williams, F. (eds) *Normal Aspects of Speech Hearing and Language:* 127-167 Englewood Cliffs, NJ: Prentice-Hall.

Broe, M. (in press) An introduction to feature geometry. in Docherty, G.J. & Ladd, D.R. (eds) *Gesture, Segment, Prosody: Papers in Laboratory Phonology II.* Cambridge: Cambridge University Press.

Browman, C., & Goldstein, L. (1986) Towards an articulatory phonology. *Phonology Yearbook,* 3:219-252.

Browman, C., & Goldstein, L. (1990) Tiers in articulatory phonology with some implications for casual speech. in Kingston, J. & Beckman, M. (eds) *Papers in Laboratory Phonology I: Between the Grammar and the Physics of Speech:* 341-376 Cambridge: Cambridge University Press.

Browman, C., & Goldstein, L. (in press) "Targetless" schwa: an articulatory analysis. in Docherty, G.J. & Ladd, D.R. (eds) *Gesture, Segment, Prosody: Papers in Laboratory Phonology II.* Cambridge: Cambridge University Press.

Brown, G. (1977) *Listening to Spoken English.* London: Longman.

Brown, W.S., & McGlone, R.E. (1969) Relation of intraoral air-pressure to oral cavity size. *Folia Phoniatrica,* 21:321-331.

Canellada, M. & Madsen, J. (1987) *Pronunciación del Español* Madrid: Castalia.

Catford, J.C. (1977) *Fundamental Problems in Phonetics.* Edinburgh: Edinburgh University Press.

Chen, M. (1970) Vowel length variation as a function of the consonant environment. *Phonetica,* 22:129-159.

Chomsky, N., & Halle, M. (1968) *The Sound Pattern of English.* New York: Harper.

Clements, G.N. (1985) The geometry of phonological features. *Phonology Yearbook,* 2:223-252.

REFERENCES

Clumeck, H. (1976) Patterns of soft palate movement in six languages. *Journal of Phonetics*, 4:337-351.

Cole, R., & Cooper, W.E. (1975) Perception of voicing in English affricates and fricatives. *Journal of the Acoustical Society of America*, 8:1286-1287.

Cooper, W. (1980) Syntactic-to-phonetic coding. in Butterworth, B. (ed) *Language Production, Vol I*: 297-333, London: Academic Press.

Daniloff, R., & Hammarberg, R. (1973) On defining coarticulation. *Journal of Phonetics*, 1:239-248.

Davidsen-Neilsen, N. (1974) Syllabification in English words with medial sp, st, sk. *Journal of Phonetics*, 2:15-45.

Delattre, P., Liberman, A., & Cooper, F.S. (1955) Acoustic loci and transitional cues for consonants. *Journal of the Acoustical Society of America*, 27:769-773.

Denes, P. (1955) Effect of duration on the perception of voicing. *Journal of the Acoustical Society of America*, 27:761-764.

Denes, P. & Pinson, E. (1963) *The Speech Chain*. New York: Bell Telephone Laboratories.

Dent, H. (1984) Coarticulated devoicing in English laterals. *Work in Progress, Reading University Phonetics Laboratory*, 4:111-134.

Diehl, R., Souther, A., & Convis, C. (1980) Conditions on rate normalisation in speech perception. *Perception & Psychophysics*, 27:435-443.

Disner, S.F. (1983) Vowel quality: the relation between universal and language-specific factors. *UCLA Working Papers in Phonetics*, 58.

Dixit, R.P. (1987) Mechanisms for voicing and aspiration: Hindi and other languages compared. *UCLA Working Papers in Phonetics*, 67:49-102.

Docherty, G. J., & Ladd, D. R. (in press) *Gesture, Segment, Prosody: Papers in Laboratory Phonology II*. Cambridge: Cambridge University Press.

Edwards, T.J., (1981) Multiple feature analysis of intervocalic English plosives. *Journal of the Acoustical Society of America*, 69:535-547.

Ferguson, G. (1976) *Statistical Analysis in Psychology Education*. New York: McGraw Hill.

Fischer-Jorgensen, E. (1980) Temporal relations in Danish tautosyllabic CV sequences with stop consonants. *Annual Report Institute of Phonetics University of Copenhagen*, 14:207-261.

Fischer-Jorgensen, E., & Hutters, B. (1981) Aspirated stop consonants before low vowels: a problem of delimitation - its causes and consequences. *Annual Report Institute of Phonetics University of Copenhagen*, 15:77-102.

Flege, J. (1982) Laryngeal timing and phonation onset in utterance initial English stops. *Journal of Phonetics*, 10:177-192.

Flege, J., & Brown, W.S. (1982) Effects of utterance position on English speech timing. *Phonetica*, 39:337-357.

Flege, J., & Eefting, W. (1986) Linguistic and developmental effects on the production and perception of stop consonants. *Phonetica*, 43:155-157.

Fletcher, J. (1988) *An Acoustic Study of Timing in French*. Unpublished dissertation, Reading University.

Fourakis, M. & Port, R. (1986) Stop epenthesis in English. *Journal of Phonetics*, 14:197-221.

Fowler, C. (1977) *Timing Control in Speech Production.* Bloomington IN: Indiana University Linguistics Club.

Fowler, C. (1980) Coarticulation, and theories of extrinsic timing control. *Journal of Phonetics,* 8:113-133.

Fowler, C. (1985) Current perspectives on language and speech production -- a critical review. in Daniloff, R. (ed) *Speech Science:* 194-278 London: Taylor and Francis.

Fowler, C., Rubin, P., Remez, R., & Turvey, M. (1980) Implications for speech production of a general theory of action. in Butterworth, B. (ed) *Language Production:* 373-420 London: Academic Press.

Fraser, H., & Docherty, G.J. (1990) On comparing acoustic and electropalatographic representations of English obstruents. *Proceedings of the Institute of Acoustics,* 12,pt10:467-474.

Fujimura, O. (1986) Relative invariance of articulatory movements: an iceberg model. in Perkell, J., & Klatt, D. (eds) *Invariance and Variability in Speech Processes:* 226-234 Hillsdale NJ: Lawrence Erlbaum Associates.

Fujimura, O. (1987) Fundamentals and applications in speech production research. *Proceedings of the Eleventh International Congress of Phonetic Sciences, Vol 6:* 10-27.

Fujimura, O., & Lovins, J.B. (1978) Syllables as concatenative phonetic units. in Bell, A., & Hooper, J.(eds) *Syllables and Segments:* 107-120 Amsterdam: North-Holland.

Gay, T. (1981) Mechanisms in the control of speech rate. *Phonetica,* 38:148-158.

Gay, T., Lindblom, B., & Lubker, J. (1981) Production of bite-block vowels: acoustic equivalence by selective compensation. *Journal of the Acoustical Society of America,* 9:802-810.

Gimson, A.C. (1980) *An Introduction to the Pronunciation of English.* 3rd edition London: Edward Arnold.

Goldsmith, J, (1990) *Autosegmental and Metrical Phonology.* Oxford: Blackwell

Goldstein, L., & Browman, C. (1986) Representation of voicing contrasts using articulatory gestures. *Haskins Labs Status Report Speech Research,* SR85:251-254.

Gracco, V., & Abbs, J. (1987) Programming and execution processes of speech movement control: potential neural correlates. in Keller, E., & Gopnik, M. (eds) *Motor and Sensory Processes of Language:* 163-201 Hillsdale NJ: Lawrence Erlbaum Associates.

Haggard, M. (1973) Abbreviations of consonants in English pre- and post-vocalic clusters. *Journal of Phonetics,* 1:9-24.

Haggard, M. (1978) The devoicing of voiced fricatives. *Journal of Phonetics,* 6:95-102.

Halle, M., & Stevens, K. (1971) A note on laryngeal features. *MIT Quarterly Progress Report, Research Laboratory of Electronics,* 101:198-213.

Hammarberg, R. (1982) On redefining coarticulation. *Journal of Phonetics,* 10:123-137.

Hanninen, R. (1979) The voiceless - voiced opposition of English consonants: difficulties of pronunciation and perception in communication between native and Finnish speakers. *Papers in Contrastive Phonetics,* 7:93-164 Jyvaskyla Cross-Language Studies.

Hardcastle, W. (1976) *The Physiology of Speech Production.* London: Academic Press.

Hardcastle, W. (1982) Constraints on coarticulatory processes. in Crystal, D. (ed) *Linguistic Controversies:* 33-49 London: Edward Arnold.

Hardcastle, W., & Clark, J. (1981) Articulatory, aerodynamic, and acoustic properties of lingual fricatives in English. *Work in Progress, Reading University Phonetics Laboratory*, 3:51-79.

Hardcastle, W., & Roach, P. (1977) An instrumental investigation of coarticulation in stop consonant sequences. *Work in Progress, Reading University Phonetics Laboratory*, 1:27-44.

Harrington, J. (1988) Automatic recognition of English consonants. in Jack, M., & Laver, J. (eds) *Speech Technology: A Survey:* 69-143 Edinburgh: Edinburgh University Press.

Harris, K.S. (1974) Physiological aspects of articulatory behaviour. in Sebeok, T. (ed) *Current Trends in Linguistics, Vol XII:* 2281-2302 The Hague: Mouton.

Harris, K.S., Tuller, B., & Kelso, J.A.S. (1986) Temporal invariance in the production of speech. in Perkell, J., & Klatt, D. (eds) *Invariance and Variability in Speech Processes:* 243-252 Hillsdale NJ: Lawrence Erlbaum Associates.

Hawkins, S. (1979) Temporal coordination in the speech of children: further data. *Journal of Phonetics*, 7:235-267.

Hawkins, S. (in press) An introduction to task dynamics. in Docherty, G.J. & Ladd, D.R. (eds) *Gesture, Segment, Prosody: Papers in Laboratory Phonology II.* Cambridge: Cambridge University Press.

Heffner, R. (1950) *General Phonetics.* Wisconsin: University of Wisconsin Press.

Henke, W. (1966) *Dynamic Articulatory Model of Speech Using Computer Simulation.* Unpublished dissertation, MIT.

Hess, W. (1982) *Pitch Determination of Speech Signals.* Berlin: Springer Verlag

Hiller, S., Laver, J., & Mackenzie, J. (1983) Automatic analysis of waveform perturbations in connected speech. *Work in Progress, Linguistics Department, Edinburgh University*, 16:40-68.

Hinkle, D., Wiersma, W., & Jurs, S. (1979) *Applied Statistics for the Behavioural Sciences.* Chicago: Rand McNally

Hirano, M. (1981) *Clinical Examination of Voice.* New York: Springer Verlag

Hirose, H. & Gay, T. (1972) The activity of the intrinsic laryngeal muscles in voicing control: electromyographic study. *Phonetica*, 25:140-164.

Holmes, J. (1973) The influence of glottal waveform on the naturalness of speech from a parallel formant speech synthesiser. *IEEE Transactions on Audio and Electroacoustics*, AU-21:298-305.

Holmes, J., Mattingly, I., & Shearme, J. (1964) Speech synthesis-by-rule. *Language and Speech*, 7:127-143.

Hombert, J-M., Ohala, J., & Ewan, W. (1979) Phonetic explanations for the development of tones. *Language*, 55:37-58.

Hooff, C.M. van, & Broecke, M. van den (1983) Assimilation of voice in Dutch at three types of linguistic boundaries. *Progress Report Institute of Phonetics University of Utrecht*, 8,1:12-23.

Hoole, P. (1987) Velar and glottal activity in a speaker of Icelandic. *Proceedings of the Eleventh International Congress of Phonetic Sciences, Vol 3:* 31-34.

Hughes, G., & Halle, M. (1956) Spectral properties of fricative consonants. *Journal of the Acoustical Society of America,* 23:303-310.

Husson, R. (1965) Sur le fonctionnement phonatoire du larynx. *Phonetica,* 13:40-42.

Hutters, B. (1985) Vocal fold adjustments in aspirated and unaspirated stops in Danish. *Phonetica,* 42:1-24.

Jassem, W. (1965) The formants of fricative consonants. *Language and Speech,* 8:1-16.

Jones, D. (1931) The word as a phonetic entity. *Maître Phonétique,* 36: 60-65.

Jones D. (1960) *An Outline of English Phonetics.* Eighth Edition, Cambridge: Heffer

Kahn, D. (1976) *Syllable-Based Generalisations in English Phonology.* Bloomington IN: Indiana University Linguistics Club.

Keating, P. (1984a) Phonetic and phonological representation of stop consonant voicing. *Language,* 60:286-319.

Keating, P. (1984b) Physiological effects on stop consonant voicing. *UCLA Working Papers in Phonetics,* 59:29-34.

Keating, P. (1985) Universal phonetics and the organisation of grammars. in Fromkin, V. (ed) *Phonetic Linguistics: Essays in Honour of Peter Ladefoged:* 115-132 New York: Academic Press.

Keating, P. (1990) The window model of coarticulation: articulatory evidence. in Kingston, J. & Beckman, M. (eds) *Papers in Laboratory Phonology I: Between the Grammar and the Physics of Speech:* 451-470 Cambridge: Cambridge University Press.

Keating, P., Linker, W., & Huffman, M. (1983)Allophone distribution for voiced and voiceless stops. *Journal of Phonetics,* 11:277-290.

Kelly, J., & Local, J. (1986) Long-domain resonance patterns in English. *Proceeedings IEE Conference on Speech I/O:* 304-309.

Kelso, J.A.S., Saltzman, E., & Tuller, B. (1986) The dynamical perspective on speech production: data and theory. *Journal of Phonetics,* 14:29-59.

Kelso, J.A.S., & Tuller, B. (1987) Intrinsic time in speech production: theory, methodology, and preliminary observations. in Keller, E., & Gopnik, M. (eds) *Motor and Sensory Processes of Language:* 203-222 Hillsdale NJ: Lawrence Erlbaum Associates.

Kelso, J.A.S., Tuller, B., & Harris, K. (1983) A 'dynamic' pattern perspective on the control and coordination of movement. in MacNeilage, P. (ed) *The Production of Speech:* 138-173 New York: Springer Verlag.

Kent, R. (1983) The segmental organisation of speech. in MacNeilage, P.(ed) *The Production of Speech:* 57-89 New York: Springer Verlag.

Kent, R., & Minifie, F. (1977) Coarticulation in recent speech production models. *Journal of Phonetics,* 5:115-133.

Kent, R., Carney, P., & Severied, L. (1974) Velar movement and timing: evaluation of a model for binary control. *Journal of Speech and Hearing Research,* 17:470-488.

Kerswill, P. (1984) Levels of linguistic variation in Durham. *Cambridge Papers in Phonetics and Experimental Linguistics,* 3.

Kerswill, P. (1985) A sociophonetic study of connected speech processes in Cambridge English: an outline and some results. *Cambridge Papers in Phonetics and Experimental Linguistics,* 4.

Kewley-Port, D. (1982) Measurement of formant transitions in naturally produced stop consonant - vowel syllables. *Journal of the Acoustical Society of America,* 72:379-389.

Kim, C. (1970) A theory of aspiration. *Phonetica,* 21:107-116.

Kingston, J. & Beckman, M. (eds) (1990) *Papers in Laboratory Phonology I: Between the Grammar and the Physics of Speech.* Cambridge: Cambridge University Press.

Klatt, D. (1973) Duration of pre-stressed word-initial consonant clusters in English. *MIT Research Lab of Electronics Quarterly Progress Report,* 108:253-260.

Klatt, D. (1975) Voice onset time, frication, and aspiration in word-initial consonant clusters. *Journal of Speech and Hearing Research,* 18:686-705.

Klatt, D. (1976a) Linguistic uses of segmental duration in English: acoustic and perceptual evidence. *Journal of the Acoustical Society of America,* 59:1208-1221.

Klatt, D. (1976b) Structure of a phonological rule component for a synthesis-by-rule program. *IEEE Transactions, Acoustics, Speech, and Signal Processing,* ASSP-24:391-398.

Klatt, D. (1979) Synthesis by rule of segmental durations in English sentences. in Lindblom, B., & Ohman, S. (eds) *Frontiers of Speech Communication Research:* 287-299 London: Academic Press.

Kohler, K. (1984) Phonetic explanation in phonology: the feature fortis/lenis. *Phonetica,* 41:150-174.

Kozhevnikov, V.A., & Chistovich, L.A. (1965) *Speech: Articulation and Perception.* Joint Publications Research Service, US Dept. of Commerce.

Ladefoged, P. (1971) *Preliminaries to Linguistic Phonetics.* Chicago: University of Chicago Press.

Ladefoged, P. (1980) What are linguistic sounds made of? *Language,* 56:485-502.

Ladefoged, P. (1988) The many interfaces between phonetics and phonology. *UCLA Working Papers in Phonetics,* 70:13-23.

Ladefoged, P., & Fromkin, V. (1967) Electromyography in speech research. *Phonetica,* 15:219-242.

Ladefoged, P., de Clerk, P., Lindau, M., & Papcun, G. (1972) An auditory-motor theory of speech production. *UCLA Working Papers in Phonetics,* 22:48-75.

Lafferière, M. (1982) Effects of stress differences on tongue blade movement in vowel consonant gestures. Unpublished paper, cited by Fujimura (1987).

Lass, R. (1984) *Phonology.* Cambridge: Cambridge University Press.

Laver, J. (1968) Assimilation in educated Nigerian English. *English Language Teaching,* 22:156-160.

Laver, J. (1970) The production of speech. in Lyons, J. (ed) *New Horizons in Linguistics:* 53-75 Harmondsworth: Penguin.

Laver, J. (1976) The semiotic nature of phonetic data. *York Papers in Linguistics,* 6:55-62.

Laver, J. (1980) *The Phonetic Description of Voice Quality.* Cambridge: Cambridge University Press.

Laver, J. (1988) Cognitive science and speech - a framework for research. *Work in Progress, Linguistics Department, Edinburgh University,* 21:83-114. [also published in Schnelle, H., & Bernsem, N.-O. (eds) (1989) *Logic & Linguistics, Vol 3:* 37-69 Hillsdale NJ: Lawrence Erlbaum Associates.]

Laver, J. (forthcoming) *Principles of Phonetics.* Cambridge: Cambridge University Press.

Lehiste, I. (1960) An acoustic-phonetic study of internal open juncture. *Phonetica,* 5, Supplement.
Lenneberg, E.H. (1967) *Biological Foundations of Language.* New York: Wiley.
Lewis, J., Daniloff, R., & Hammarberg, R. (1975) Apical coarticulation at junctural boundaries. *Journal of Phonetics,* 3:1-7.
Liberman, A., Cooper, F.S., Shankweiler, D., & Studdert-Kennedy, M. (1967) Perception of the speech code. *Psychological Review,* 74:431-461.
Liberman, M. (1983) In favour of some uncommon approaches to the study of speech. in MacNeilage, P. (ed) *The Production of Speech:* 265-274 New York: Springer Verlag.
Liljencrants, J., & Lindblom, B. (1972) Numerical simulation of vowel quality systems: the role of perceptual contrast. *Language,* 48:839-862.
Lindau, M., & Ladefoged, P. (1986) Variability of feature specifications. in Perkell, J., & Klatt, D. (eds) *Invariance and Variability in Speech Processes:* 464-477 Hillsdale NJ: Lawrence Erlbaum Associates.
Lindblom, B. (1963) Spectrographic study of vowel reduction. *Journal of the Acoustical Society of America,* 35:1173-1181.
Lindblom, B. (1983) Economy of speech gestures. in MacNeilage, P.(ed), *The Production of Speech:* 217-245 New York: Springer Verlag.
Lindblom, B. (1987) Adaptive variability and absolute constancy in speech signals: two themes in the quest for phonetic invariance. *Proceedings of the Eleventh International Congress of Phonetic Sciences, Vol 3:* 9-18.
Lindblom, B. (1990) Explaining phonetic variation: a sketch of the H & H theory. in Hardcastle, W., & Marchal, A. (eds) *Speech Production and Speech Modelling:* 403-439 Dordrecht: Kluwer.
Lindblom, B., Lubker, J., & Gay, T. (1979) Formant frequencies of some fixed mandible vowels and a model of speech motor programming by predictive simulation. *Journal of Phonetics,* 7:147-162.
Lindblom, B., & MacNeilage, P. (1986) Action theory: problems and alternative approaches. *Journal of Phonetics,* 14:117-132.
Lindqvist, J. (1972) Laryngeal articulation studied on Swedish subjects. *Speech Transmission Laboratory, Quarterly Progress and Status Report,* 2-3:10-27.
Lindsey, G., Davies, P., & Fourcin, A. (1986) Laryngeal coarticulation effects in English VCV sequences. *Speech Hearing and Language: Work in Progress Department of Phonetics and Linguistics, University College London,* 2:167-176.
Lisker, L. (1974) On time and timing in speech. in Sebeok, T.(ed) *Current Trends in Linguistics, Part 4:* 2387-2418 The Hague: Mouton.
Lisker, L., & Abramson, A. (1964) A cross-language study of voicing in initial stops: acoustic measurements. *Word,* 20:384-422.
Lisker, L., & Abramson, A. (1967) Some effects of context on voice onset time in English stops. *Language and Speech,* 10:1-28.
Lisker, L., Abramson, A., Cooper, F.S., & Schvey, M.H. (1969) Transillumination of the larynx in running speech. *Journal of the Acoustical Society of America,* 45:1544-1546.

REFERENCES

Local, J. (in press). Modelling assimilation on non-segmental, rule-free synthesis. in Docherty, G.J. & Ladd, D.R. (eds) *Gesture, Segment, Prosody: Papers in Laboratory Phonology II.* Cambridge: Cambridge University Press.

Löfqvist, A. (1980) Interarticulator programming in stop production. *Journal of Phonetics*, 8:475-490.

Löfqvist, A. (1986) Commentary on paper by Harris et al (1986). in Perkell, J., & Klatt, D. (eds) *Invariance and Variability in Speech Processes:* 254-256 Hillsdale NJ: Lawrence Erlbaum Associates.

Löfqvist, A. (1990) Speech as audible gestures. in Hardcastle, W., & Marchal, A. (eds) *Speech Production and Speech Modelling:* 289-322 Dordrecht: Kluwer.

Löfqvist, A., & McGarr, N. (1986) Laryngeal dynamics in voiceless consonant production. *Working Papers in Logopedics and Phoniatrics, Lund University Hospital*, 3:49-65.

Löfqvist, A., & Yoshioka, H. (1981) Interarticulator programming in obstruent production. *Phonetica*, 38:21-34.

Löfqvist, A., & Yoshioka, H. (1984) Intrasegmental timing: laryngeal-oral coordination in voiceless consonant production. *Speech Communication*, 3:279-289.

Lorge, B. (1967) A study of the relationship between production and perception of initial and intervocalic /t/ and /d/ in individual English speaking adults. *Haskins Labs Status Report Speech Research*, SR-9:3.1-3.18.

Lubker, J. (1981) Representation and context - sensitivity. in Myers, T., Laver, J., & Anderson, J.(eds) *The Cognitive Representation of Speech:* 127-131 Amsterdam: North Holland.

Lubker, J., & Gay, T. (1982) Anticipatory labial coarticulation: experimental, biological, and linguistic variables. *Journal of the Acoustical Society of America*, 71:437-448.

Lubker, J., & Lindgren, R. (1983) The perceptual effects of anticipatory coarticulation. Unpublished Manuscript.

Mack, M. (1982) Voicing dependent vowel duration in English and French monolingual and bilingual production. *Journal of the Acoustical Society of America*, 73:173-178.

MacNeilage, P. (1970) The motor control of serial ordering in speech. *Psychological Review*, 77:182-196.

MacNeilage, P. (1972) Speech physiology. in Gilbert, J.(ed), *Speech and Cortical Functioning:* 1-72 New York: Academic Press.

Malecot, A. (1969) The lenis-fortis opposition: its physiological parameters. *Journal of the Acoustical Society of America*, 47:1588-1592.

Markel, J. (1972) The SIFT algorithm for fundamental frequency estimation. *IEEE Transactions*, AU-20:367-77.

Massaro, D., & Cohen, M. (1977) Voice onset time and fundamental frequency as cues to the /zi/-/si/ distinction. *Perception Psychophysics*, 22:373-382.

McClean, M. (1973) Forward coarticulation of velar movement at marked junctural boundaries. *Journal of Speech and Hearing Research*, 16:286-296.

McGlone, R.E, & Shipp, T. (1972) Comparison of subglottal air pressures associated with /p/ and /b/. *Journal of the Acoustical Society of America*, 51:664-665.

McInnes, F., & Jack, M. (1988) Automatic speech recognition using word reference patterns. in Jack, M., & Laver, J. (eds) *Speech Technology: A Survey:* 1-68 Edinburgh: Edinburgh University Press.

Menyuk, P., & Klatt, D. (1975) Voice onset time in consonant cluster production by children and adults. *Journal of Child Language,* 2:223-231.

Miller, J., Green, K., & Reeves, A. (1986) Speech rate and segments: a look at the relation between speech production and speech perception for the voicing contrast. *Phonetica,* 43:106-115.

Moll, K., & Daniloff, R. (1971) Investigation of the timing of velar movements in speech. *Journal of the Acoustical Society of America,* 50:678-684.

Moll, K., Zimmerman, G., & Smith, A. (1977) The study of speech production as a human neuromotor system. in Sawashima, M., & Cooper, F.S. (eds) *Dynamic Aspects of Speech Production:* 107-127. Tokyo: University of Tokyo Press.

Nakatani, L., & Dukes, K. (1977) Locus of segmental cues for word juncture. *Journal of the Acoustical Society of America,* 62:714-719.

Nespor, M., & Vogel, I. (1986) *Prosodic Phonology.* Dordrecht: Foris.

Netsell, R. (1969) Subglottal and intraoral air pressures during the intervocalic /t/ and /d/. *Phonetica,* 20:68-73.

Ní Chasaide, A. (1979) The laterals of Gaoth-Dobhair and of Hiberno-English. *Occasional Papers in Linguistics and Language Learning (New University of Ulster),* 2:64-78.

Ní Chasaide, A. (1987) Glottal control of aspiration and of voicelessness. *Proceedings of the Eleventh International Congress of Phonetic Sciences, Vol 6:* 28-31.

Nolan, F. (1982a) The nature of phonetic representations. *Cambridge Papers in Phonetics and Experimental Linguistics,* 1:1-12.

Nolan, F. (1982b) The role of Action Theory in the description of speech production. *Linguistics,* 20:287-308

Nolan, F. (1983) *The Phonetic Bases of Speaker Recognition Cambridge.* Cambridge: Cambridge University Press.

Nolan, F. (1987) The limits of segmental description. *Proceedings of the Eleventh International congress of Phonetic Sciences, Vol 5:* 411-414.

Noll, A.M. (1967) Cepstrum pitch determination. *Journal of the Acoustical Society of America,* 41:293-309.

Ohala, J. (1974) Experimental historical phonology. in Anderson, J., & Jones, C. (eds) *Historical Linguistics II: Theory and Description in Phonology:* 353-389 Amsterdam: North Holland.

Ohala, J. (1978) The production of tone. in Fromkin, V. (ed) *Tone: A Linguistic Survey:* 5-39 New York: Academic Press.

Ohala, J. (1981) Articulatory constraints on the cognitive representation of speech. in Myers, T., Laver, J., & Anderson, J.(eds) *The Cognitive Representation of Speech:* 111-122 Amsterdam: North Holland.

Ohala, J. (1983) The origin of sound patterns in vocal tract constraints. in MacNeilage, P.(ed) *The Production of Speech:* 189-216 New York: Springer Verlag.

Ohala, J., & Jaeger, J. (eds) (1986) *Experimental Phonology.* New York: Academic Press.

REFERENCES

Perkell, J. (1969) Physiology of speech production. *Research Monograph,* 53. Cambridge Ma.: MIT Press.

Perkell, J. (1980) Phonetic features and the physiology of speech production. in Butterworth, B. (ed) *Language Production, Vol 1:* 337-372 London: Academic Press.

Perkell, J., & Klatt, D. (eds) (1986) *Invariance and Variability of Speech Processes.* Hillsdale NJ: Lawrence Erlbaum Associates.

Peterson, G., & Lehiste, I. (1960) Duration of syllable nuclei in English. *Journal of the Acoustical Society of America,* 32:693-703.

Pisoni, D. (1977) Identification and discrimination of the relative onset time of two component tones: implications for voicing perception in stops. *Journal of the Acoustical Society of America,* 61:1352-1361.

Port, R. (1986) Translating linguistic symbols into time. *Research in Phonetics and Computational Linguistics,* 6:156-173 Indiana University Department of Linguistics.

Port, R., & Mitleb, F. (1980) Phonetic and phonological manifestations of the voicing contrast in Arabic-accented English. *Research in Phonetics,* 1:137-165 Indiana University Department of Linguistics.

Port, R., & O'Dell, M. (1984) Neutralisation of syllable final voicing in German. *Research in Phonetics,* 4:93-133 Indiana University Department of Linguistics.

Port, R., & Rotunno, R. (1979) Relation between voice onset time and vowel duration. *Journal of the Acoustical Society of America,* 66:654-662.

Port, R., Al-Ani, A., & Maeda, S. (1980) Temporal compensation and universal phonetics. *Phonetica,* 37:235-252.

Prosek, R.A., & House, A.S. (1975) Intraoral air pressure as a feedback cue in consonant production. *Journal of Speech and Hearing Research,* 18:133-147.

Quarmby, D. & Holmes, J. (1984) Implementation of a parallel-formant speech synthesiser using a single-chip programmable signal processor. *IEE Proceedings,* 131, pt. F:563-569.

Rabiner, L. (1968) Speech synthesis-by-rule: an acoustic domain approach. *Bell System Technical Journal,* 47:17-32

Rabiner, L. (1969) A model for synthesising speech by rule. *IEEE Transactions Audio and Electroacoustics,* AU-17:7-13.

Rabiner, L., & Schafer, L. (1978) *Digital Processing of Speech Signals.* Englewood Cliff, NJ: Prentice-Hall.

Randolph, M., & Zue, V. (1987) The role of syllable structure in the acoustic realisation of stops. *Proceedings of the Eleventh International Congress of Phonetic Sciences, Vol 2:* 360-363.

Raphael, L. (1972) Preceding vowel duration as a cue to the perception of the voicing characteristic of word-final consonants in American English. *Journal of the Acoustical Society of America,* 51:1296-1303.

Repp, B. (1984) Categorical perception: issues, methods, findings. in Lass, N. (ed) *Speech and Language: Advances in Basic Research and Practice, Vol. 10:* 243-335 New York: Academic Press.

Roach, P. (1973) Glottalisation of English - a re-examination. *Journal of the International Phonetics Association,* 3:10-21.

Roach, P. (1980) Reaction time measurements of laryngeal closure. *Journal of Phonetics*, 8:305-315.

Roach, P. (1983) *English Phonetics and Phonology*. Cambridge: Cambridge University Press.

Rosenburg, A. (1971) Effect of glottal pulse shape on the quality of natural vowels. *Journal of the Acoustical Society of America*, 49:583-590.

Rothenburg, M. (1968) The breath stream dynamics of simple-released-plosives. *Bibliotecha Phonetica*, 6 Basel: Karger.

Saltzman, E., & Kelso, J.A.S. (1987) Skilled action: a task-dynamics approach. *Psychological Review*, 94:84-106.

Sawashima, M., & Hirose, H. (1983) Laryngeal gestures in speech production. in MacNeilage, P. (ed) *Speech Production:* 11-38 Hillsdale NJ: Lawrence Erlbaum Associates.

Scully, C. (1987) Linguistic units and units of speech production. *Speech Communication*, 6:77-42.

Scully, C. (1990) Articulatory synthesis. in Hardcastle, W., & Marchal, A. (eds) *Speech Production and Speech Modelling:* 151-186 Dordrecht: Kluwer.

Scully, C. & Allwood, E. (1985) The production and perception of an articulatory continuum for fricatives of English. *Speech Communication*, 4:237-245.

Shadle, C. (1990) Articulatory and acoustic relationships in fricative consonants. in Hardcastle, W., & Marchal, A. (eds) *Speech Production and Speech Modelling:* 187-209 Dordrecht: Kluwer.

Slis, I. (1970) Articulatory measurements on voiced, voiceless, and nasal consonants. *Phonetica*, 21:193-210

Slis, I. (1986) Assimilation of voice in Dutch as a function of stress, word boundaries, and sex of speaker and listener. *Journal of Phonetics*, 14:311-326.

Smith, B. (1978) Effects of place of articulation and vowel environment on 'voiced' stop consonant production. *Glossa*, 12:163-175.

Smith, T. (1971) A phonetic study of the function of the extrinsic tongue muscles. *UCLA Working Papers in Phonetics*, 18.

Snedecor, G., & Cochran, W (1980) *Statistical Methods*. 7th edition, Ames, Iowa: Iowa State University Press.

Sock, R., & Benoit, C. (1986) VOTs et VTTs en français. *Proceedings of the 15ème Journées d'Etudes sur la Parole:* 307-310.

Stathopoulos, E., & Weismer, G. (1983) Closure duration of stop consonants. *Journal of Phonetics*, 11:395-400.

Sternberg, S., Monsell, S., Knoll, R., & Wright, C. (1978) The latency and duration of rapid movement sequences: comparisons of speech and typewriting. in Stelmach, G. (ed) *Information Processing in Motor Control and Learning:* 117-152 New York: Academic Press.

Stevens, K., & House, A. (1963) Perturbation of vowel articulations by consonantal context. *Journal of Speech and Hearing Research*, 6:111-128.

Stevens, K., & Klatt, D. (1974) Role of formant transitions in the voiced-voiceless distinction for stops. *Journal of the Acoustical Society of America*, 55:653-659.

Strevens, P. (1960) The spectra of fricative noise in human speech. *Language and Speech,* 3:32-49.

Subtelny, J., Worth, J., & Sakuda, M. (1966) Intra-oral air pressure and rate of flow during speech. *Journal of Speech and Hearing Research,* 9:498-518.

Summerfield, Q. (1975) Aerodynamics versus mechanics in the control of voicing onset in consonant-vowel syllables. *Speech Perception,* 2(4):61-72 Department of Psychology, Queen's University, Belfast.

Suomi, K. (1980) Voicing in English and Finnish stops. *Publications of the Department of Finnish and General Linguistics of the University of Turku,* 10.

Tatham, M. (1984) Towards a cognitive phonetics. *Journal of Phonetics,* 12:37-47.

Thorsen, N. (1971) Voicing in British English /t/ and /d/ in contact with other consonants. *Annual Report Institute of Phonetics University of Copenhagen,* 5:1-39.

Uldall, E.T. (1957) *Vocal cord action in speech: a high speed study.* Film. Swiss Federal Institute of Technology.

Umeda, N. (1977) Consonant durations in American English. *Journal of the Acoustical Society of America,* 61:846-858.

Voiers, W. (1983) Evaluating processed speech using the diagnostic rhyme test. *Speech Technology,* Jan/Feb 1983:30-39.

Wang, W. S-Y., & Fillmore, C. (1961) Intrinsic cues and consonant perception. *Journal of Speech and Hearing Research,* 4:130-136.

Warren, D. (1976) Aerodynamics of speech production. in Lass, N. (ed) *Contemporary Issues in Experimental Phonetics:* 105-137. New York: Academic Press.

Watson, I. (1983) Cues to the voicing contrast: a survey. *Cambridge Papers in Phonetics and Experimental Linguistics,* 2.

Weismer, G. (1979) Sensitivity of voice onset measures to certain segmental features in speech production. *Journal of Phonetics,* 7:194-204.

Weismer, G. (1980) Control of the voicing distinction for intervocalic stops and fricatives: some data and theoretical considerations. *Journal of Phonetics,* 8:427-438.

Wells, J. (1982) *Accents of English* 3 Volumes Cambridge: Cambridge University Press.

Westbury, J. (1979) *Aspects of the Temporal Control of Voicing in Consonant Clusters in English.* Unpublished dissertation, University of Texas at Austin.

Wickelgren, W. (1969) Context-sensitive coding, associative memory, and serial order in (speech) behaviour. *Psychological Review,* 76:1-15.

Windsor-Lewis, J. (1987) The teaching of English pronunciation: the model accents. *Journal of the International Phonetics Association,* 17:139-141.

Wingate, A. (1982) A phonetic answer to a phonological question. *UCLA Working Papers in Phonetics,* 54:1-27.

Wolf, J. (1972) Efficient acoustic parameters for speaker recognition. *Journal of the Acoustical Society of America,* 51:2044-2056.

Yoshioka, H., Löfqvist, A., & Hirose, H. (1979) Laryngeal adjustments in the production of consonant clusters and geminates in American English. *Haskins Labs Status Report on Speech Research,* SR-59/60 :127-151.

Yoshioka, H., Löfqvist, A., Hirose, H., & Collier, R. (1986) How voiceless sound sequences are organised in terms of glottal opening gestures. *Annual Bulletin of the Research Institute for Logopedic and Phoniatrics, Tokyo,* 20:55-67.

Zemlin, W.R. (1968) *Speech and Hearing Sciences: Anatomy and Physiology.* Englewood Cliff, NJ: Prentice-Hall inc.

Zlatin, M. (1974) Voicing contrast: perceptual and productive voice onset time characteristics of adults. *Journal of the Acoustical Society of America,* 56:981-994.

Zue, V. (1976) *Acoustic Characteristics of Stop Consonants.* Bloomington IN: Indiana University Linguistics Club.

Name Index

Abbs, J. 56, 57, 63, 64, 77, 95, 204
Abercrombie, D. 20, 39, 40, 53, 229
Abramson, A. 13, 16, 25, 26, 27, 28, 29, 31, 52, 130, 132, 140, 141, 143, 174, 199, 206
Al-Bamerni, A. 15, 42, 45, 46, 54, 75, 153, 189, 225
Allen, J. 235, 236, 237, 255
Allwood, E. 38, 39, 168
Anderson, S. 78, 94
Arkebauer, J. 159
Armstrong, L. 175
Askenfelt, A. 103
Baer, T. 61
Baken, R. 93
Baran, J. 25, 26, 27, 140, 173
Barry, M. 77
Barry, W. 42, 47, 151
Batliner, A. 256
Beckman, M. 1, 77
Bell-Berti, F. 10, 50, 65, 206
Bellugi, U. 95
Benguerel, A-P. 72, 73
Benoit, C. 16
Bickley, C. 18, 132, 175
Bladon, A. 15, 42, 45, 46, 54, 75, 153, 189, 225
Broad, D. 4, 50
Broe, M. 84, 201
Browman, C. 58, 72, 80, 84, 89, 90, 96, 175, 200, 201, 213, 223
Brown, G. 45, 46, 47, 110, 112, 177
Brown, W. 8, 34, 159
Canellada, M. 152
Catford, J. 4, 5, 9, 27, 95, 137, 230
Chen, M 35

Chen, M. 75
Chistovich, L. 57
Chomsky, N. 72, 73, 81
Clark, J. 39, 119
Clements, G.N. 84
Clumeck, H. 75
Cochrane, W. 113
Cohen, M. 53
Cole, R. 53
Cooper, W. 53, 178
Cowan, H. 72, 73
Daniloff, R. 63, 70, 72, 94
Davidsen-Nielsen, N. 48
Delattre, P. 17
Denes, P. 1, 35, 53, 248
Dent, H. 42, 45, 46, 152, 154, 180, 186, 189
Diehl, R. 52
Disner, S. 230
Dixit, P. 18
Docherty, G. 1, 9, 119
Dukes, K. 189
Edwards, T. 24, 33, 34
Eefting, W. 229
Eilenberg, G. 57, 63
Ferguson, G. 172
Fillmore, C. 95
Fischer-Jorgensen, E. 24, 38, 52, 102, 132
Flege, J. 34, 52, 117, 206, 229
Fletcher, J. 59, 210
Fourakis, M. 74, 75, 94, 213, 217
Fowler, C. 57, 66, 68, 94, 95, 204, 224
Fraser, H. 9, 119
Fromkin, V. 93
Fujimura, O. 57, 60, 77, 78, 79, 93, 95, 189, 223, 225

INDEX

Gay, T. 18, 66, 67, 75, 174
Gimson, A. 41, 45, 46, 47, 48, 50, 54, 110, 155, 174, 177, 189
Goldsmith, J. 84, 201
Goldstein, L. 58, 72, 80, 84, 89, 90, 96, 175, 200, 201, 213, 223
Gracco, V 64
Haggard, M. 15, 39, 53, 146, 150, 154, 163
Halle, M. 9, 72, 73, 81, 95
Hammarberg, R. 57, 63, 70, 94
Hanninen, R. 15, 34, 38, 39, 40, 52, 232
Hardcastle, W. 9, 39, 70, 94, 119
Harrington, J. 53
Harris, K. 57, 62, 78
Hawkins, S. 15, 25, 26, 42, 44, 57, 84, 133, 146, 154, 224, 230
Heffner, R. 51
Henke, W. 72, 73
Hess, W. 102, 103, 171
Hiller, S. 61
Hinkle, D. 113
Hirano, M. 4, 18, 93
Hirose, H. 4, 7, 18, 50, 51
Holmes, J. 235, 236, 237, 244
Hombert, J-M. 62
Hoole, P. 146
House, A. 8, 63, 159
Hughes, G. 9
Husson, R. 50
Hutters, B. 24, 38, 52, 102, 172, 217
Isard, S. 144
Jack, M. 254
Jaeger, J. 1
Jassem, W. 9
Jones, D. 35, 39, 41, 42, 45, 47, 51, 177
Kahn, D. 45, 177
Keating, P. 33, 65, 72, 73, 75, 78, 79, 80, 87, 88, 89, 90, 94, 95, 96, 104, 132, 163, 164, 167, 169, 214, 230
Kelly, J. 66, 75
Kelso, J.A.S. 57, 68, 84, 204, 224, 230
Kent, R. 62, 70, 72, 94, 152, 230
Kerswill, P. 41, 231

Kewley-Port, D. 173
Kim, C. 7, 18, 19
Kingston, J. 1
Klatt, D. 1, 12, 15, 24, 25, 26, 28, 29, 31, 38, 42, 44, 104, 128, 130, 132, 137, 143, 144, 146, 154, 173, 174, 211, 224, 229, 230, 236
Kohler, K. 13, 80, 88, 90, 96, 174, 230
Kozhevnikov, V. 57
Kunzel, H. 42, 47, 151
Ladd, D.R. 1
Ladefoged, P. 51, 57, 66, 72, 73, 93, 94, 95, 198, 229
Laferrière, M. 77
Lass, R. 45
Laver, J. 1, 4, 5, 6, 7, 10, 12, 40, 50, 57, 58, 60, 61, 68, 94, 95, 209
Lehiste, I. 24, 25, 26, 47, 133
Lenneberg, E. 207
Lewis, J. 179
Liberman, A. 70, 95
Liberman, M. 78
Liljencrants, J. 82, 95
Lindau, M. 72
Lindblom, B. 63, 66, 67, 68, 69, 82, 95, 100, 141, 142, 207, 230
Lindgren, R. 75
Lindqvist, J. 18
Lindsey, G. 103
Lisker, L. 13, 15, 18, 25, 26, 27, 28, 29, 31, 52, 78, 94, 130, 132, 140, 141, 143, 161, 174, 206
Local, J. 66, 75
Löfqvist, A. 7, 18, 19, 20, 78, 156, 161, 173
Lovins, J. 57, 60
Lubker, J. 70, 75
Mack, M. 75
MacNeilage, P. 66, 67, 68, 94, 229
Madsen, J. 152
Malecot, A. 13
Markel, J. 102
Massaro, D. 53

McGarr, N. 18, 161
McGlone, R. 8, 159, 173
McInnes, F. 254
McLean, M. 179
Menyuk, P 25
Miller, J. 52
Minifie, F. 70, 94, 230
Mitleb, F. 71, 75, 76, 227
Moll, K. 57, 72
Nakatani, L. 189
Nespor, M. 45
Netsell, R. 175
Ní Chasaide, A. 18, 19, 20, 75
Nolan, F. 5, 27, 57, 59, 65, 66, 72, 77, 78, 87, 94, 189, 203, 204, 209, 225, 230
Noll, A. 102
O'Dell, M. 54, 77
Ohala, J. 1, 26, 62, 74, 143, 144, 161, 174, 175
Perkell, J. 1, 57, 66, 72, 84
Peterson, G. 24, 25, 26, 133
Pinson, E. 1
Pisoni, D. 12, 229
Port, R. 24, 25, 26, 27, 28, 29, 52, 54, 71, 74, 75, 76, 77, 78, 94, 143, 211, 213, 217, 224, 227, 230
Prosek, R. 8, 159
Quarmby, D. 237, 244
Rabiner, L. 102, 236
Randolph, M. 12, 46, 189
Raphael, L. 35, 53, 248
Repp, B. 246
Roach, P. 35, 53, 70, 110, 207
Rosenburg, M. 235
Rothenburg, M. 7, 18, 206
Rotunno, R. 24, 25, 26, 27, 28, 29, 143, 211, 224, 230
Saltzman, E. 57
Sawashima, M. 4, 7, 18, 50, 51
Schafer, L. 102
Schieffer, L. 256
Scully, C. 9, 38, 39, 64, 132, 168

Shadle, C. 9
Shipp, T. 175
Shockey, L. 157
Shoji, A. 77
Slis, I. 13, 16
Smith, B. 29, 31, 167
Smith, T. 63
Snedecor, G. 113
Sock, R. 16
Stathopoulos, E. 172
Sternberg, S. 95
Stevens, K. 12, 18, 63, 81, 95, 128, 132, 175, 229
Strevens, P. 9
Studdert-Kennedy, M. 95
Subtelny, J. 159
Summerfield, Q. 26, 52, 144, 174
Suomi, K. 15, 25, 26, 32, 33, 34, 52, 119, 121, 130, 133, 138, 146, 163
Tatham, M. 94
Thorsen, N. 42, 165
Tuller, B. 57, 222, 228
Uldall, E. 5
Umeda, N. 150, 154
van den Berg, R. 4, 5
van den Berg, R.J. 16, 165
van den Broecke, M. 190
van Hoof, C. 190
Vogel, I. 45
Voiers, W. 255
Wang, S-Y. 95
Warren, D. 50
Watson, I. 16, 27, 51, 205
Weismer, G. 7, 15, 18, 19, 24, 25, 26, 27, 28, 29, 51, 130, 132, 138, 139, 143, 172, 173, 204
Wells, J. 50, 110
Westbury, J. 10, 25, 26, 28, 29, 31, 32, 33, 34, 42, 104, 163, 165, 206, 229
Wickelgren, W. 57
Windsor-Lewis, J. 50
Wingate, A. 54
Wolf, J. 52

Yoshioka, H. 7, 18, 19, 156, 161
Zemlin, W. 50
Zlatin, M. 23, 25, 26, 31, 51
Zue, V. 7, 8, 12, 15, 24, 25, 26, 31, 42, 44, 46, 189

Subject Index

Abduction of the vocal folds (*see* laryngeal mechanisms: voicelessness)
Action Theory 57-59, 67-68, 84, 87, 88-89, 95n, 224
Aerodynamic-myoelastic theory of phonation (*see* laryngeal mechanisms: voicelessness)
Allophonic variability (*see* phonetic variability)
Articulatory compensation 69, 94n
Articulatory economy (*see* phonetic variability)
Articulatory efficiency (*see* phonetic variability)
Articulatory plasticity (*see* phonetic variability)
Aspiration 12, 229n (*see also* voice onset time)
    in voiceless fricatives 38
Assimilation
    of place 77
    of voicing in consonant sequences 40-41 (*see also* timing of voicing)
        in Durham English 41
        in Dutch 165, 190n
        in Nigerian English 41
        in Scottish English 40
'Bite-block' speech 69
Coarticulation (*see also* phonetic variability) 69-70, 71, 94n, 178-179
    coarticulation resistance 225
Consonant sequences (*see also* assimilation, timing of voicing in consonant sequences,).

criteria for identification in the acoustic signal 106-107
Coordination of laryngeal and supralaryngeal gestures 10 (*see also* medial voicing, timing of voicing, timing of voicing in fricatives, timing of voicing in stops, voice onset time)
    relative independence of laryngeal and supralaryngeal articulators 10
    strategies for maintaining voicing during articulatory occlusion 10, 206
Coordinative structures 58, 67-68, 88-89
Danish 217
Description of the timing of voicing 11-14, 191-201
    general requirements of descriptive framework 11, 191
    parametric description 20-21, 37, 192
    'template' approach to description of timing of voicing 192-201
    terminology definition and usage 11-14
        'aspirated' 12
        'devoiced' 13, 51n
        'Fortis/Lenis' 13
        'Tense/Lax' 13
        'unaspirated' 12
        'voiced' 11
        'voiceless' 11
Detection of voicing in speech waveform (*see* experimental method)
Dutch 165, 200n
Experimental method 97-112, 179-182
    description of database 110-112, 181
    detection of voicing 102-103

linguistic material 97-98, 179-180
measurement consistency 109
measurement criteria 103-109
reading task 99-100, 180
recording and analysis 100-110, 181-182
statistical analysis 113, 172n, 182
subjects 98-99, 181
'Extrinsic' allophones 95n
'Flapping' rule in American English 77
Fortis vs lenis (*see also* description of the timing of voicing) 87-89
French 175n
Fricatives (*see also* timing of voicing in fricatives)
articulatory and acoustic characteristics 8-9
criteria for identification in the acoustic signal 106, 172n,
perceptual cues to the voicing contrast 53n
German 76
Gestural score 71
role of in an account of the timing of voicing 83-87
Gestures (*see* gestural score)
Glottal 'attack' 50n
Glottal reinforcement of stop closures 53n, 110-112, 184-186
'Intrinsic' allophones 95n
'Intrinsic' timing 58, 224
Japanese (devoicing of vowels) 77
Laryngeal mechanisms: voicing 4-6
aerodynamic-myoelastic theory of phonation 4-5
gradual onset of voicing 5
voiced-voiceless 'continuum' 5-6
Laryngeal mechanisms: voicelessness 6-7,
timing of abduction gesture 19-20, 133-139, 146-148, 156-157, 160-162, 174n
Mechano-inertial constraints 62-65
Medial Voicing

effect of manner of articulation 157-163
effect of phonetic environment 164-166
effect of phonological voicing category 32-35, 38-40, 119-130
effect of place of articulation 163-164
effect of position in word 166-167
in mixed consonant sequences 42-43
inter-speaker variability 167-169
Micro-variability 94n (*see also* phonetic variability)
Motor equivalence 67-68
'Neurochronaxic' theory of vocal fold vibration 50n
Neutralisation (of German voicing contrast) 76
Obstruents (articulatory characteristics of) 7 (*see also* fricative consonants, stop consonants)
Phonetic representation 55, 71-78 (*see also* phonetic variability)
Phonetic variability (*see also* timing of voicing)
accounting for general characteristics of variability of 59-79, 90-91. 94n
factors inherent in motor programming 66-71
articulatory economy 68-69, 207
articulatory efficiency 69-70
articulatory plasticity 69, 141-142, 174n
motor equivalence 67-68
factors inherent in utterance execution 61-66
'dynamic' and 'configurational' constraints of the speech production mechanism 203 208
mechano-inertial constraints 62-65

role of the phonetic representation 71-78
      implementation rules 211-213, 223-224
      limitations of feature-matrix representation 72-73
      need to account for non-universal variability 74-76
      non-discrete nature of allophonic variability 76-78, 189-190, 208
   language-specific characteristics 55, 74-76, 208
   random variability 60-61
Pre-aspiration 12
Segment 50n, 208
Sign language (parallels to speech production) 95n
Southern British English (definition of) 50n
Spanish 152, 174n, 217
Speech production modelling (see also action theory, phonetic variability, timing of voicing)
   'predictive simulation 67
   'translation' model 57-59
   typical modelling strategies 56-5
Stops (see also timing of voicing in stops)
   articulatory and acoustic characteristics 7-8
   criteria for identification in acoustic signal 104-105
   incomplete occlusion 112, 184-186
   intra-oral pressure in 159-160
   sub-glottal pressure in 175n
Stop epenthesis 74-75, 112
Systematic phonetic representation 71
Task dynamics 57-59, 84, 87, 224
Timing of voicing
   accounting for variability in the timing of voicing 79-90, 91-92, 202-228
      Browman & Goldstein's gestural score approach 83-87, 90, 223

      critique of some previous proposals 90
      Keating's (1984a) model 80-83, 90, 169, 223
      Kohler's (1984) model 87-89, 90
      'window' model 213-228
   limitations of previous studies 14-17
   method in present study (see experimental method)
   motivation for an acoustic study (as opposed to articulatory) 92-94
   'physiological' studies of 18-20, 51n
   rules for a speech synthesis-by-rule system Appendix A
Timing of voicing in consonant sequences
   Effect of medial boundary status 45-48, 157, 182-190
   Medial voicing 42-43, 164-165
   Voice onset time 41-42, 44-48, 117-118, 130-131, 149-157, 182-187
Timing of voicing in fricatives
   'Aspiration' 38
   Medial voicing 38-40, 122-127, 157-169
   Voice onset time 118-119
Timing of voicing in stops
   Medial voicing 32-35, 119-122, 157-169
   Voice onset time 21-32, 113-118, 130-149
Typewriting (parallels to speech production) 95n
Voice onset time 13-14, 15-16, 21-32
   effect of adjacent vowel quality 26-27, 31, 133, 142-144
   effect of following consonants 28-29
   effect of medial boundary status 45-47, 48, 182-190
   effect of no. of syllables in word 28
   effect of phonological voicing category 113-117, 127-130,140
   effect of place of articulation 25-26, 31-32, 52n, 130-140, 173n, 174n

effect of position of stop 27-28
effect of speech rate 23, 52n
effect of stress 28
effect of utterance type 140-142
in /s/-stop sequences 155-157
in English stops produced by native Arabic speakers 76
in fricative-sonorant sequences 149-154
in single stops as opposed to stop-sonorant sequences 145-149
inter-speaker variation in 29, 117, 140-141, 167-169
measurement criteria 24, 52n, 54n
use as a parameter in automatic speaker recognition 52n
use as a parameter in automatic speech recognition 172-173n
voicing 'lead' 29

Voicing 'lead' (*see* voice onset time)

Whisper 6, 53n

Stig Johansson
Anna-Brita Stenström (Editors)

English Computer Corpora
Selected Papers and Research Guide

1991. VII, 402 pages. 75 illustrations. Cloth.
ISBN 3 11 012395 9
(Topics in English Linguistics 3)

The contributions in this collection show the wide range of current work on machine-readable texts in English language research. The contributors discuss grammar, syntax, lexis, speech, dialects, specialized corpora and software.

Most of the papers report on descriptive studies, but more general topics such as probabilistic grammar study and quantitative versus qualitative analysis are also covered.

The volume also contains a detailed survey of English machine-readable corpora and a full bibliography of publications drawing on some major computer corpora (primarily the Brown Corpus, the LOB Corpus and the London-Lund Corpus), and thus serves both as a research guide and a description of the state of the art in English corpus work.

mouton de gruyter
Berlin · New York